FINANCIAL SERVICES

The American Assembly, *Columbia University*

FINANCIAL SERVICES:
THE CHANGING INSTITUTIONS AND GOVERNMENT POLICY

Prentice-Hall, Inc., *Englewood Cliffs, New Jersey*

Library of Congress Cataloging in Publication Data
Main entry under title:

FINANCIAL SERVICES.

At head of title: The American Assembly, Columbia University.
"A Spectrum Book."
Background papers prepared for a meeting convened by the American Assembly at Arden House, Harriman, N.Y., Apr. 7-10, 1983; edited by George J. Benston.
Bibliography: p.
Includes index.
1. Financial institutions—United States—Congresses. 2. Banks and banking—United States—Congresses. 3. Banking law—United States—Congresses. I. Benston, George J. II. American Assembly.
HG181.F6435 1983 332.1'0973 83-13995
ISBN 0-13-316513-2
ISBN 0-13-316505-1 (pbk.)

This book is available at a special discount when ordered in bulk quantities. Contact Prentice-Hall, Inc., General Publishing Division, Special Sales, Englewood Cliffs, N. J. 07632.

Editorial/production supervision by Betty Neville
Cover design © 1983 by Jeannette Jacobs
Manufacturing buyer: Cathie Leonard

10 9 8 7 6 5 4 3 2 1

ISBN 0-13-316513-2
ISBN 0-13-316505-1 {PBK.}

PRENTICE-HALL INTERNATIONAL, INC. *(London)*
PRENTICE-HALL OF AUSTRALIA PTY. LIMITED *(Sydney)*
PRENTICE-HALL OF CANADA, INC. *(Toronto)*
PRENTICE-HALL OF INDIA PRIVATE LIMITED *(New Delhi)*
PRENTICE-HALL OF JAPAN, INC. *(Tokyo)*
PRENTICE-HALL OF SOUTHEAST ASIA PTE. LTD. *(Singapore)*
WHITEHALL BOOKS LIMITED *(Wellington, New Zealand)*
EDITORA PRENTICE-HALL DO BRASIL LTDA. *(Rio de Janeiro)*

Table of Contents

Preface

Financial services, particularly banking, have always attracted a strong public interest in the United States. Throughout our history, many of the monumental legislative battles in our republic have been fought over issues concerned with the regulation of the financial industry.

In the wake of the Great Depression, the legislators of the New Deal created a rather comprehensive framework designed to stipulate public mores for those in this country who engage in banking, securities, and other related financial services. The edifice of regulation resulting from this legislation, built upon earlier governmental action at both the federal and state level, has shaped the nature and the practices of the financial services industry over the past fifty years.

Recently, however, significant changes have taken place in that industry. These have resulted in part from technological advances, in part from innovative practices, and in some measure from adjustments in governmental oversight. Their net effect has been to render obsolete many of the laws and regulations governing the industry and to make it imperative to modernize the regulatory framework.

In order to seek some consensus among various interested groups and institutions on the best way to proceed with the process of modernization, The American Assembly convened a meeting at Arden House, Harriman, New York, from April 7 to 10, 1983. Participants attended from the Congress, the executive branch, the regulatory agencies, the full spectrum of the financial services industry, the law, the universities, and the communications media. In preparation for that meeting, the Assembly retained Dr. George J. Benston of the University of Rochester as editor and director of the undertaking. Under his editorial supervision, background papers on various aspects of the American financial services industry were prepared and read by the participants in the Arden House discussions.

The participants, in the course of their deliberations, achieved a substantial consensus on recommendations for public policy. Their proposals, which call for significant measures of deregulation and for greater competition in the industry, also stipulated the need for reasonably priced insurance to protect depositors and for disclosure actions to assure responsible management. Copies of their report, entitled *The Future of American Financial Services Institutions,* can be obtained by writing directly to The American Assembly, Columbia University, New York, New York 10027.

The background papers used by the participants have been compiled into the present volume, which is published as a stimulus to further thinking and discussion about this subject among informed and concerned citizens. We hope this book will serve to provoke a broader national consensus for action to renovate the oversight apparatus for our nation's financial services industry.

Funding for this project was provided by Citicorp, the American Bankers Association, the U.S. League of Saving Institutions, Chase Manhattan Bank, the Bank of America, Beneficial Finance, Merrill Lynch, the Independent Bankers Association, the Securities Industry Association, CIGNA, Lehman Brothers Kuhn Loeb Inc., Chemical Bank, the "Temp Fund," and Marine Midland Bank. The opinions expressed in this volume are those of the individual authors and not necessarily those of the sponsors nor of The American Assembly, which does not take stands on the issues it presents for public discussion.

William H. Sullivan
President
The American Assembly

George J. Benston 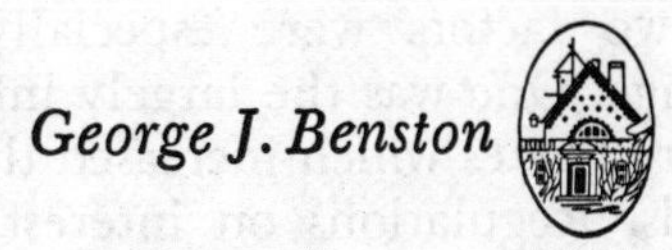

Introduction

Not too many years ago, few books would have had the title "financial services." Rather, the emphasis would have been on financial institutions, and financial services would have been considered as their output. In large measure, this emphasis reflected the specialized nature of the institutions. For example, until recently, savings and loan associations and savings banks (thrifts) in most states were constrained to offer only savings deposits services and mortgages and other loans related to real estate. They were not permitted to offer checking accounts, consumer cash loans, and general business loans. Consumer cash loans were offered only by commercial banks and consumer finance companies. Commercial banks could not (and still cannot) underwrite and deal

---

GEORGE J. BENSTON *is professor of accounting, economics, and finance at the Graduate School of Management of the University of Rochester and is a visiting scholar at the Federal Reserve Bank of Atlanta. Previously he taught at the University of Chicago and at Georgia State College and has lectured at the London School of Economics, the London Graduate School of Business Studies, and Hebrew University of Jerusalem. Dr. Benston has consulted for many institutions, including the Federal Reserve Board, the Office of the Comptroller of the Currency, the FDIC, the Federal Home Loan Bank Board, and the National Commission on Consumer Finance, and has acted as expert witness on regulation, SEC, and antitrust cases. The author of numerous books and monographs, he has published widely in professional journals and publications.*

in most securities issues, while investment bankers could not (but now do) offer checking accounts. Thus, one could describe and analyze financial services and institutions concurrently.

Two factors were especially important for bringing about change. One was the largely inflation-caused increase in nominal interest rates which increased the opportunity value of depository funds. Regulations on interest rates, on services that could be offered, and on entry and expansion prevented the traditional institutions from competing for depositors' funds. This gave others an incentive to bid for the funds with alternative services. The second factor was the reduced cost of effecting financial transactions as computer facilities became better and less expensive. These factors—the higher opportunity value of competing with traditional institutions and the lower cost of doing so—resulted in an influx of new institutions and services into the market.

As a consequence of these changes, the structure of regulations and institutional arrangements that have characterized the U.S. market for financial services is changing—some might say crumbling. But change rarely occurs in sharp jumps; rather, the future tends to evolve from the past. Hence it is important to understand the history and present positions of the institutions that provide financial services as a means of predicting their future, as well as that of the market itself.

Thomas Huertas's chapter, "The Regulation of Financial Institutions: A Historical Perspective on Current Issues," provides a brief overview of the regulatory structure of U.S. financial institutions. He describes the three regimes of regulation—chartered banking (through 1837), free banking (1838–1933), and cartel banking (1934–1983). In this review, he considers the solutions to past problems that our predecessors attempted. These experiences provide us with lessons that we would be well advised to learn in facing our current problems.

My chapter considers "The Regulation of Financial Services" first by delineating the types of services provided and then by specifying the ways that the different providers of these services are extensively and inconsistently regulated. (These sections also serve as an outline of the subject of this book.) After this, the rationale for regulation is examined, from which I assess the prospects for change in the regulatory structure and give my suggestions for reform. In brief, I suggest that, with the exception of deposit insurance, most regulations are not useful except for those who benefit from constraints on competition.

"Payments System Developments and Public Policy" are discussed by Paul Horvitz. He sketches the history and describes the present status of the U.S. payments system. He points out that, despite some dire prediction to the contrary, the system has stood up well to the increasing demands placed upon it. From his review of the system and its evolution, he concludes that "there is little reason for public concern with its development." However, high nominal interest rates, together with regulatory constraints, have disrupted the system. Horvitz delineates and reviews the problems that are likely to affect the payments system. He observes that while these problems will affect individual participants and groups of institutions, "there is little justification for increased government intervention into the evolution of the system."

Commercial banks are the principal institution providing payments services. Their future in the financial services industry is considered by George Kaufman, Larry Mote, and Harvey Rosenblum. They first describe recent developments, pointing out that interest-sensitive funds have become an increasingly important part of banks' liabilities. Legal and regulatory changes have permitted a greater diversification in their activities. Then they analyze the courses of changes and show how the banks have fared in the face of these changes. The authors find that the future for commercial banks depends in part on legislation and regulation, but largely on the actions taken by the banks and their competitors.

In "Bank Holding Companies and Public Policy," Robert Eisenbeis examines the dominant form of banking organization. He first sketches the evolution of holding companies, particularly as they were influenced by laws and regulations. The present regulatory structure also is delineated. Holding companies, he finds, were created largely to avoid restrictions on desired geographic and product diversification that commercial banks could not undertake directly. Tax considerations also play a role. This analysis provides the basis for Eisenbeis's consideration of public policy alternatives, particularly with respect to supervision of holding companies and banks.

"The Role of Government in the Thrift Industry's Net-worth Crisis" is considered by Edward Kane. He first reviews the history and present financial and regulatory status of thrift institutions. Their specialization in long-term assets (mortgages) and short-term liabilities (savings) has made them particularly vulnerable to capital losses caused by unexpected increases in interest rates. Kane shows that this type of risk-taking is due, in large measure, to the way government deposit insurance is priced. He then considers the ways in which the thrifts' problems have been addressed, finds these approaches wanting, and makes some suggestions for reform.

Another important financial service, "Consumer Finance," is analyzed by Richard Peterson. He reviews the history of consumer credit, particularly its regulation, and then describes and evaluates the regulations, which include usury laws, the Truth-in-Lending Act, the Equal Credit Opportunity Act, the Fair Credit Billing Act, consumer bankruptcy laws, and other legislation. He finds that the effect of these laws (each of which Peterson analyzes) on consumer markets has been substantial and generally not salutary.

"Financial Innovation" is described by Stuart Greenbaum and Bryon Higgins as "a process by which the financial system adapts to environmental shocks in the form of changes in technology, demand, and public regulation." Though the preceding chapters deal with financial innovation and its effects on the institutions analyzed, this chapter considers the effects of the adaptation process on the entire financial market. To this end, the authors first describe the traditional function of the financial system and then assess the profound effects of inflation on the system. The effect of the other principal motivator of financial innovation, government regulation, is considered next. In particular, they examine the government's role as guarantor of the financial system. The authors then apply their analysis to an assessment of three theories of financial innovation, from which they draw conclusions about future developments.

In the last full chapter, Almarin Phillips and Donald Jacobs reflect on their experiences as codirectors of the 1971 Hunt commission (the Presidential Commission on Financial Structure and Regulation). They describe the process by which the recommendations presented in the commission's report were agreed to and the problems in getting the recommendations adopted legislatively. In particular, they identify the sources of resistance to reform legislation. Finally, they assess the considerable costs of the failure to deregulate.

As can be seen from these very brief summaries, the chapters of this book are designed to provide descriptions of the histories and present status of the institutions that supply financial services. The regulations that constrain and govern the institutions and the forces that affect them and result in changes are delineated. Since each chapter was written and can be read independently of the others, some descriptions and analyses of these regulations, institutions, and changes necessarily are repeated. The authors also drew their policy conclusions independently, some of which are in conflict (though most are not). Hence, the book concludes with a listing of key public policy issues, set forth in the form of questions, rather than with policy prescriptions. How these questions are answered, together with ongoing environmental forces and gradually changing institutional structures, will determine the way financial services are provided to the American public.

Thomas F. Huertas

1

The Regulation of Financial Institutions:

A Historical Perspective on Current Issues

The task of regulating financial institutions is not new. In the first decades after independence no question in American politics inspired more controversy than banking. It symbolized larger issues, the type of society the United States should become: a powerful nation-state or a nation of states, a merchant aristocracy or a yeoman democracy. All agreed that banking was a public trust, requiring some form of regulation via a corporate charter. But who should receive charters, and who should charter banks? What should banks do, and where should they be permitted to do it?

The answers to these questions, adopted then and in subsequent generations, influence the choices open to the country in the 1980s. They have not only shaped the financial system, but they color the views of every participant in the debate concerning what reforms, if any, are desirable. This chapter reviews the

---

THOMAS F. HUERTAS *has a Ph.D. in economics from the University of Chicago. He is vice president of Citibank, where he currently heads an economics department special projects section that analyzes the economics of strategic and regulatory issues facing Citicorp. He has written for* Foreign Affairs *and the* Journal of Economic History *and is coauthor of the forthcoming book* The Bank for All: A History of Citibank, 1812–1968.

solutions of our predecessors and draws some lessons from their experience.

During its history the nation has employed three regimes to regulate its financial system. The first, chartered banking, ended in 1837. The second era, free banking, the longest to date, lasted from 1838 until the end of the Great Depression in 1933. The third system, cartel banking, began with the New Deal legislation on banking and securities. By 1983 it was in its death throes.

Each of these three regimes has balanced three objectives—structure, safety, and stability. The first concerns the degree of competitiveness in the industry; the second, the risk associated with a bank's liabilities, either notes or deposits; and the third, the effect of the financial system on the development and stability of the economy as a whole.

Like other types of regulation, financial regulation is determined in a political marketplace. Each regulatory regime has balanced structure, safety, and stability in a way that reflects the relative strength of the constituencies affected by financial regulation—financial firms, their customers, the public, and the regulators themselves. No regulatory regime is ever static. Like the economic marketplace, the political market operates continuously. Constituents constantly seek to obtain in the political marketplace objectives not obtainable in the economic marketplace. Conversely, constituents innovate in the economic marketplace to offset the adverse impacts of regulations crafted in the political marketplace.

Major changes in the system of financial regulation have followed crises in the industry and the economy. These convulsions alter drastically the relative strength of constituencies affected by financial regulation, undermining the economic and political assumptions underlying the regulatory regime. The new regime establishes new ground rules, strengthening some constituencies at the expense of others. This makes regulatory reform a slow and contentious process.

Chartered Banking (through 1837)

In the chartered banking era, structure was the dominant concern. From this era the United States has inherited a prohibition against nationwide banking—a banking structure that distinguishes it from practically every other nation. This prohibition resulted from a squabble over states' rights. Although the Constitution gave the federal government the right to issue currency, it left open the question of whether the states or the federal government could charter banks with the power to issue notes, a close substitute for currency. Initially, both the states and the federal government claimed and exercised this right. The states chartered many banks; the federal government, just two, the First (1791–1811) and Second (1816–1836) Banks of the United States.

This was a crucial difference, for the federally chartered banks aroused intense opposition among their state chartered rivals. In its time, each of the federal banks had several advantages, born of its mandate to help the government manage its finances and to promote the nation's economic growth and development. Each bank had the federal government's deposit account, the right to circulate its own notes as legal tender, and a nationwide system of branches. Moreover, each exercised some control over its state chartered competitors by refusing to accept their notes unless convertible into specie, which limited the state chartered banks' ability to expand their note circulation and loans. With these advantages, the branches of both the First and the Second Banks of the United States became leading commercial banks in the cities in which they were located. Together the branches made each federally chartered bank a colossus, far outranking state chartered rivals in capital and assets.

Success proved the undoing of both the First and the Second Banks of the United States. Their charters were not perpetual, but limited to twenty-years duration, as were the charters of most state banks. The First Bank was killed in 1811 when Congress refused to renew its charter. Following the War of 1812 and the general suspension of specie payments by state chartered banks, Congress reconsidered its decision. In 1816 it chartered the Second Bank of the United States to help the federal government manage its finances and to help restore specie convertibility.

Once again, however, the federal bank proved too successful. Under Nicholas Biddle, president from 1823 to 1836, the Second Bank was not only the largest commercial bank in the United States, but something of a central bank as well. Its power earned it enemies, most formidable among them the president of the United States, Andrew Jackson. To Jackson, the Second Bank was a symbol of corporate power, monopoly and privilege, political corruption, and social inequality, as well as an institution of doubtful constitutionality. It was also a useful political issue. With the 1832 election approaching, Jackson vetoed the bill extending the bank's charter, thereby establishing himself as the champion of the people against the money power. With the demise of the Second Bank, the federal government in fact ceded to the states the right to determine where banks could branch, a right that the states have exercised ever since.

Although opposed to the "monopoly" power of the federally chartered bank, state chartered banks were not themselves innocent of trying to use the power of the state to exclude others from the business of banking. In fact, no sooner did a bank obtain a charter than it sought to close the door to others behind it. Despite the country's rapid economic growth, existing banks uniformly maintained that the banking market was saturated and that new banks would endanger the solvency of the old. This was the start of another American banking tradition—invoking concern for safety as a means of stifling competition.

Frequently the only path to a banking charter was bribery or chicanery, particularly in the first decade of the nineteenth century, when economic growth was rapid and the number of banks small. The correspondingly high value of a banking charter escaped neither the politicians granting it nor the bankers seeking it, for both were generally merchants. Ultimately they struck deals profitable to all. The state received a bonus or loan at low interest; the legislators, financial support; and the bankers, the right to borrow from the public by issuing bank notes.

As more banks began operation, the resistance to new charters died down. Each existing bank had less and less to fear from a new entrant, and the costs of organizing opposition to a new bank rose as the number of banks increased. As a result, banking became more and more competitive, weakening the presumption that chartered banks would necessarily be profitable and, therefore, safe banks.

Following the failure of several small banks, New York State took measures to protect noteholders in the case of bank failure. In 1829 it passed the Safety Fund Act—the nation's first experiment with the insurance of bank liabilities. It failed, for the act was ill-designed for the intended purpose and probably increased the probability that a bank would fail. The establishment of the insurance fund lowered the risk of bank notes and enhanced banks' ability to keep them in circulation. At the same time, however, the act taxed a bank's capital rather than its outstanding note circulation. It thereby encouraged banks to increase their leverage, a clear example of the phenomenon known as "moral hazard" that afflicts any type of insurance scheme.

Free Banking (1838 through 1933)

The Panic of 1837 ushered in the free banking era. This regime separated the three concerns of regulation—safety, stability, and structure—and developed rules to address each. To make notes safe, regulators forced banks to post collateral against their outstanding circulation. To ensure stability the government largely relied on the gold standard, although following the Panic of 1907 a lender-of-last-resort was created with ultimately disastrous effects. The structure of the banking industry promoted efficiency. Entry was free. Prospective bankers no longer needed special acts of the legislature to start operations as they had in the chartered banking era. Although charters were required, these were freely available to bankers who met certain minimum requirements. Within this context banks participated in the trend toward nationwide, department store finance—the very trend emerging in the 1980s and the phenomenon that the post–1933 regulatory system of cartel banking was designed to prevent. We therefore examine the free banking regime in some detail.

SAFETY

New York State began the movement toward free banking in 1838, when it completely revised its banking law. The failure of many banks in the Panic of 1837 made safety of bank notes the key concern. The new code dropped the idea of insurance for noteholders and forced banks to post collateral for the notes that they issued to the public. If the bank failed, the collateral could be sold and the noteholders reimbursed from the proceeds. Securing notes by bonds removed the chief rationale for the alternative of limiting entry into banking, and the new act eliminated the requirement for each bank to obtain a charter from the legislature. Instead, entry into banking became free, subject only to the bank's meeting a minimum capital requirement.

From New York and Michigan (which had passed a similar law in 1837), the revolution in banking regulation spread quickly to other states. By 1860, eighteen of the nation's thirty-three states had adopted free banking, and these included the most populous and heavily industrialized states. During the Civil War free banking received a further boost, when the federal government created a new national banking system modeled on that of New York. Thereafter, the country had a dual banking system. Except for restrictions on branching, entry was completely free, and prospective banks could choose either a federal or state charter. After 1866 notes became completely safe. State bank notes were taxed out of existence, and national bank notes were backed by the bonds of the federal government.

STABILITY

Initially, stability was not a major concern of the free banking regime. It was considered more of a currency question than a banking question. Following the demise of the Second Bank of the United States, the federal government became its own banker. The Independent Treasury System, created in 1846, managed the government's finances. The ultimate guarantor of economic stability was to be the smooth operation of the gold standard. The government was to ensure that the dollar would remain convertible into gold at a fixed price.

The government assumed no responsibility for the solvency of individual banks or for the stability of the banking system. Each bank had to maintain its own liquidity and reserves. Individual banks could and did fail. In some cases depositors suffered losses, for there was no federal deposit insurance. Depositors therefore considered risk as well as return in deciding where to place their funds.

Banks themselves, especially the members of the New York Clearing House, assumed responsibility for the stability of the banking system. To preserve the system they sometimes suspended the rules regarding reserve requirements and the convertibility of deposits into currency at par. Although these measures were effective in halting panics once they had started, after the Panic of 1907 banks lobbied for the creation of a bankers' bank that would serve as a lender-of-last-resort.

This was the Federal Reserve, created in 1913. Its chief purpose was to put an end to banking panics. Its mechanism was the discount window. The Federal Reserve stood ready to lend to member banks, on the basis of "real bills," short-term, self-liquidating commercial loans. This would permit solvent, but temporarily illiquid, banks to obtain cash in a crisis. It would also encourage banks to hold "productive" paper in their portfolios rather than "speculative" paper, such as corporate bonds or call loans collateralized by securities. According to the real-bills doctrine, such a portfolio shift by banks would reduce the probability of a banking panic occurring at all.

However, the Federal Reserve quickly became more than a bankers' bank. Soon after its establishment, World War I broke out, suspending the international gold standard, whose continuing operation the Federal Reserve Act had implicitly assumed. The United States emerged from the war as the world's dominant economic power. It also held the major portion of the world's gold stock. The world went onto a dollar standard, and the Federal Reserve inherited the responsibility of running it—a responsibility that its creators had never envisaged. This conflicted with the more limited aims originally assigned the Federal Reserve and with the tenets of the real-bills doctrine embodied in the Federal Reserve Act.

Disaster was the consequence. In the years 1929 to 1933 the Federal Reserve let the nation's money supply fall by 33 percent. This produced the Great Depression. After nearly a decade of monetary and price stability, the abrupt, massive, and unexpected decline in the nation's money stock induced firms and individuals across the country to slash their spending. As they did, output and employment fell; bankruptcies rose. As firms failed, so did their banks. From 1930 through 1933, over 9,000 banks, more than 33 percent of those in existence at the end of 1929, suspended operations, most of them never to resume.

None of this was intentional. Indeed, the calamity resulted from policy makers' rigid adherence to the two precepts thought to guarantee stability: the real-bills doctrine and the gold standard. The former made the Federal Reserve unable to extend credit to banks without eligible paper, and the latter made it unwilling to engage in large-scale, open-market purchases, lest it fail to maintain the gold backing for its notes at the minimum required by law. As a result, the Federal Reserve failed to prevent the worst banking panic in the nation's history.

BRANCH BANKING

The tradition of state control over branching, established during the chartered banking era, continued throughout the free banking period. Although the National Banking Act contained no explicit provisions regarding branching, the Office of the Comptroller of the Currency (OCC) ruled soon after the establishment of the national banking system in 1864 that national banks should be unit banks.

At the time this made little difference; though most states prohibited it, branching within states was unattractive economically. By the end of the nineteenth century, however, the inability of national banks to branch put them at a competitive disadvantage vis-à-vis state chartered banks. Increasing urbanization and the advent of new communication technologies, such as the telephone, made branching within states attractive. State chartered banks began to develop branch systems within and around major metropolitan centers in states, such as California and New York, which allowed limited branching.

Greater branching powers added to the advantages of lower reserve and capital requirements that state chartered banks enjoyed relative to national banks. Owners of national banks partially offset this disadvantage in a variety of ways (also employed by state banks in states with restrictive branching laws). Some acquired interests in other banks, creating chains of banks which they operated approximately like a branch system. Other national banks established state chartered banks as affiliates or employed holding companies to acquire control of other banks. However, none of these devices was as efficient as a branch system.

The advent of chain banking concerned the OCC, which chartered and supervised the national banks, as did the growing numbers of national banks converting to state charters. As early as 1896, the OCC recommended repeal of the unit banking rule for national banks, but only in 1913 did national banks receive authority under the Federal Reserve Act to open branches, but only outside the United States. The road to domestic branches for national banks would be long and bitterly contested by state chartered banks and small, rural national banks who feared competition from big-city giants.

The first step toward domestic branching by national banks came in 1918, when a national bank became able to acquire the existing branches of a state bank, if it could persuade the state bank to convert itself to a national bank and then merge. This device did not, however, permit a national bank to open *de novo* branches. Further progress came in 1922. After Congress had again failed to act on the OCC's recommendation that the National Banking Act be amended to allow *de novo* domestic branching, the OCC reversed a long-standing policy and allowed national banks to establish offices in areas where state banks were allowed to branch. These offices, known as "teller's windows," could accept deposits but could not make loans. Full-service offices, however, were definitively prohibited by a 1924 Supreme Court decision.

Only in 1927 did national banks gain the right to establish *de novo* branches. The McFadden Act represented a compromise between those concerned about the safety and stability of the banking system and those opposed to branching. Failures of hundreds of banks in the west and south had weakened the opposition to branch banking. So had the increase in the number of national banks converting to state charters to obtain greater branching powers. Once a bank had obtained a state charter, it could also leave the Federal Reserve System. Many did so, thus reducing the Fed's control over the banking system. To counter this trend the Federal Reserve recommended, and Congress approved, greater branching powers for nationally chartered banks. By allowing national banks to branch within their headquarters' city (providing state banks were permitted to do so), the act put nationally chartered banks more on a par with state chartered banks.

Pressure soon arose for further liberalization of the branching laws. In California, A.P. Giannini had succeeded in building a statewide branching system through a concerted acquisition program and deft use of the holding company device. Giannini then proposed to do across the nation what he had done in California.

In 1928 his holding company acquired a new name, Transamerica Corporation, and a new bank, the Bank of America of New York, to go along with the Bank of Italy in California. From its bases on each coast Transamerica was poised to acquire banks in other states. By 1929, the United States was on the verge of nationwide banking.

COMPREHENSIVE FINANCE

Transamerica Corporation also typified a second phenomenon characteristic of the free banking era—the trend toward comprehensive finance. Modeling themselves on department stores, financial firms, especially the largest ones, sought to offer individuals and institutions a full array of financial services, including deposits, credit, fiduciary, investment, and insurance services. The trend toward comprehensive finance arose in response to market forces and came despite the opposition of firms who sought regulation as protection for their niches in particular product or geographic markets. With economic development came greater sophistication and a wider variety of financial instruments, each with its own risk, return, and liquidity characteristics. As a customer's demands became more diverse, financial firms had a clear incentive to make their service more comprehensive. Knowledge of the customer's financial situation necessary to sell and manage commercial banking, investment banking, and trust or insurance services could be used to sell and manage all financial services.

At first, however, insurance and trust companies pointed the way toward comprehensive finance. In the early nineteenth century many insurance companies conducted a banking as well as an insurance business. At the turn of the century the leading insurance companies underwrote securities and owned banks and trust companies. Potentially, they could have integrated these services into a comprehensive package. It was not to be. New York State's Armstrong Investigation of 1905 exposed potential and actual conflicts of interest in the simultaneous conduct of the investment banking and insurance businesses. Rather than regulate these businesses jointly, New York State chose to segment the two. A 1906 law prohibited insurance companies operating within New York State from underwriting securities and forced them to divest their holdings of stock, including stock in commercial banks and trust companies.

Trust companies also provided comprehensive financial service. Generally, these state chartered firms provided commercial and investment banking services in addition to the fiduciary and investment management services implied by the trust company label. This ability to offer comprehensive financial service, coupled with tax advantages and lower reserve requirements, enabled trust companies to gain ground in underwriting and commercial lending in the late nineteenth century at the expense of other financial firms.

Initially, banks stood at a competitive disadvantage relative to trust and insurance companies, which were able to offer a full line of financial services to customers directly or through subsidiaries. This was especially true of national banks, whose investment banking, trust, and insurance powers were limited by the National Banking Act and rulings of the OCC. The problem facing national banks became acute at the turn of the century, with the shift from owner to management control. Prior to 1900, the owners of large national banks often also had owned and operated trust companies, underwritten securities, and helped manage insurance companies. As individuals, therefore, they were in a position to offer comprehensive financial service to their customers. The shift to management control and widely dispersed stock ownership—the hallmark of the modern corporation—threatened to destroy this coordination, unless some way could be found for the firm to do what its owners had done as individuals.

In 1902 the OCC further aggravated the problem facing national banks by restricting their existing investment banking powers. From their inception American banks had underwritten and traded government bonds and provided long-term credit to corporations by repeatedly renewing short-term credits as they came due, a form of credit so common as to earn a name—accommodation paper. When a market for railroad and industrial bonds developed during the latter half of the nineteenth century, banks followed, and in some cases led, their customers to the bond market, trading, underwriting, and buying bonds for their own portfolios. In most respects the bond was equal to the accommodation paper it replaced. It had the same credit risk and the same effective maturity. In one respect, however, the bond was superior—it had greater liquidity, and in the last decade of the nineteenth century banks began to use corporate bonds as a secondary reserve.

This alarmed the OCC, which ruled in 1902 that a national bank's holdings of a corporation's bonds would henceforth be included in the calculation of the assets subject to the legal limit of 10 percent of the bank's capital and surplus for loans to a single borrower. This placed national banks at a disadvantage relative to other underwriters, such as state chartered banks and trust companies, private banks, and insurance companies, that were subject to less stringent lending limits or to none at all. In response to this ruling and to the problems posed by the shift to management control, national banks engaged in underwriting securities created the security affiliate, a separately incorporated company subject to state law and linked by common ownership to the bank. This affiliate conducted underwriting activities, the risks of which were borne by the stockholders alone. After New York State's Armstrong Law (1906) limited the underwriting activities of insurance companies, national banks picked up much of the slack, directly or through affiliates. Although the Pujo committee (1912) decried the practice of investment banking by commercial banks, Congress as a whole condoned it, refusing to prohibit it in either the Federal Reserve (1913) or the Clayton Antitrust (1914) Acts. Indeed, the Federal Reserve Board went a step further, allowing state chartered banks and trust companies to become members without giving up their investment banking powers. National banks interpreted this as a sign that they too could continue to engage in investment banking activities, either directly or through affiliates. Congress confirmed this in 1927. The McFadden Act codified the investment banking powers of national banks and formally recognized their security affiliates, authorizing the OCC to determine what securities affiliates might underwrite. Although the comptroller restricted the bank itself to debt issues, he granted affiliates the power to underwrite equity issues as well.

Thus, by the end of the 1920s, national banks were at the forefront of the trend toward "department store" finance. The union between commercial and investment banking remained intact. Leading underwriters had extensive deposits and commercial loans. Leading commercial lenders underwrote and distributed securities through affiliates.

Trust services were also provided by these firms. Although the National Banking Act did not permit national banks to provide trust services, owners of national banks overcame this disadvantage by acting as individual trustees or by acquiring control of a trust company and running it in conjunction with the bank, or after 1903, by forming affiliates to conduct trust operations. In 1913, the Federal Reserve Act granted national banks trust powers, but a clarifying amendment was required before national banks began to engage in trust business on a large scale. Starting in 1919, they began to open their own trust departments. Further impetus was given to trust banking by national banks in 1927, when the McFadden Act granted them perpetual charters, placing them on a par with state chartered trust companies. In response, many national banks transformed their affiliates into trust departments or merged with leading trust companies. By the end of the 1920s, the specialized trust company was becoming a thing of the past. Trust services were increasingly provided together with commercial and investment banking.

In some cases these financial department stores provided insurance as well. Although banks were generally prohibited from engaging directly in the underwriting or distribution of insurance, holding companies could and did acquire banks and insurance companies. One of the most prominent was Transamerica Corporation, which, in 1930, acquired Occidental Life Insurance to complement its interests in commercial, investment, and trust banking. Other firms, large and small, were following Transamerica's example, and these diversified intermediaries were providing a growing proportion of the nation's commercial, investment, and trust banking services. Plainly, the department store approach to finance seemed the wave of the future.

Cartel Banking

Then came the Great Depression. Commercial banks, in particular large banks with security affiliates, were made scapegoats for the worst economic disaster in the nation's history. Regulation became punitive. The efficiency of the financial system was sacrificed to the aims of safety and stability.

According to Congress, stability depended on a safe banking system, and this required that each bank be safe. That in turn implied that each bank should be consistently profitable. The solution was to limit the risk to which a bank could expose itself and to restrict the competition to which a bank could be exposed. In practical terms this meant two things: first, segmenting banking from other forms of finance, and, second, creating a cartel among the banks that had survived the Great Depression.

GLASS-STEAGALL AND THE SEGMENTATION OF THE FINANCIAL SERVICES INDUSTRY

Segmentation of commercial and investment banking was the first priority. The Banking Act of 1933, popularly known as the Glass-Steagall Act, reflected the general conviction that the banking practices of the 1920s, identified as speculative, had caused the banking panics and the depression. In the vocabulary of 1933, "speculation" meant primarily the activity of banks and their affiliates as investors, underwriters, and distributors of securities. It followed logically enough that if banks had been forbidden to invest in securities, to finance such investments by others, or otherwise to participate in the securities markets—if, in other words, they had been confined to commercial banking and bank assets had been limited to short-term commercial loans and government bonds as the real-bills doctrine demanded—there would have been no depression. Thus, the main thrust of the 1933 legislation was to separate commercial and investment banking. Department store finance was to end. Firms were to choose whether they wanted to be commercial banks or investment banks. Each type of firm would be regulated separately.

Investment banks came under the regulation of a new agency—the Securities and Exchange Commission (SEC). The Securities Act of 1933 and the Securities Exchange Act of 1934 revamped the entire process of underwriting, distributing, and trading securities. The emphasis of the new regime was on disclosure. Together the acts required full and prompt dissemination of information considered by the SEC to be relevant to a company's prospects. Strict controls were imposed on the use of inside information; the formation of pools to manipulate stock prices was prohibited. The legal liability of accountants, corporate officers, brokers, and others who participated in security transactions was defined and extended. It was presumed that investors in the securities markets were sophisticated enough to make and live with their own decisions. Ostensibly, the government's role was simply to ensure that relevant information be accurate and available. Therefore, the actual operation of the exchanges and the structure of the investment banking industry continued to be characterized by self-regulation. In practice, this meant fixed brokerage commissions, a cartel device which limited the operational efficiency of the securities markets and resulted in higher prices to investors until removed in 1975.

Subsequent legislation further extended the segmentation principle. The Bank Holding Company Act of 1956 brought all bank holding companies under the supervision of the Federal Reserve Board and limited the activities in which multibank holding companies could engage to those that were closely related and properly incident to banking. The law reflected the Federal Reserve's longstanding concern about the tendency of holding companies in general to unite banking and commerce and about Transamerica in particular, which continued after 1933 to own and add to its stock holdings in financial services companies, including insurance and banks in several western states. In 1970, Congress amended the Bank Holding Company Act, extending it to one-bank holding companies in response to a movement by major banks to use the holding company device as a means of entering other financial businesses. The 1970 amendments also defined a bank as an institution that makes commercial loans and accepts demand deposits. This was consistent with the basic premise of the cartel banking system—banking was a unique line of commerce, whose conduct affected the stability of the entire economy.

LIMITS TO COMPETITION AMONG BANKS

This rationale dictated that commercial banks be subjected to extensive and detailed regulation. Banking had to be made fail-safe, and a cartel, policed and controlled by the regulatory agencies, was the answer. The rules of the cartel, the nation's banking laws, were to have but one purpose—to prevent banks from competing too much either against each other or against other financial intermediaries. Moreover, banks were to be protected against the judgment of the bankers who ran them; they were to restrict their activities to a set of "safe," low-risk activities.

To secure safety the New Deal banking legislation reduced efficiency. The cardinal precept of the chartered banking regime—limited entry—was applied with a vengeance. According to the Banking Act of 1935, applications for new banking charters became subject to a "needs" test, and other laws prohibited nonbanks, such as thrift institutions, from offering demand deposits and other commercial banking services. This practically closed entry into banking and, in effect, created a cartel among the 14,000 banks that survived the Great Depression. Competition among these banks was limited by restrictions on branching, the rates payable on deposits, and by deposit insurance.

The Banking Act of 1933 retained the prohibition against interstate branching. Each state determined where the banks within it could branch; however, a national bank could thereafter branch anywhere that a state bank could. In theory, the restrictions on branching gave each bank a protected local market. In practice, holding companies evaded these restrictions by acquiring banks in more than one state until prohibited by the Bank Holding Company Act of 1956. One exception was made. The so-called Douglas Amendment allowed states to override the prohibition on interstate acquisitions. A state could enact specific legislation permitting out-of-state bank holding companies to acquire banks within the state.

Competition within banking markets was limited by restrictions on the interest rates payable on bank deposits. It was commonly but incorrectly believed that excessive competition by banks for deposits in the 1920s had forced up their costs, propelling them into securities-related activities and from there into receivership. To prevent this from recurring, the Banking Acts of 1933 and 1935 prohibited the payment of interest on demand deposits and empowered the Federal Reserve Board to set ceilings on the interest rates payable on time deposits.

Deposit insurance provided a safety net. It was intended to prevent panics by convincing the small, unsophisticated depositor that the failure of one bank did not mean that all banks were in danger of failing. His own deposits were guaranteed; there was no need to start a run. However, deposit insurance restricted competition as well, as the small banks who supported its passage were well aware. It tended to make the deposits of one bank equivalent to the deposits of any other and made a small bank as safe as a large, geographically diversified (branch) bank. Thus, deposit insurance prevented banks from competing for funds by offering deposits with lower risk and blunted the movement toward branch banking.

A strong central bank was to be the final guarantor of economic stability. New Deal legislation broadened the powers of the Federal Reserve and concentrated the authority to use those powers in the hands of the Federal Reserve Board. In line with the theory that the depression was caused by excessive credit creation and extensive credit diversion to the securities markets, the new powers accorded the Federal Reserve were largely aimed at controlling the amount and use of credit.

Broadest in scope was the power granted to the Federal Reserve Board by the Securities and Exchange Act of 1934 to set margin requirements for loans on the collateral of securities, whether granted by banks or by securities dealers. This extended the Federal Reserve's bailiwick from participants in the securities market (member banks) to the market itself. This would be the precursor of later regulations and legislation empowering the board to regulate consumer credit and the use of credit generally.

Within its traditional banking domain, the Federal Reserve also received broader powers. The Banking Act of 1935 granted the board the authority to vary reserve requirements, a tool thought necessary to control the total volume of bank credit. The Banking Act of 1933 made permanent the power of the Federal Reserve to grant member banks credit on the basis of any of its assets rather than just government securities or "real bills." Coupled with deposit insurance, this enabled the regulatory authorities to prevent, or at least delay, the failure of any bank.

In sum, segmentation and sedation were the guidelines of the New Deal financial system. In order to preserve stability, it was thought necessary to ensure the safety of not only the banking system, but of each individual bank. This demanded a less competitive, and hence less efficient, banking system—in fact, a cartel.

THREE CRISES

A cartel carries within it the seeds of its own destruction. By attempting to mandate extraordinary profits for the industry as a whole, a cartel spurs each of its members to incur extraordinary costs. Firms will spend in order to increase their market share at the expense of others, using product and service improvements to evade the cartel's restrictions on price competition. Thus, cartels do not eliminate competition, but distort it. In the long run members do not earn superprofits, but a normal rate of return.

Even this may be threatened. No market is an island, and no cartel can prevent nonmembers from designing and offering close substitutes at a competitive price. If these substitutes prove attractive to consumers, cartel members may find themselves in a situation where costs are abundant, but customers scarce. If this occurs, the rules of the cartel will not coddle members, but condemn them to extinction as business flows to the unregulated market. If its members are to survive, a cartel must adapt, either by embracing the interlopers or by permitting more open competition. If the cartel does neither, it may spark the very crisis it was intended to prevent.

In broad outline, this has been the history of the nation's financial system since the New Deal. Competition has continued within the segments of banking, securities, and insurance, as well as across their boundaries. The result of regulation has been a succession of crises, each of which has weakened the structure of the cartel system.

In banking, these crises go by the name "disintermediation." The first arose in the late 1950s in connection with corporate deposits. In response to rising interest rates, corporations had begun to economize on interest-free demand balances at commercial banks. Large New York City banks were affected particularly severely, for they depended on such deposits for a major portion of their funding. If they were to survive, the cartel had to allow them to meet the competition from the securities market for corporate cash balances. It did. With the encouragement and approval of the Federal Reserve, the negotiable certificate of deposit (C/D) was introduced in 1960. This allowed banks to compete openly in the marketplace for corporate funds on the basis of price.

This was the beginning of liability management. Until the introduction of the C/D, banks had to limit their assets to their demand and savings deposits and structure their portfolios in anticipation of large and sudden withdrawals. For the first time the C/D gave banks a true time deposit, enabling them to bid for funds to finance loans and other asset acquisitions and to stretch out the effective maturity of their liabilities.

Liability management revolutionized the business of banking. Traditionally, banks had lumped together their two primary activities: the management of risk, or financial intermediation in the broadest sense, and the manufacture of financial transactions, particularly the execution of third-party payments by check. Banks conducted business on the basis of relationships, pricing credit and third-party payment services at levels which compensated customers for the noncompetitive rate of interest paid on deposits. The C/D changed that. Henceforth, the growth in loans, particularly at large banks, would be fueled by C/Ds, a liability that contains no obligation to provide payment services. As a result, banks increasingly became pure financial intermediaries; the relative importance of their depository activities—the reason why banks are regulated differently from other firms—declined.

Disintermediation also sparked the second crisis in the New Deal banking system, centered on the liquidity crunches of 1966 and 1969–70. In order to arrest the growth in bank credit, the Federal Reserve allowed the ceilings on time deposit interest rates to become effective. As rates rose above the ceilings, corporations and consumers began to withdraw deposits from banks and to invest directly in money market securities.

To this crisis the regulatory authorities reacted in two different ways. In 1970, interest rate ceilings were suspended for time deposits of more than $100,000; large depositors simply had too many alternatives (including the Eurodollar market) to make interest rate ceilings effective. This accelerated the revolution in liability management.

With small depositors the regulatory authorities took a different tack. Instead of allowing banks to compete openly for funds, they decided to make the cartel more effective by making disintermediation more difficult and by broadening the cartel's scope to include thrift institutions. The Treasury Department handled the first task by raising the minimum denomination of Treasury bills to $10,000. Congress handled the second, subjecting savings and loan institutions for the first time to interest rate ceilings in the Interest Rate Adjustment Act of 1966.

Savings and loan associations were another example of segmented finance. The Federal Home Loan Bank Act of 1932 provided for the federal chartering of such associations and granted them tax incentives to specialize in home mortgage finance. The National Housing Act of 1934 created a separate deposit insurance corporation, the Federal Savings & Loan Insurance Corporation (FSLIC), to insure savings and loan associations. At first the FSLIC offered less protection to depositors than the Federal Deposit Insurance Corporation did to depositors of commercial banks, making savings and loan deposits somewhat riskier than deposits at commercial banks. In 1950, however, insurance coverage was equalized. Partly as a result, savings and loan associations grew rapidly thereafter relative to commercial banks, for they were able to pay slightly higher rates on deposits of equal risk. In 1966, the Interest Rate Adjustment Act cemented this custom, mandating that thrift institutions be allowed to pay higher rates than commercial banks.

Implicitly, the Interest Rate Adjustment Act also buried concern for bank safety as the reason for restricting competition. In its place the act substituted a new reason—credit allocation. Since savings and loan associations extended a major portion of the country's mortgages, it was reasoned that assuring a steady flow of deposits to these associations at low rates would produce an abundant supply of mortgages at low rates. In effect, the saver was asked to subsidize the builder and the borrower.

This sowed the seeds for the type of crisis that the New Deal legislation was intended to prevent. Starting in 1979, interest rates again soared above Regulation Q ceilings on savings and time deposits. New entrants appeared, ready to compete on the basis of price for consumer deposits. Their device was the money market mutual fund, an instrument that looks and acts like a deposit but pays a market rate of return. Customers flocked to the new instrument, drawing funds from thrift institutions and banks. Thrifts were particularly hard hit, for regulations had induced them to take a large interest rate risk—their fixed-rate, long-term mortgages were funded with short-term deposits. (See chapter 6 for a more extended analysis.) As these deposits left for the money funds, thrifts' earnings were squeezed. For the first time since the Great Depression, the nation was faced with the prospect that large numbers of depository institutions would fail. Instead of preventing disorder, the New Deal legislation had created it.

In response to the crisis, regulators further dismantled rules of the cartel. Restraints on price competition were practically eliminated. The Depository Institutions Deregulation and Monetary Control Act of 1980 provided for the phase-out of Regulation Q ceilings on all time deposits and established an interagency committee to oversee the process. In late 1982 the committee eliminated interest rate ceilings on most deposits of over $2,500, practically establishing free and open price competition for deposits. Congress also expanded the powers of thrift institutions, making them more like commercial banks, and introduced a special form of capital assistance, net-worth certificates, to keep failing thrift institutions in operation.

Considerations for Reform

The crises in cartel banking demonstrated that the New Deal regulations are rules without reason. They did not prevent chaos; instead they promoted it.

From modern intellectual standpoints the New Deal banking legislation appears largely irrelevant to its intended purpose of preventing depressions. Since the early 1930s, views about the role of banks in business fluctuations have changed. Keynesian theories attribute the business cycle to autonomous changes in the public's propensity to invest and consume. Monetary theories trace it to changes in the quantity of money created by the central bank. These theories have largely replaced the notion embodied in the New Deal legislation that the business cycle is driven by the autonomous expansion and contraction of bank credit. Banks, according to modern theories, are transmission belts for disturbances originating elsewhere. They assume risk, but they do not create it, at least not for the economic system as a whole. Creation of risk is largely a product of fiscal and monetary policy.

Sweeping reform of financial regulation is needed. Removing rate ceilings on deposits did not destroy the cartel banking system; it merely repealed its most destructive element. Other elements remain, foremost among them the segmentation of banking from other financial services, the barriers against interstate branching, and deposit insurance. Without further reform, further crises can be anticipated.

A new system of financial regulation is needed. Its concerns should remain the same—a stable economy, safe financial products, and an efficient financial structure. However, the means to these ends should change. Each should be pursued directly. While stability should be the primary concern, society need not promulgate extensive regulations to achieve it. Quite the contrary; stable policies will produce a stable economy. Nothing else will.

What the regulation of financial institutions can do is assure that financial products are "safe" and that the financial system is efficient. How "safe" is a matter for serious debate. Financial institutions manage risk. They bring together savers and investors, acting as an intermediary between the two. They acquire assets suited to the preferences of investors and issue liabilities suited to the preferences of savers. Through diversification and the investment of their own capital, financial institutions are able to assume risks which neither savers nor investors wish to bear. For this they earn a profit. In so doing, they make economic life more certain for both savers and investors. But they do not, and cannot, make it absolutely certain.

George J. Benston

2
The Regulation of Financial Services

Introduction and Overview

Financial services are produced in great variety by a large number of firms and individuals. Some of these services and their producers are regulated by the federal and state governments, while others are not. As a means of establishing the scope of the regulations, brief descriptions of the types of financial services that are the subject of this analysis are presented in the next section. Following this, the types of regulations that pertain to some of these products and some of the producers, as well as a delineation of those products and producers that are not regulated, are given. The rationale for these regulations are then considered. The historical reasons for regulation are given and assessed first, and then the forces that support or explain regulation are specified. This analysis is followed by a brief assessment of the benefits and costs of regulation. Finally, conclusions and recommendations are presented.

Dr. Benston gratefully acknowledges helpful comments and suggestions by Robert Eisenbeis, Thomas Huertas, Edward Kane, George Kaufman, Larry Mote, and Richard Peterson.

Types of Financial Services

The range of financial services is very wide and seems to be widening. To reduce the list to manageable proportions, the services can be categorized as follows: (1) transactions deposits, including demand deposits and negotiable order of withdrawal (NOW) accounts; (2) savings (investments); (3) short-term borrowing; (4) long-term borrowing; (5) equity securities; (6) other financial transfers; and (7) financial planning and advice. Financial services also can be dichotomized into those provided to consumers and to business and those provided domestically and internationally. However, the categories and dichotomies suggested cannot be precisely delineated. For example, the distinction between transactions and savings deposits is becoming blurred; the dividing point between a short- and a long-term loan never was clear; some consumer loans are made for business reasons; and funds flow across or around national boundaries. Nevertheless, at least the seven-part categorization suggested above allows one to make a reasonably compact and concise description of the products provided by the industry. It also demonstrates that the differences among the products often are slight, which makes it difficult, and often fruitless, to maintain distinctions among institutions that provide these nominally different products.

TRANSACTIONS DEPOSITS

The transfer of funds with negotiable instruments, such as checks, is one of the most useful of financial services. It reduces considerably the transactions costs of making fund transfers over alternatives such as currency or other property. Transfers by check also provide the parties with control over the amounts and timing of the transactions and with a record that can be used as legally admissible evidence. Funds also are transferred electronically, with a printout provided as a record of the transaction. This form of transfer is often less expensive than paper check transfers, particularly for large amounts when the opportunity value of time is an important cost consideration, and it is becoming still less expensive as technological improvements are made and adopted. Other relatively recent developments are transfers by telephone and by automatic teller machines (ATMs). (See chapter 3 of this volume.) But, for many consumers, the advantages of paper check transfers are likely to persist at least for several years.

SAVINGS (INVESTMENTS)

Dollar-denominated savings accounts give people the opportunity to invest in the amounts and for the periods they wish at very low transactions costs. The investments usually are placed in a portfolio of assets and usually are insured by a federal agency. Time deposits are similar, but the period to maturity is specified. These deposits can be represented by a certificate of deposit (C/D), which may be negotiable. Shares in money market mutual funds are very similar to savings accounts, except that they represent a claim on specified market-valued assets. However, since these assets, generally commercial bank C/Ds and U.S. Treasury bills, tend to be almost risk-free and of short maturity, the differences between the funds and savings accounts are small.

People also may invest in a portfolio of assets by purchasing a share of the market value of the portfolio. Open-end mutual funds, pension funds, and, to a large extent, life insurance contracts are the principal types of this form of saving. The funds offer investors diversification and professional management. The open-end funds permit them to invest and withdraw the amount they wish, when they wish. The money market mutual funds even permit withdrawal by check, usually if over a specified amount. The pension and life insurance funds and contracts offer a combined product of annuities and life insurance and tax-sheltered income.

SHORT-TERM BORROWING

Two forms characterize the borrowing of funds for relatively short periods. One is loans by such lenders as banks and finance companies. The amounts lent and repayment terms are tailored to the demands of the borrower and the concerns of the lender. For most individuals and smaller enterprises, information that allows the lender to assess the probability of nonrepayment is a major concern. Borrowers and lenders benefit from a reasonably close, personal relationship which reduces the cost of information and permits flexibility in the amounts, repayment schedules, and other terms of the loans. The second form, direct borrowing and lending via commercial paper, takes advantage of positive public knowledge about the borrower and the preference of borrowers and lenders for dealing in relatively large dollar amounts. Commercial paper also permits borrowers and lenders to avoid the costs of federal regulations, particularly the prohibition of interest payments on demand deposits, and taxes in the form of non-interest-bearing required reserves on deposits.

LONG-TERM BORROWING

When the interest rate on long-term debt varies with the market rate of interest, it is very similar to short-term debt that is renewed periodically. Fixed interest rate long-term debt, on the other hand, is riskier, since its value can change considerably with unexpected changes in interest rates. Long-term borrowing generally is otherwise distinguishable from short-term borrowing principally as regards the instruments that represent the indebtedness. Relatively few lenders provide individuals or businesses with debt maturing in more than four or five years that is not represented by a formal, often marketable, instrument. For individuals, these loans usually are secured with real property (mortgages). For businesses, the instruments usually are bonds that often are secured and that are not fully marketable unless they are registered with the Securities and Exchange Commission (SEC). Bonds not registered under the Securities Act of 1933 may be directly placed, usually with an insurance company.

Although the loans made by regulated institutions and those made by other institutions and individuals are almost indistinguishable, they are treated differently in that commercial banks may make and hold short-term loans and commercial paper and can hold bonds, but they are forbidden by the Glass-Steagall Act from underwriting and dealing in corporate bonds.

EQUITY OBLIGATIONS

Equities represent residual claims against income and assets. Though equities generally are thought of as ownership claims, debt also is a contingent ownership claim. However, the tax treatment of equity and debt differs considerably. In particular, interest on debt is a deductible expense for corporate income taxes while a dividend on equity is not. Regulations also differ; in particular, the Glass-Steagall Act forbids commercial banks from underwriting and dealing in equities. However, they can advance funds to businesses in this form; this usually is done through venture capital subsidiaries because this form offers tax and regulating benefits.

OTHER FINANCIAL TRANSFERS

Financial intermediaries provide the service of facilitating a wide range of financial transfers, such as dividend payments, confirmation of bills of lading, acceptances of notes given in exchange for goods, foreign exchange, and note collection. These transactions are enhanced by the expertise of the intermediary in checking, recording, and transferring trade and other legal documents and in the expectation by the parties that the institution will stand behind its promises and representations.

FINANCIAL PLANNING AND ADVICE

Financial institutions often have a comparative advantage over others in providing technical expertise to individuals and businesses on financial matters. These include the timing and form of financing for projects, choices among investment alternatives, and trustee services for trusts and estates. The institutions' comparative advantages come from their familiarity with financial instruments and markets, their knowledge about customers' business affairs, and the expectation of their customers that the institutions are trustworthy and enduring.

From this very brief listing of products, it should be evident that not only is the range of services great, but also that distinctions among types of services and the institutions that provide them cannot be drawn unambiguously. This situation necessarily complicates, if not completely frustrates, attempts to regulate the industry. At the very least, it results in inconsistent regulation, as is shown below.

Types of Regulation

Producers of financial services are extensively and inconsistently regulated. The regulations affect the following aspects of business behavior: (1) entry; (2) expansion, including type of service offered; (3) contraction, including mergers; (4) prices paid for funds; (5) prices and other terms on loans; (6) supervision of management (financial and performance); and (7) customer relations. The regulating is done by five federal agencies and well over fifty state agencies. In addition, financial institutions are subject to the laws and regulations, such as those promulgated by the SEC and the Federal Trade Commission (FTC), to which most enterprises are subject. But not all suppliers of financial services are specially regulated, and the regulations are applied unevenly to the regulated institutions. The reasons for this state of affairs and its implications are a major concern of this chapter. (Also see chapter 1 of this volume.) But first, each of the forms of regulation, the producers regulated, and the agency that administers the regulations are outlined briefly. Each of the seven types of regulation is discussed as each applies to providers of depository funds transfer services, other savings and investment services, and loans and other forms of indebtedness and equity. This discussion illustrates the inconsistencies with which the alternative suppliers are regulated.

ENTRY

Depository Funds Transfer Services—Most institutions that accept and process transactions deposits and other funds subject to third-party transfers and savings deposits that are essentially transferable on demand are required to get a charter from a state or from the federal government. For the federal government, the Office of the Comptroller of the Currency (OCC) grants national charters to commercial banks; the Federal Home Loan Bank Board (FHLBB) charters savings and loan associations and savings banks; and the National Credit Union Administration (NCUA) charters credit unions.

Prior to 1837, bank charters often were difficult to get since each required a special act by a state legislature; national charters were not an option. Beginning in 1837, many states enacted "free" bank chartering statutes that made charters relatively easy to obtain (by 1860, eighteen of the thirty-three states had enacted such laws). The National Bank Act of 1863, which established federal chartering, continued the relatively unrestrained issuing of charters. But, after the massive failures of the early 1930s, bank charters became very difficult to obtain. These constraints continued until 1962, when Comptroller of the Currency James Saxon liberalized the procedures. In the four years 1962–1965, 515 national banks were chartered, more than double the number chartered over the twelve preceding years. Subsequently, as the opportunity cost of non-interest-bearing reserves that national banks and state chartered Federal Reserve member banks were required to hold increased, so did the number of state chartered nonmember banks, which did not need to join the Federal Reserve System which required them to hold non-interest-earning deposits as reserves.

Thrift institutions, which now can offer transactions as well as time deposits, were chartered essentially by the states until the FHLBB was established in 1932 for savings and loan associations and the Federal Credit Union Act in 1934 for credit unions. Federal mutual savings and loan charters were made rather freely available in the 1930s as a means of encouraging the flow of funds into housing. Beginning in 1978, Title XII of the Financial Institutions Regulatory and Interest Rate Control Act (FIRA) provided for federal chartering by the FHLBB of mutual savings banks. As of 1982, stockholder-owned savings and loan associations can be federally chartered and established in several states, principally California and Illinois. Since 1970, federally chartered mutual credit unions have been supervised by the NCUA.

Chartered depository institutions generally must obtain deposit insurance from a federal agency. The only exceptions are a few hundred banks and savings and loan associations chartered by some states. Commercial banks' and most mutual savings banks' deposits are insured by the Federal Deposit Insurance Corporation (FDIC); savings and loan associations' and some mutual savings banks' deposits are insured by the Federal Savings and Loan Insurance Corporation (FSLIC); and credit unions' deposits are insured by the National Credit Union Share Insurance Fund

(NCUSIF). Some states also operate insurance funds for thrift associations (most notably, Massachusetts).

However, not all acceptors of depository funds are chartered or must carry deposit insurance. The cash management accounts established by some brokerage firms have all of the attributes of transactions deposits, but not federal deposit insurance. Except for federal deposit insurance, money market mutual funds are similar to demand or savings deposits (depending on how the customer views the requirement by most funds that amounts transferred be no less than $500). But, the SEC requires money market mutual funds to restrict their investment to short-term, relatively riskless money market obligations. In addition, neither brokers nor money market mutual funds are required to obtain charters.

Other Savings and Investment Services—Mutual and pension funds are chartered only in the sense that they must be registered with the SEC. Insurance companies are chartered by the states. The states' concern is primarily with the companies' insurance activities and the maintenance of sufficient assets to satisfy the potential claims of policyholders.

Loan and Equity Fund Providers—Banks, thrift institutions, and life insurance companies are chartered, and they are very important providers of loans. Consumer finance companies also are chartered by the states, principally as a consequence of small loan laws that permit higher-than-usury-ceiling interest rates to be charged. All other lenders do not need government permission to lend funds or otherwise invest in enterprises, but they are potentially subject to the usury and securities laws. These unfettered lenders and types of obligations include mortgage companies that make mortgages, usually Federal Housing Administration (FHA) and Veterans Administration (VA) guaranteed; sales finance companies that make loans to purchasers of specified assets; small business finance companies that make loans to enterprises; factors (companies that lend funds to their customers via accounts and notes receivable); and individuals. These lenders also may be affiliates of a one-bank holding company.

Providers of equity capital and of services related to issuing equity and debt need not obtain charters as a prerequisite for offering their services to the public. These providers include brokerage firms, venture capital funds, and individuals. Insurance companies also are important investors in equities and debt obligations, particularly directly placed, not SEC-registered, obligations. Mutual savings banks can hold corporate debt and equities, and commercial banks can invest in corporate debt. But commercial banks are forbidden by the Glass-Steagall Act from directly underwriting or dealing in these obligations, and the National Banking Act and state statutes prevent them from investing in equities. However, with the permission of the Federal Reserve, bank holding companies can acquire brokerage firms that do no underwriting or give investment advice. Banks also can contract with brokers to provide services to the banks' customers, or national banks can provide discount brokerage services directly or through a subsidiary.

EXPANSION

Depository Fund Transfer Services—Expansion can take two forms: locational and functional. Locational expansion of commercial banks and state chartered thrift institutions is limited by state laws that restrict branching. Presently, twelve states prohibit branching, fifteen allow limited branching, and twenty-three permit statewide branching. The McFadden Act, enacted in 1927 and extended by the Banking Act of 1933, and all states prohibit banks that are chartered in another state from operating depository branches in the state. The 1956 Douglas Amendment to the Bank Holding Company Act requires a holding company with bank subsidiaries in one state to obtain the permission of other states in which it wants to have bank subsidiaries. Several states (e.g., Maine, New York, and, by purchase of an existing bank, Alaska) have passed laws giving such permission on a reciprocal basis. Some states (e.g., Massachusetts) have given reciprocal permission only to holding companies domiciled in other states in their region (e.g., New England). Banks legally circumvent this prohibition against nationwide depository banking by operating customer service offices in many cities around the country. While these offices cannot accept deposits directly, they provide almost all other services. Furthermore, banks, as well as thrift institutions, can solicit funds anywhere by mail and through brokers.

There is no federal statutory prohibition against intrastate and interstate branching by federally chartered savings and loan associations and mutual savings banks. Prior to the mid-1970s, the FHLBB followed state laws on branching as a matter of policy. Thereafter, the board increasingly approved branches for federally chartered institutions until, by 1983, branching within states was not constrained. The FHLBB also has permitted—indeed, encouraged—some financially troubled associations that are located in different states to merge, thus establishing interstate institutions.

Functional expansion has been constrained in several ways. Commercial banks are prohibited by the Glass-Steagall Act from underwriting and dealing in corporate bond issues and equities. The act has been interpreted to restrict them from offering full brokerage services to their customers and even from maintaining joint equity mutual funds for trust accounts. Until passage of the Depository Institutions Deregulation and Monetary Control Act of 1980 (DIDMCA), thrift institutions were prohibited in most states from offering transactions deposits, consumer direct cash loans, and services to businesses that were not related to real estate. Since enactment of the Garn–St Germain Depository Institutions Act of 1982, there are no banking services that the thrift institutions cannot legally provide, though they are limited to stated percentages of total assets. More important, however, is the cost of entering already serviced markets, which severely constrains their diversification.

Commercial banks are legally prohibited from offering nonbanking-related (congeneric) products, either directly or indirectly via affiliates. The permitted activities are defined by the Federal Reserve Board. But a holding company with a savings and loan, rather than a commercial bank, subsidiary is not restricted. However, if a bank does not either hold demand deposits or make commercial loans, it is not legally considered a bank and could avoid the restrictions.

Brokerage firms and money market mutual funds that also provide fund transfer and savings services are not legally restricted from establishing branches wherever they wish.

Other Providers of Savings, Loans, and Equities—Except for consumer finance companies, which are restricted by some states from opening offices, there are no restrictions on intrastate or interstate branching for these providers. Nor are they prohibited from providing other financial services, including depository services, such as the cash management accounts offered by brokers.

CONTRACTION

Depository Funds Transfer Services—Chartered financial institutions require the permission of their chartering agency to close branches or merge with another institution. In addition, the Federal Reserve, the FDIC, FSLIC, or NCUSIF must approve the change. The Community Reinvestment Act of 1977 requires that the agencies consider the service rendered to its community by an institution before a change is approved. (As is the case for other enterprises, the Department of Justice also may object to a merger.) Commercial banks generally may not merge with thrift associations, particularly when the thrifts are mutuals. However, in the case of institutions in severe financial difficulties, the Garn–St Germain Act allows for exceptions, and a mutual can own the stock of a commercial bank. But state laws that restrict branching act to prevent mergers of commercial banks in different states.

Other Providers of Savings, Loans, and Equities—No special regulations restrict these suppliers.

PRICES THAT CAN BE PAID FOR FUNDS

Depository Funds Transfer Services—The Banking Act of 1933 and the Federal Deposit Insurance Act prohibit the explicit payment of interest on demand deposits held at chartered financial institutions with insured deposits. The acts also require the Federal Reserve to set ceilings on the interest rates that could be paid on savings and time accounts (Regulation Q). The Interest Rate Adjustment Act of 1966 extended Regulation Q to federally insured thrift institutions. Although the DIDMCA called for a gradual phasing-out of the Regulation Q restrictions by 1986, the ceilings were effectively lifted by regulations adopted by the Depository Institutions Deregulation Committee, established under DIDMCA, in December 1982. Chartered financial institutions were permitted to pay market rates of interest on nonbusiness savings and checking accounts (effectively, to all except corporations). Although some important restrictions still apply (principally on the minimum balances, but also on the number of transactions per month that can be made and the exclusion of corporate accounts), the almost fifty-year experiment with deposit interest rate controls appears to have ended.

However, DIDMCA extended the federal reserve requirements previously imposed only on Federal Reserve member banks to all except very small chartered depository institutions. Non-interest-bearing reserves now are required against all transactions deposits; the required reserve ratios are lower for smaller institutions, but they are to be scaled up over several years. In effect this requirement is a tax on transactions balances in the amount of the interest that the institutions forego on the reserves. It necessarily is passed on to the users of the affected institutions' services.

Other providers of depository and savings services were not legally constrained from offering people the market rate for their funds. Consequently, as inflation pushed up the nominal interest rate beyond the rates that depository institutions could pay (either in interest on savings and time deposits or in "free" services on demand deposits), depositors turned to these other providers to obtain market yields for their funds. Thus, money market mutual funds grew as they provided savers the market rate of interest less the funds' management fees. Similarly, brokers' cash management accounts offered depositors close-to-market rates. Banks and thrifts attempted to meet the competition with such devices as NOW accounts (that were constrained by Regulation Q ceilings), procedures to "sweep" balances above some level into market-interest-bearing instruments, and short-term investment of deposits via repurchase agreements. But these devices were only partially effective in meeting the attraction of market rates of interest. The consequence was the considerable growth of these unregulated alternatives to regular transactions and savings deposits. The regulatory change in December 1982, permitting chartered depository institutions to offer money market fund equivalents, has reversed this movement of funds, since the institutions can offer depositors the advantages of convenience and the safety of deposit insurance.

Other Providers of Savings, Loans, and Equities—The prices that other institutions and individuals can pay for the funds they lend to or invest in enterprises and to people are not legally regulated. However, the interest that can be charged is limited by state usury laws. And the cost of publicly issuing debt and equity is increased by the requirement that they be registered with the SEC. Generally, securities involved in offerings confined to a single state, or made only to "sophisticated" investors and/or a limited number of others, or consisting only of financial instruments that are not regarded as "securities" or that are specifically exempted, are not required to be registered.

PRICES AND OTHER TERMS ON LOANS

Depository Funds Transfer Services—The loans made by chartered depository institutions have been regulated as a means of controlling the risk these investments pose to depositors and the deposit insurance agencies. Institutions are prohibited from making loans to any borrower that amount to over 15 percent of their capital and surplus. Loans to officers and directors also are constrained. In the past, mortgage loans could not be made on properties located more than a specified distance from the institution's offices, and mutual savings banks were prohibited in the late 1800s from making commercial loans because these were considered to be unsafe and subject to possible conflicts of interest. However, these restrictions have been removed. Otherwise, no special regulations on loan prices and other terms have applied to chartered depository institutions.

Other Savings and Investment Services—No special regulations apply, except that the Glass-Steagall Act forbids commercial banks from directly providing investment advisory services.

Loan (and Equity) Fund Providers—State usury laws put ceilings on the rates that can be charged for loans to specified borrowers. These laws date back to ancient religious prohibitions against the charging of interest. The English law (the Statutes of Queen Anne) was copied by the colonies and continued by the states even though England repealed its usury laws in the late eighteenth century. These laws apply to all lenders, with higher ceilings permitted for small consumer loans made by licensed companies. The obvious effect of the ceilings (when they are below the rate that would have been charged in an unregulated market) is to reduce the supply of funds to riskier borrowers, except in two instances. One is where there is little competition in the supply of loans and the ceiling is close to the competitive rate. This situation is rarely, if ever, found. The second is where the threat of political penalties and/or economic subsidies is used to get institutions to lend at less than market rates. This method has been effective in getting some thrift institutions (e.g., mutual savings banks in New York State) to make some mortgage loans when the usury ceilings were binding. At present, state usury ceilings on mortgages are suspended by DIDMCA. Beginning in 1983, state legislatures have three years to legislatively reinstate the usury ceilings, if they wish.

Other loan terms have been regulated at various times. The states specify the minimum down payments on mortgage loans. The states also have specified maximum rates that insurance companies could charge on policyholder loans. The Federal Reserve has been given, and has used, authority to limit the maturity on consumer installment loans and establish margin requirements for loans secured by securities. Moral suasion also has been applied to get Federal Reserve member banks to forego lending to "unworthy" borrowers.

SUPERVISION OVER MANAGEMENT

Depository Funds Transfer Services—The managers of chartered depository institutions are subject to extensive regulatory supervision. The assets in which they can invest, the liabilities they can incur, the business that can be conducted in their offices (including the hours and days of operation), the location of offices, the security arrangements that must be maintained, the capital that must be invested, the character of the organizers, and the transfer of shares among principal owners are regulated in varying degrees by the state and/or federal authorities that granted the institutions their charters and by the deposit insurance agencies. In addition, field examinations of the institutions are conducted by the supervising agencies, usually once every year or two times in three years or more often if considered necessary. Federally chartered institutions are examined by only one agency, by agreement among the agencies. This extensive supervision is undertaken to protect the uninsured depositors from having the bank's assets dissipated and to reduce the losses that the deposit insurance agency might have to incur. It also is argued that the requirement protects the nation's money supply and community well-being from the effect of multiple bank failures as well as the public from abuses of power by bankers. The validity of these concerns is considered below.

Other depository funds transfer service providers, such as brokers' cash management accounts, are not similarly supervised. While they are subject to the SEC's regulations, these are limited to capital requirements, record keeping, and, for money market funds, type of assets held. Detailed supervision and field examinations are not imposed on these suppliers. The rationale for this difference is that, although these deposits are not insured, the present SEC regulatory structure is considered sufficient to protect the investors from fraud and from the gross mismanagement of their investments.

Other Providers of Loans and Equities—Insurance companies are state supervised primarily to protect the holders of insurance contracts and their beneficiaries from imprudent, incompetent, or dishonest managers who might dissipate or divert the assets required to meet the companies' obligations. This supervision includes regulations specifying the types of assets that can and cannot be held for investment, the reserves that must be maintained, the filing of reports with state insurance commissioners, and occasionally field examinations when considered necessary. Pension funds are subject to the reporting requirements of the Employee Retirement Income Security Act (ERISA). State licensed small loan companies have to file annual reports. Except for the reporting requirements of the SEC, the managers of these and other suppliers of savings and investment services are not otherwise supervised.

CUSTOMER RELATIONS

Depository Funds Transfer Services—Customers of a chartered depository financial institution who are dissatisfied with the service they receive may complain to the institution's supervising agency. Unless the complaint clearly is unjustified, and particularly if it alleges invidious discrimination, the institution will be asked to explain its action. Field examinations also are conducted by the supervising agencies to see that the institutions have complied with the laws and regulations that forbid specified types of invidious discrimination and business practices.

The Electronic Fund Transfer Act (Title IX of the Consumer Credit Protection Act—CCPA), enacted in 1978, requires disclosure to the customer of account terms, documentation of transfers, and prompt resolution of errors. It also limits the consumer's liability for unauthorized transfers and imposes liability for unauthorized transfers by financial institutions. The Currency and Foreign Transactions Reporting Act, enacted in 1970 and upheld by the Supreme Court in 1974, requires financial institutions to file a report (IRS Form 4789) on each deposit, withdrawal, exchange of currency, or other transfer exceeding $10,000. Individuals also are required to file reports of large transfers.

Several states have enacted "truth in savings" laws that specify how institutions should inform savers about the ways interest is compounded and recorded, the fees that are charged, penalties for early withdrawal that are charged, and so forth.

Other Savings and Investment Services—No special laws or regulations govern the relationship of these enterprises and their customers.

Loan and Equity Fund Providers—A fairly large number of federal and state laws govern the practices of lenders. The Fair Housing Act of 1968 prohibits lenders from denying mortgages or house improvement loans due to a person's race, color, religion, sex, or national origin. The Equal Credit Opportunity Act (Title VII of the CCPA), enacted in 1974 and amended in 1976, added prohibitions against all credit discrimination on the grounds of age, race, religion, national origin, receipt of welfare benefits, and exercise of rights under the CCPA. Regulations written under the dictate of the community Reinvestment Act of 1977 forbid the alleged practice of denying mortgage and home improvement loans on properties solely because they are old or are located in older urban areas—a practice known as redlining. The Home Mortgage Disclosure Act, enacted in 1975, requires federally chartered financial institutions to report publicly the location of the properties on which they make mortgages and other information about the mortgages.

Other laws provide borrowers with information and forbid

certain practices by lenders. The Truth-in-Lending Act of 1968 (Title I of the CCPA) requires disclosure of a standard interest rate and other terms on consumer loans and long-term leases of consumer goods. It also regulates the content of credit advertising and credit card distribution, terms, and liabilities. The Real Estate Settlement Practices Act, enacted in 1974 and amended in 1976, requires mortgage lenders to provide borrowers with a statement of actual charges, forbids kickbacks of settlement fees and tie-ins of sales of title insurance, and limits escrow for taxes and insurance.

Some lending and collection practices of creditors also are constrained or prohibited by various laws. The Fair Credit Reporting Act (Title VI of the CCPA), passed in 1970, regulates the content, accuracy, and disclosure of credit and investigative reports furnished to creditors, employers, and insurers in connection with consumer transactions. Title III of the CCPA establishes a minimum level of wages that are exempted from garnishment and prohibits an employer from firing an employee because of a single garnishment. The Fair Debt Collections Practices Act (Title VIII of the CCPA), enacted in 1977, prohibits abusive and coercive collection practices and requires bill collectors to provide debtors with certain information. It applies to banks and thrift institutions only insofar as they collect the debts of other lenders. The Federal Trade Commission's holder-in-due-course rule, issued in 1975, effectively abolished this protection for financial institutions that discounted consumers' notes made to retailers.

In addition, the states have enacted laws that similarly regulate credit practices. Some of these parallel the federal Truth-in-Lending and Equal Credit Opportunity Acts. In several states, notably California, the antiredlining regulations are more severe than the federal regulations. As noted above, most states have usury statutes that stipulate the maximum interest rate that can be charged on various types of loans. These laws are quite diverse and complex. The Uniform Consumer Credit Code, promulgated in 1969, has been adopted by only six states, and they changed various provisions. In contrast, the Uniform Commercial Code has been adopted virtually intact by almost all states. Finally, the laws of various states restrict creditors' collection remedies more severely than do the federal statutes. These restrictions on contractual provisions include prohibitions against confession of judgment clauses or cognovit notes, restrictions on collateral available as security, restrictions on deficiency judgments following repossession, and limitations on cosigner agreements.

While these laws apply to all lenders, only those supervised by the federal and state chartering authorities are subjected to detailed regulations enforced by field compliance examinations.

SUMMARY

From the financial services and regulations outlined above, it should be clear that neither all financial services nor all providers of financial services are equally regulated. The principally regulated services are (1) depository fund transfers, when provided by chartered depository institutions; (2) dollar denominated savings (investments), when provided by chartered financial institutions; and (3) short-term lending, particularly to consumers.

The institutions regulated and the types of regulations imposed are (1) depository institutions with respect to entry, geographic and product line expansion, contraction, prices that can be paid for funds, prices that can be charged for loans, supervision of management, and customer relations and (2) licensed small consumer loan lenders with respect to entry, expansion, and prices that can be charged for loans.

Rationale for Regulation

Financial institutions have been regulated almost from their beginnings. Government control of one sort or another pervades this segment of the economy in most countries. This situation obtained even when most other enterprises were not subject to government intervention. Therefore, the usefulness of regulations should not be dismissed lightly.

Two ways of analyzing the rationale for regulation are employed here. One is to consider the specific reasons upon which the regulation of financial institutions and services has been based historically, from which the applicability of regulation to the current situation in the United States can be derived. The second is to explore the forces that support regulation. Both of these perspectives are examined, in turn, in this section.

HISTORICAL REASONS FOR REGULATING FINANCIAL INSTITUTIONS AND SERVICES

Elsewhere (Benston, 1983A), nine historical reasons are delineated for the regulation of financial institutions. These are: (1) taxation of banks as monopoly suppliers of money, (2) prevention of centralized power, (3) maintenance of bank solvency and avoidance of the negative effects of failures on the economy, (4) the provision of banking services as a social goal, (5) support of housing and other attempts to allocate credit as social goals, (6) the prevention of invidious discrimination and unfair dealings against persons, (7) control of the money supply, (8) protection of the deposit insurance funds, and (9) protection of some suppliers of financial services from competition. An analysis of the situation that pertained when the regulations previously discussed were adopted leads to the conclusion that the first six listed reasons are not presently valid for the United States.

Taxation of Banks—The desire of monarchs and those in power to tax the seigniorage derived from money creation is largely responsible for their limiting the creation of private banks. Thus, those in power could enhance the monopoly, or quasi-monopoly, bank's profits from seigniorage. The profits then were appropriated with taxation, forced loans, and/or returns on their personal investments in the bank's equity shares. In the United States, as in most other countries today, government-owned central banks control the money supply, and bank money is taxed via non-interest-bearing required reserves. Restraints on entry would only reduce competition among bank money providers, thereby reducing the government's revenues from this source. The provisions of DIDMCA are consistent with this taxation goal of government, since thrift institutions were permitted to offer transactions deposit services, but all chartered depository institutions now must maintain reserves at the Federal Reserve banks. At present, the other providers of third-party transfers are exempt from this tax.

Prevention of Centralized Power—The prevention of centralized power was, and probably still is, an important popular rationale for regulating financial institutions, particularly with respect to intrastate and interstate branching. But there is little reason to fear centralized power if all regulatory constraints were removed.

First, there are no meaningful regulatory constraints on loans. Borrowers can obtain funds from a very wide range of intermediaries, including commercial banks, thrift institutions, insurance companies, pension funds, finance companies, mortgage companies, and venture capital companies. Or funds can be obtained directly from individuals and companies, in the form of accounts and notes payable, and with commercial paper, long-term debt, securities, and equities. Large businesses can obtain funds internationally as well as from almost any part of the United States. Smaller businesses have access to banks throughout the country, either through brokers or direct contacts with the lending offices that banks have set up in major cities. Even small businesses do not appear to be lacking for alternative sources of finance, as indicated in a recent study by the Interagency Task Force on Small Business Finance (1982).

Second, centralized control of the money supply is in the hands of the Federal Reserve. Regulatory constraints on bank charters, branching, and mergers cannot adversely affect the Federal Reserve's control, except perhaps in the very short run.

Third, the available data indicate no significant operations-cost economies of scale in banking beyond the smallest size of bank (Benston, Hanweck, and Humphrey, 1982). Nor is there reason to believe that regionwide, or even nationwide, financial institutions would have a necessary advantage in risk reduction or other scale economies over smaller institutions. Hence, fears that a few large banks would dominate the nation were there no constraining laws and regulations are not based on evidence. The situation in other countries, such as Canada and the United Kingdom, is unlikely to be duplicated in the United States for several reasons. One is that the phenomenon of a relatively few dominant banks in these countries was due, in large measure, to government policy that encouraged consolidations and discouraged entry. A second, corollary reason is that our antitrust laws would prevent mergers that work to restrict competition.

Finally, neither evidence nor reasoning supports continuation of the Glass-Steagall Act prohibition against chartered depository institutions engaging in securities underwriting and sales. No evidence was put forth at the time the legislation was enacted showing that depository banks that dealt with securities did so to the detriment of their customers or to others as compared to underwriters and brokers who were not associated with banks. Senator Glass's concern was derived from his acceptance of the real-bills doctrine, under which banks were asserted to be safely managed when they were restricted to "self-liquidating" loans rather than long-term obligations and equities. Subsequent studies only pointed out the *possibilities* of self-dealing and abuses of power that might occur should banks both lend to, market the securities of, and invest in the equities of companies. But no evidence has been presented nor is it logical to expect that any bank in the United States could have this power, particularly given the present existence of the securities acts.

Maintenance of Solvency and Avoidance of the Negative Effects of Failures on the Economy—The maintenance of bank solvency has been a serious problem in the United States, where 1,084 banks were suspended between 1890 and 1899; 1,789, between 1900 and 1920; 5,712, between 1920 and 1929; and 9,096, from 1930 through 1933. Although the creation of the Federal Reserve in 1913 was supposed to have changed this situation, it clearly did not. In part, this was because they could not prevent the failure of banks that were legally restricted to a single office, or even a single state, when the economy of its region and the value of its assets collapsed. Nor could the Federal Reserve alone prevent mismanagement and fraud by bankers. However, the large number of failures that occurred as a consequence of money supply decreases could have been largely mitigated, if not entirely prevented, by Federal Reserve open-market operations, by reductions in required reserves, and/or by more liberal discount window policies, as was expected of the lender-of-last-resort.

In any event, the federal deposit insurance agencies now protect most depositors and largely obviate bank runs. Furthermore, the failure of individual financial institutions, while serious for stockholders and employees, has relatively little disruptive effect on other persons or enterprises. Unlike many other enterprises, financial institutions produce products that have many close substitutes. Employees of a failed institution have skills that are readily transferable to other financial institutions or businesses. And there are few specialized assets that would become worthless. Consequently, the costs borne by the failure of a financial institution are borne principally by the deposit insurance agency, contract holders of insurance companies and pension funds, and stockholders or debenture holders, including shareholders of money market mutual funds. Risk-bearing by owners is a necessary and desirable aspect of a private property, free enterprise system. Insurance and pension funds are supervised by state agencies and the SEC, primarily by required reporting and occasional direct intervention. The deposit insurance agencies use direct field examinations and supervision, as is discussed below.

Provision of Banking Services as a Social Goal—The social goal of providing banking services was supported by the creation of the Federal Reserve and its improvement of the national payments system. But the goal has been met completely. People who still do not have a financial service and are able to pay for it are the objects of search by a large number of potential suppliers. In any event, laws and regulations that restrict entry, expansion, contraction, and the types of products that particular institutions may offer can only work against fulfillment of this social goal.

Support of Housing and Other Attempts to Allocate Credit as Social Goals—The social goal of supporting housing has been expressed in the requirement that thrift institutions specialize in mortgages, thereby subsidizing these investments, and in holding down the interest rate that may be paid on savings. Whether or not this is a desirable goal, it seems clear that it has not been helped much by the regulations. Mortgage funds are available from a very large number of suppliers of many types, including commercial banks, thrift associations, mortgage companies, credit unions, consumer finance companies, federal agencies, and individuals. Furthermore, funds borrowed with a house as collateral can be used for many purposes. As Jaffee (1975) concludes from his review of the relationship between mortgage finance and housing: "The main effect of developed policies [subsidies and interventions in the mortgage market] has been to extend greatly the use of mortgage debt in the U.S., but without any appreciable pay-off in terms of housing investment" (p. 119). And, as is clear from recent history as well as from a host of studies, Regulation Q ceilings on savings interest rates have resulted in disintermediation and short-run shortages of mortgage funds. In addition, the thrifts' previously enforced specialization in mortgages and savings subjected them to losses caused by unexpected nominal interest rate increases. The resulting financial problems they experienced made them less supportive of housing.

Other attempts to allocate credit via laws and regulations also have not been very successful. Mayer (1975) surveys a number of studies on governmental credit-directing attempts and concludes: "Credit allocation is not an efficient system. The shifts in the distribution of credit which it tries to bring about are of doubtful value, and, in any case, credit allocation would be ineffective in the long run" (p. 91).

Prevention of Invidious Discrimination and Unfair Dealings Against Persons—Laws forbidding invidious discrimination against specified groups of people are another important aspect of social policy. These laws, enacted by Congress, and the associated regulations, drawn up by the agencies that supervise the chartered depository institutions, are enforced by periodic, generally annual, field examinations of all institutions, supplemented by investigations into specific complaints. This general enforcement procedure must be based on the assumption that more than a few institutions engaged in the forbidden practices, since all institutions are examined.

There is very little evidence that the alleged practices occurred in the years immediately preceding passage of the legislation. With respect to discrimination against women, the only evidence on which the legislation was based is testimony describing incidents of invidious discrimination in lending to women presented at hearings before congressional committees and the National Commission on Consumer Finance (1972A). This perception of unfair treatment by a number of people is further revealed in a systematic survey conducted by Shay, Brandt, and Saxon (1981). They found that 12 percent of people interviewed in 1977 believed that they had been discriminated against in purchasing consumer goods. But the amount of credit they held relative to their incomes and other relevant variables was no different than the other 88 percent.

Studies of lending practices in the years immediately prior to passage of the legislation found no evidence of invidious discrimination against women. One study (Chandler and Ewert, 1976) examined the records of 2,000 credit card applications at a major metropolitan bank between 1971 and early 1974. The researchers found that women tended to be better risks, and the Equal Credit Opportunity Act prohibition against using gender as a discriminating variable was likely to result in fewer loans made to women and more bad loans. Another (Peterson, 1981) studied small loans made at thirty banks in five major metropolitan areas plus surrounding environs and found no evidence of discrimination against females. A third study (Shay, Brandt, and Saxon, 1981) examined the records of a national retailer and a large finance company. The researchers found that an "analysis of acceptances and rejections of applications revealed no evidence of credit discrimination based on age, sex, or marital status in the pre–ECOA [Equal Credit Opportunity Act] period" (p. 236).

Allegations of mortgage lender discrimination against home owners whose properties are located in older, declining urban areas—redlining—led to passage of the Home Mortgage Disclosure Act in 1975 and the Community Reinvestment Act in 1977. However, only anecdotal evidence and data showing that some chartered depository institutions made relatively more mortgages on suburban than on central city properties were presented at the congressional hearings that preceded passage of the legislation. Since then, a large number of studies have been conducted, several of which are sufficiently well done to allow meaningful conclusions to be drawn. None of these studies finds evidence of redlining with respect to the location of the properties on which mortgages were made or sought. (See Benston, 1981, for a review of these studies.) Though two studies found some evidence that blacks had higher rates of loan application denials than whites, these findings contradicted two other (I believe much better conducted) studies (see Benston, 1981, and Schafer and Ladd, 1981). In other studies, when the apparently racially denied applications were examined closely, valid economic reasons were found for the denials (King, 1980; JBR Associates, 1982). However one study (reported in Schafer and Ladd, 1981) found that single males, not single or married females, appear to be discriminated against. Thus the evidence does not support the allegations on which the legislation was based. Nor have subsequent compliance examinations of chartered financial institutions revealed any but minor possible violations of the laws (JBR Associates, 1982; Canner and Cleaver, 1980).

The laws that constrain creditors from collecting defaulted loans also are justified primarily with anecdotal evidence. However, an extensive survey (Peterson and Falls, 1981) of consumers and creditors in four states that had widely varying restraints found that

> the market will adjust to consumers' attitudes toward remedies. Creditors will not use remedies strongly disliked by consumers unless those remedies have great value to them as collection tools. . . . However, if creditors continue to use unpopular remedies, such as garnishments and attorney's fees clauses, the banning of such remedies through legislation may lead to welfare losses because credit availability will contract (p. iii).

Finally, the Truth-in-Lending (TIL) Act appears to have improved information to borrowers somewhat (see Shay and Brandt, 1981). But it also has resulted in increased costs for creditors. For example, the United Bank of Denver found that the costs of consumer-oriented regulations amounted to $2.6 million in 1979, or 7.2 percent of before tax net profit (Darnell, 1982). Of the regulations, Darnell reports, "Regulation Z, dealing with truth-in-lending, was singled out by department managers as the regulation which requires the greatest expenditure of bank resources to satisfy. It also is the one that customers find most inconvenient" (p. 14). Interpretations and rulings on the Federal Reserve's Regulation Z occupy several volumes, and cases based on creditors' violations of TIL make up a large proportion of the dockets of the federal courts. McAfee (1981) reports:

> By early 1980 more than 1,500 interpretations [of Regulation Z] had been published by the Federal Reserve Board and staff, with varying degrees of legal authority. In addition, by June 30, 1978, more than 13,000 TIL lawsuits had been filed in federal courts, representing 2 percent of the federal civil case loads but up to 50 percent of the cases in some districts (p. 3).

Much, and probably most, of this litigation is undertaken as a means of voiding contracts or obtaining damages. Violations of the spirit of TIL appear to be unusual. According to Shay and Brandt (1981), a compliance survey of cash loans revealed that "well over 90 percent of the 1,080 institutions interviewed were in compliance with TIL with respect to oral A.P.R. [annual percentage rate] disclosure" (p. 180). Since the costs of lawsuits, compliance audits, training credit officers, designing and reprinting forms, etc. must be borne essentially by borrowers, it is questionable whether consumers are net beneficiaries of the legislation.

Control of the Money Supply—The laws and regulations outlined earlier do not increase, nor were they designed to affect, the government's control over the money supply. It is only necessary that velocity and the effect of open-market operations on changes in bank money (transactions deposits) be predictable. Reporting to the Federal Reserve by financial institutions of their outstanding deposit balances also is desirable. While the requirement that suppliers of bank money maintain reserves with the Federal Reserve banks may enhance the Fed's control over monetary aggregates, it is not necessary. Control could be affected with open-market operations alone, though the result might be more variable. But, if reduced variability is a goal, interest should be paid on the banks' required reserves and on their customers' transactions deposits to reduce the opportunity value of the customers' transferring funds to interest-bearing accounts. In that way, erratic changes in interest rates would have less of an effect on velocity. In any event, effective control of the money supply does not necessitate reserves being required against substitutes for transactions deposits, such as money market funds or time deposits, unless these become such close substitutes that switches between these assets and that which is defined as money significantly reduce the ability of the monetary authorities to predict velocity.

Protection of the Deposit Insurance Funds—From logic and past experience, it should be clear that once deposits are insured by a trusted insurer, such as a federal government agency, some sort of monitoring of the insured depository institutions is necessary. If this were not done, bankruptcies would result from at least some of the institutions' owners having the incentive to take risks that they would not take in the absence of the insurance. Were there no deposit insurance, depositors would have reason to fear such risk-taking, and the institutions' owners would have a considerable incentive to assure the depositors of the safety of their funds or to compensate them for the risks. In the absence of monitoring by uninsured depositors, the insurance agency bears the monitoring cost.

The deposit insurance agencies could follow one or a combination of the following procedures to control the risks that the insured institutions might take. First, they could require a capital investment by the owners to give them a sufficient incentive to avoid bankruptcy. Second, the particular assets and liabilities in which an institution invests could be constrained to ensure adequate collateral for deposits and diversification with respect to expected cash flows and changes in interest rates. Third, rules could be promulgated to reduce the possibilities of self-dealing and fraud. Fourth, the extent to which an institution was investing in risky assets and liabilities could be evaluated with field examinations and controlled with suggestions for improvement or cease-and-desist orders. The institution's compliance with other rules and regulations must be monitored. Fifth, an insurance rate could be charged that reflects the risk taken by an institution. The federal agencies have followed all of these procedures, with the exception of risk-variable insurance rates. But the rules have not always been applied consistently and the agencies' records on the effectiveness of field examinations leave much to be desired (see Benston, 1973B, and Flannery and Guttentag, 1980).

Though federal deposit insurance is firmly entrenched as a feature of the U.S. financial system, alternatives to the present system may be preferable. These include risk-related insurance premiums, private insurance, 100 percent insurance of all deposit accounts, and more limited or even no insurance. Considering the importance of this issue, a further analysis and some specific suggestions for changes are presented below.

Restraints on Competition—Those who are established often seek to prevent others from offering services to their customers. Consequently, it is not surprising to find the power of government brought to bear for this purpose. The necessity for potential bankers to obtain charters before they can offer deposit services has been used as a means of restraining competition. Laws that prohibit or limit branching also serve this purpose. Other examples are the (recently removed) prohibition of thrifts offering checking accounts; consumer loans, except those related to real estate and education; and services to businesses. The prohibition of interest payments on transactions deposits and the

Regulation Q limitation on the interest rate that could be paid on savings and time deposits are additional examples of laws that limit competition. Others are the Glass-Steagall Act prohibition against corporate security dealings and the Bank Holding Company Act prohibition against affiliates that are not engaged in activities considered by the Federal Reserve to be closely related to banking. It is interesting to note that those who object to a bank's supplying a product almost always are those who supply that product, not its consumers.

However, many laws and regulations are supported on other grounds. Bank charters and branching restrictions are said to be necessary to promote soundness and limit the growth of large banks. Mutual savings banks were not permitted to deal with businesses because this was believed to be too risky. The mission of the savings and loan associations was to support the housing industry; hence they should not divert their funds to consumer loans. Dealings in corporate securities were said by Senator Glass to be incompatible with commercial banking. And banks might risk insolvency or become too powerful if they engaged in non-banking-related activities. But, even though aspects of these arguments may be valid, it seems clear that the effect, if not the purpose, of many, perhaps most, of the laws and regulations related to banking serve to restrain competition among bankers or others who might compete with them. The present effectiveness of these legal constraints on competition is considered below.

FORCES THAT SUPPORT REGULATION

As a means of summarizing the nine reasons for regulation discussed above, they are reconsidered under four, not mutually exclusive, rationales or explanations for regulation: (1) the public interest, (2) private interest, (3) special conditions, and (4) continuing constituency—a combination of the previous (2) and (3).

The Public Interest Rationale—Proponents of most laws and regulations usually assert that they are needed to serve the public interest. In the case of financial services, the public's interests are said to include safety for the funds of people who are unable to determine the risks to which they may be subject, a solvent banking system, prevention of centralized power, and support of other social objectives, such as greater amounts of housing and the availability of financial services without invidious discrimination.

Safety for the depositor's funds and the solvency of the banking system have been achieved by the creation of federal deposit insurance. While this need not be the only way of fulfilling these goals, it has been effective. But it brings with it the necessity of supervising or monitoring the risks accepted by insured depository institutions. The ultimate solvency of the banking system, though, rests on the Federal Reserve's control of the money supply. This control, however, does not rest on laws and regulations that constrain the activities in which financial institutions may engage.

The voters' desire to prevent the amassing of centralized financial power, cultivated by those who want to reduce competition, probably is responsible for much legislation that restricts banks' activities. However, as argued above, the basis for this fear is conceptually weak and is not empirically supported. Furthermore, the laws have the effect of restraining competition, which is likely to be detrimental to the goal of preventing centralized power. There also is little reason to expect that the present regulatory constraints would benefit housing or other social goals. Whether the present methods of preventing invidious discrimination are sufficiently effective to be worth their cost is considered below.

The Private Interests Rationale—Laws may be thought of as commodities that, like other goods, are bought and sold to benefit the parties that have the power to get them enacted and enforced. Owners of smaller banks, for example, might fear competition from larger banks that could open branches in their market areas. One way of dealing with this situation is to get a law enacted that makes branching illegal. This requires the expenditure of resources for organization, a campaign to convince the voters that branch banking is against their interests, and contributions to legislators in favor of antibranching law and opposition to those against it. A law that prohibits or constrains chartered depository institutions from paying interest on deposits also benefits the institutions at the expense of consumers. It is expensive and individually not very beneficial for consumers to oppose such legislation. Consequently, the desire of competitors to restrain competition explains much regulatory legislation.

But restrictive regulation often does not benefit all producers. Commercial banks gain from restrictions on thrifts, but thrifts lose. Owners of smaller banks gain from branching restrictions, except for those who want to sell out to larger banks. Money center banks gain from the prohibition of interest on bankers' balances, but country banks lose. Consequently, laws often are modified. For example, branching is permitted in several states only when a bank is acquired by another bank. Alternative institutional arrangements also arise to get around the restrictions. For example, banks pay interest on deposits in the form of "free" services, and companies practice cash management to avoid keeping nonearning balances. A market for interest-bearing obligations serves the demand of country banks for short-term investments. Money market funds were expanded and established to offer consumers market rates of interest on their savings. Eventually, when the benefits from avoiding the regulation become sufficiently great, the regulations become obsolete, and the producers may support repeal. Occasionally, when the cost to consumers becomes sufficiently large and visible, politicians are able to gain or keep office by opposing the producers.

Thus, the private interests rationale explains regulation as an interplay between the benefits to private interests from legislation, the breakup of coalitions as individual producers seek to benefit by avoiding the regulations, and the efforts of outsiders to offer consumers better and unregulated substitute products as the costs to consumers of the regulations and technological change increase the profitability of innovations.

The Special Conditions Explanation—Legislation also might be due to pressures on or by legislators to enact laws because of a crisis or to fulfill the strongly felt convictions of a powerful person or group. These special conditions, together with the efforts of private interests, probably explain the passage of at least some important laws. One example might be the separation of investment banking from commercial banking mandated by the Glass-Steagall Act. Senator Glass strongly believed that commercial banks should be restricted primarily to short-term, self-liquidating loans—the real-bills doctrine. The Great Depression, together with the Federal Reserve's failure to prevent a precipitous decline in the money supply, resulted in the failure of thousands of banks. Prior to this time, investment brokers had been suffering from competition from commercial banks and their affiliates, whose share of bond issues had grown from 37 percent in 1927 to 61 percent in 1930. Representative Steagall favored federal deposit insurance, which small banks desperately wanted. Large banks wanted interest on demand deposits prohibited by law. The combination of the historical accident of a large number of bank failures, the philosophy of powerful legislators, and the private interests of suppliers gave birth to the Banking Act of 1933.

This history is important in that it should lead one to question the present usefulness of our laws. A major reason that such laws often continue to be supported long after they have outlived their original purpose is considered next.

The Continuing Constituency Rationale—Once a law has been enacted it gains a constituency that participates in and benefits from its enforcement. This is particularly the case when an agency is given the responsibility and authority for writing and administering regulations under the legislation. A subset of legislators then specializes in overseeing the agency and in working with its "clients." The agency's officials and employees become committed to the legislation. They not only come to believe in the desirability of the regulation—if not, they tend to leave—but they also benefit financially and politically from its continuation and expansion. In addition, since they become expert at working with the regulations, should they leave their agency, they are likely to get jobs or consulting assignments with the regulated firms. Officials of the regulated firms also become expert at working in the regulated market and, if successful, they learn to use the regulatory structure to benefit their firms. Consequently, many people benefit from the legislation—they become its constituents. This makes repeal of regulatory laws difficult to achieve, should this be desired by those who are not part of the constituency.

The Benefits and Costs of Regulation

BENEFITS

The analysis presented above leads to the conclusion that the present regulation of financial services yields the following benefits to some persons: (1) prevention of bank runs and avoidance of the resulting losses to depositors and to those associated with competently managed institutions; (2) reduction of fraud, gross mismanagement, and excessive risk-taking by some managers of financial institutions; (3) possible reduction of invidious discrimination and/or a greater allocation of resources than would be forthcoming in the absence of laws to people who appear to be, but actually are not, invidiously discriminated against; (4) reduction of competition by chartered financial institutions with investment brokers and dealers and with suppliers of noncongeneric financial services that the institutions might have a comparative advantage in supplying, by branch banks with unit banks, and, when interest rate ceilings are effective, by suppliers who can compete by offering locational convenience with those who cannot; (5) reductions of some possible aspects of centralized power and self-dealing should this occur were banks unconstrained as to location and products offered to the public; and (6) personal advantages to regulators, managers who are skilled at working with regulators and regulations, and some legislators.

COSTS

Consumers tend to be the principal losers. They bear the cost of reduced competition (benefit 4 above) in the form of higher prices and/or worse service. In addition, since the higher operating expenses caused by the antidiscrimination laws and regulations (benefit 3 above) must be borne by someone, once the capital markets have adjusted to the situation, these costs are borne by consumers. Consumers who would find the costs of learning about the risk of bank failure and of absorbing the consequence of errors in judgment excessive would benefit from federal deposit insurance (benefit 1 above); but holders of large deposits generally pay more for the insurance than it is worth to them. Nevertheless, all consumers tend to benefit from the prevention of bank runs that would result in economic collapse.

Some producers of financial services also bear costs. This is particularly so for those who are prevented or constrained from competing with established institutions. The regulated institutions bear costs as well, from two sources. One is the cost of complying with the regulations, such as supervision and examination, particularly compliance examinations conducted pursuant to the antidiscrimination laws. The second is the cost of being prevented from organizing their activities efficiently and offering products that consumers want.

Whether the benefits from regulation exceed the costs depends on who one is with respect to the benefits and costs and on one's assessment of the relative magnitudes.

Conclusions and Recommendations

Evidence supports the following conclusions as to the benefits and costs of regulation: (1) deposit insurance is desirable for transactions deposits; (2) constraints on competition are not desirable, even if removing the constraints results in the failure of some institutions or in the loss of benefits to some persons; (3) price controls, whether on deposits, loans, or other services, are harmful to most consumers and most suppliers; (4) centralized power is unlikely to occur as a result of the removal of all regulations on the provision of financial services; (5) if there are benefits from the antidiscrimination laws, it seems logical that the laws should be applied equally to all suppliers of credit (see chapter 7 in this volume); and (6) there is no reason to tax users and suppliers of bank money differently than other suppliers of transactions deposits and their customers.

Consequently, the following changes in the laws and regulations affecting the provision of financial services are suggested.

DEPOSIT INSURANCE

1. All suppliers of transactions deposits (those withdrawable on demand, in person, or by order) must obtain deposit insurance from an insurer approved by their chartering agency. De-

mand deposits balances should be 100 percent insured to prevent bank runs; but time-dated deposits or deposits secured by shares in short-term, time-dated market instruments (e.g., money market funds) need not be insured, since holders of these liabilities cannot cause a run. However, nonmarketable time deposits below a specified amount (e.g., $10,000) could be insured to provide consumers with a convenient way to invest in a default-free asset.

2. The insurance agency cannot cancel its insurance without a one-year notice.

3. Beneficial competition among deposit insuring agencies would be possible if the OCC and a unit split off from the Federal Reserve were established to provide insurance to the institutions they presently examine. The FDIC insurance fund should be allocated to the two new agencies in proportion to the total demand deposits of the banks insured. The FSLIC and these three other federal agencies should remain separate, and any institution with transaction accounts should have the right to be insured by any of the agencies, if the agency accepts it as a client. In addition, any institution may purchase some or all of its insurance from a private insurer, including a bank, if the insurer is approved by the institution's chartering agency and if the institution clearly informs depositors of the insurer's identity.

4. In any event, combining the FDIC and FSLIC, as has been proposed, would reduce severely the possibility of competition with few offsetting advantages. The direct costs also would be great, since the examination staffs of these agencies and the OCC would have to be combined. Against these costs there are not likely to be economies of scale.

5. The deposit insurance agency or company—and only the agency or company—should be empowered to impose whatever rules or monitoring procedures on its depository institutions and on its parent corporation, if it is a subsidiary of a holding company, that it believes are necessary to protect its interests; this is similar to the situation for other types of insurance. It should also establish and negotiate an insurance rate structure with the depository institutions, as long as all institutions that offer equal degrees of risk are treated equally. (See Benston, 1983B, for further amplification on deposit insurance.)

SPECIFIED RESERVES ON TRANSACTIONS DEPOSITS

If reserves are required, they should be required only against transactions deposits and held at the Federal Reserve Banks solely as a means of enhancing the Fed's control over the money supply. The required reserves should bear interest at the opportunity value of the funds. Borrowing from the Federal Reserve should be permitted at a penalty rate by all institutions with reserves at the Fed.

PROVISION OF FINANCIAL SERVICES

All firms that want to offer financial services should be allowed to do so, with one exception. Those offering deposits withdrawable on demand would have to obtain a charter and insurance on these deposits. The only reason for the charter requirement is to assure the public that deposit insurance has been secured from, and is being maintained with, a responsible insurer.

Space limitations did not permit presentation of evidence and reasoning supporting the following changes. However, the suggested changes follow as corollaries to the conclusions from the analysis. (See Benston, 1983A, for a fuller discussion.)

FEDERAL REGULATORY AUTHORITIES

The Federal Reserve should be responsible only for the conduct of monetary policy; its check clearance facilities should be spun off or sold as a private corporation, the stock of which could be owned initially by the present member banks. (Chapter 7 reaches a somewhat different conclusion.) The Federal Home Loan Banks also should become stockholder-owned institutions. The Federal Home Loan Bank Board and National Credit Union Administration would exist only as residual supervisors of mutual thrift institutions. The Office of the Comptroller of the Currency would only be a passive issuer of bank charters.

STATE REGULATIONS

The states should no longer supervise financial institutions. With deposit insurance protecting depositors, and with other providers of savings deposit and loan services not specially regulated, there is no reason to regulate and tax one segment of the market differently. But states still would charter depository institutions, subject to their obtaining satisfactory transactions deposit insurance, as an alternative to federal chartering.

TAXATION OF FINANCIAL SERVICES SUPPLIERS

All suppliers of financial services should be equally taxed. In particular, interest should be paid on reserves (as discussed above) and, as is required of other taxpayers, interest and other operating costs expended to acquire funds should not be deducted to the extent that an institution invested these funds in obligations (e.g., state and municipals) yielding tax-free interest.

OTHER LEGAL CONSTRAINTS

All other laws and regulations that especially constrain the provision of financial services and the merger of financial institutions, such as the Bank Holding Company Act and restrictions on the merger of thrifts and commercial banks, would be repealed. (See chapter 5 in this volume.)

These changes are suggested in consideration of the diversity of financial services, the perversity of the present regulatory scheme, and the conclusion that the costs to the public of regulators far outweigh the benefits. While the rationale for regulation, particularly the private interest and continuing constituency rationale, are likely to work against the suggestions, there is reason to believe that they have weakened considerably. High nominal interest rates and technological change have led to the development of unregulated alternatives. The unexpected increase in interest rates also has weakened many regulated institutions, which, in turn, has forced the regulatory and legislative authorities to reconsider the desirability of the present system. For the first time in over fifty years the number of institutions and individuals that benefit from deregulating the financial services industry is sufficient to make deregulation a realistic possibility. The public certainly would benefit.

Paul M. Horvitz

3

Payments System Developments and Public Policy

Economic historians have always placed great emphasis on the invention of money as a necessary step in allowing a primitive economy to develop into one based on exchange in which specialization is feasible. As an economy becomes more complex, the existence of money is not sufficient: an efficient mechanism for transferring money—a payments system—is essential.

Even in advanced economies, most small payments will be made with coin and currency, but security considerations make this less desirable for larger transactions and not feasible when payments must be made at a great distance. Further, when large transactions are involved, the time and risk involved in moving coin and currency (or other paper-based means of payment) may represent a significant cost.

PAUL M. HORVITZ *is the Judge James A. Elkins Professor of Finance at the University of Houston. Dr. Horvitz was previously with the Federal Deposit Insurance Corporation where he was director of research and assistant to the chairman. Prior to joining the FDIC, he was associate director of the department of banking and economic research for the Office of the Comptroller of the Currency. The author of several books and monographs, Dr. Horvitz has also written numerous articles for professional journals and business publications. He has served on several national advisory committees and is a consultant to financial institutions and government agencies.*

For the first hundred years of U.S. history, coin and currency—much of it issued by private banks—was the primary payments medium. Over the last hundred years, we have seen the development of an efficient payments system based primarily on the paper check. It has become increasingly common to make large payments, particularly involving financial transactions, through the use of electronic communications systems, and we are moving toward greater use of electronic means of handling consumer payments.

The writing of checks on commercial bank demand deposits became a significant payments system in the U.S. in the 1870s and has developed since that time in response to initiatives taken by individual banks, by banker associations and committees, and as a result of policies adopted by the federal government. Development of an efficient check payments system was more difficult in the United States than in other countries. As distinct from other countries, the U.S. banking system consisted of a very large number of banks, most of them very small, spread across a very large area. During the last half of the nineteenth century a number of clearing houses developed where local banks could exchange checks on each other promptly and cheaply. Collection of intercity checks was slower and more cumbersome. Banks developed networks of correspondent relationships to facilitate collections, though a number of banks imposed exchange charges on checks delivered to them by mail. While improvement was steady, roundabout and inefficient means of collecting checks persisted into this century.

The establishment of the Federal Reserve System in 1913 represented a quantum leap forward. Though the emphasis today is on the monetary policy responsibilities of the Federal Reserve, a major purpose of the Federal Reserve Act was the creation of a national check collection and settlement system. Federal Reserve member banks were able to deposit checks with their Federal Reserve Bank for collection (including checks drawn on nonmember banks), receiving credit in accord with a firm schedule. Nonmember banks were able to obtain such services indirectly by arrangements with a correspondent bank that was a Federal Reserve member.

Over the next forty years there was further improvement in the speed and efficiency of the check collection system. The volume of check payments grew at an annual rate of about 7 percent (except for the interruption of the Great Depression), and the number of checks handled by the Federal Reserve System grew at a somewhat faster rate, representing an increase in its role in the check payments system. Handling the growing volume of checks has always required the use of the most modern equipment available. But because checks generally pass through more than one bank, a decision on processing methods and equipment frequently involves agreement among all participants in the system. During the 1950s representatives of the commercial banking industry, the Federal Reserve, and equipment manufacturers agreed on magnetic ink character recognition (MICR) as the standard for automated check handling. The agreement was rapidly implemented, and by 1963 almost 85 percent of all checks handled by the Federal Reserve carried MICR encoding. The use of high-speed check sorters based on MICR greatly reduced the time and cost of check processing at both commercial banks and the Federal Reserve, with an estimated doubling of the productivity of such operations from the 1960s to 1979.

Despite the improved productivity in handling paper checks, concern was expressed during the 1960s and early 1970s about the ability of the banking system to handle the ever increasing volume of checks. Check volume was continuing to increase at about a 7 percent annual rate, which implies a doubling in about ten years. Analogies were frequently drawn with the securities industry which came close to a breakdown in the 1960s as increased stock trading volume threatened to swamp back-office capabilities. Several efforts at developing electronic payments systems were justified on the basis of fears that the paper-based check payments system would not be able to handle the growth in volume, though there is some dispute about the reality of that fear. Thus, one expert on the payments system, Edwin Cox (1974) of Arthur D. Little, stated at a Federal Reserve Bank of Boston Conference that "concern with the payment system was rooted in the fear that growing check volumes posed a threat to the continued satisfactory performance of the system" (p. 16). Similarly, at the same conference, John Reed of Citicorp referred to "the driving force of many involved in the early EFTS (Electronic Funds Transfer System) efforts to seek an alternative to the check processing system based on the view that the system was potentially fragile."

On the other hand, Robert H. Long (1974) of the Bank Administration Institute argued that, "Since the implementation of MICR, I have found no EFTS implementor who believed that check volume was a serious problem. Rather, I believe this fear was and is a straw man, a useful prod that EFTS promoters used to arouse some degree of cooperation and support from the industry at large" (p. 32). In any case, subsequent developments have tended to support the views of those who believe that the banking system will be able to keep up with the increasing volume of paper checks. Basic change in the system has not seemed to be required to keep up with normal growth.

In recent years, however, several major changes have occurred in the economy and the financial system which have profound impacts on the payments system. These changes in the economy suggest that major changes in the payments system are inevitable and that these changes may have public policy implications. That is, it may not be appropriate to allow the payment system to evolve solely in accord with the needs and interests of the providers of payments services.

The purpose of this chapter is to describe briefly the present payments system of the United States, to describe the forces impinging on the payments system and the changes they are likely to bring to it, to discuss the public policy issues raised by these changes, and to consider the appropriate public response to these problems.

The Present U.S. Payments System

CURRENCY

Payments are made in a variety of ways in the U.S. economy. Obviously a very large number of transactions are made with currency. This is now and will remain the principal means of payment for the majority of small transactions made by consumers. For such transactions this is convenient and efficient. While good data exist on the volume of currency in circulation, there are no reliable data on the actual volume of transactions, though there is some evidence of an increase in the use of currency for larger transactions. The lack of data on currency transactions, reflecting the anonymity of such transactions, may be related to the possible increasing use of currency for illegal transactions (particularly drug trafficking) and its use in the "underground economy," where otherwise legal transactions involve payment in cash to evade income taxes. While there are some public policy issues involved in the growing use of currency for these purposes, they are not related to the efficiency of the payments mechanism itself. Consequently, these issues are not discussed further in this chapter.

CHECKS

Apart from payments made with currency, nearly all payments in the United States at the present time are made by check. Recent intensive study of the check payment system conducted by the Federal Reserve Bank of Atlanta and the Bank Administration Institute found that 32 billion checks were written on commercial banks in 1979, with an additional 1 billion government checks and money orders. The annual rate of growth in the number of checks written has been declining over the past decade, from slightly above 7 percent ten years ago to about 5 percent in 1982. Over 70 percent of all checks require processing by more than one bank, with the average check handled by 2.4 institutions.

While most checks are handled efficiently on an automated basis, some items, such as NSF checks (drawn on accounts with insufficient funds), involve hand processing with higher labor costs and long delays. The danger of losses from acceptance of bad checks adversely affects the willingness of merchants and others to accept checks. Further, despite extensive automation of the process, paper checks still involve significant labor, transportation, and space costs. Some of these costs could be avoided if it were not necessary to return checks to the original writer of the check. A number of banks, and many thrift institutions with checking accounts, have truncated the process by holding the checks rather than returning them to their depositors. This saves postage and some sorting costs, though the bank must be able to retrieve the check at a customer's request if needed for proof of payment. These savings are modest as compared with the potential of truncation at the bank of first deposit. If such a system were in effect, the information from the check would be moved electronically, but physical transportation of checks would no longer be necessary. Consumers seem reluctant to give up the security of the paper check as a legal receipt, but this is the direction in which the system is moving.

An important attribute of the paper check system is that the collection of checks takes time. This gives rise to "float"—a difference between the time a check is presented in payment of an obligation and the time at which the payee actually receives good funds. All during that time one party to the transaction is, in effect, providing free credit to another party. There has been much conflict over the years among depositors, their banks, correspondent banks, and the Federal Reserve as to who will reap the benefit from that float. Part of the consumer's reluctance to adopt electronic payments devices is concern that he will lose the float he had previously been enjoying. While float is frequently treated as an inefficiency in the system, it should be noted that it involves no net cost to society—one party's loss is someone else's gain—and reducing float through use of more labor, equipment, or transportation facilities involves real social costs. (Of course, float can involve some real costs. An increase in the length of time it takes to collect a check increases the risk that the check writer will fail before the check is collected. The greater the volume of checks in the collection pipeline, the greater the total risk in the system.)

The current state of the checking system was accurately summed up in a study of the payments system conducted by Arthur D. Little, Inc. (1982) for the Association of Reserve City Bankers: "Checking services are . . . reliable, accurate, and timely. It is a readily accepted means of funds transfer in most sectors of society. As such, it acts as a standard against which other payments systems are and will continue to be measured" (p. 114). The check payment system has been firmly established in our legal system, which means that the allocation of risks in the system is well understood by all participants in the process. While this is easily taken for granted, the allocation of risks is not settled in all electronic systems.

WIRE TRANSFERS

There are several systems by which funds can be transferred by wire. The oldest and largest is the Fed Wire system, which began with a leased telegraph system linking Federal Reserve Banks and branches in 1918 and has been upgraded several times since. In 1980, $80 trillion was transferred over the Fed Wire in 43 million transactions (an average of over $1.8 million per message). While the number of transactions is a small fraction of the 34 billion checks written during the same period, the dollar amount of wire transfers greatly exceeded the $19 trillion of check payments.

An important feature of the Fed Wire system from the point of view of participating commercial banks is that it is the only element of the payment system on which all transactions are instantaneous and final. A bank receiving funds via this means knows that the transaction cannot be reversed because of the failure to deliver by any participant in the system. The bank receiving a paper check cannot be certain that the funds are good because of the possible failure of the writer of the check or the bank on which the check is written. Probably the Federal Reserve is the only institution that can make such a guarantee.

The New York Clearing House Interbank Payments System (CHIPS) began operations in 1970 to facilitate transfers of funds for international customers of the members of the New York Clearing House. Banks other than clearing house members, both domestic and foreign, are now participants in the system. In 1980 CHIPS handled about 13 million transactions involving $37 trillion, and system volume has been growing at a rate of about 20 percent per year. Settlement of net debits and credits among the participants is handled at the close of business each day. This "same-day" settlement was designed to minimize risks to participants, but some risk remains. Consider the bank that receives a message with a credit for a customer of the bank. If the customer is allowed immediate use of the funds, and the sending bank fails before the settlement at the end of the day, then the receiving bank is at risk. While these risks are extremely small on an individual basis, the volume of transactions is very high, with amounts equal to many times the bank's total capital flowing into and out of the bank in the course of a single day.

There are two other operating communications networks—BankWire and the Society of Worldwide Interbank Financial Telecommunication (SWIFT). BankWire was organized in 1952 by a group of large commercial banks. SWIFT includes about 900 members in 39 countries. Up to now, these systems have been for communication rather than funds transfer, though the majority of messages relate to the transfer of funds. Actual transfer requires a means of settlement which, for all practical purposes, requires Federal Reserve participation and agreement. BankWire has negotiated such arrangements with the Federal Reserve and will soon begin operating a network that will be a full competitor of the Fed Wire System.

While the wire systems have agreements among their members with respect to the allocation of risks and potential losses, the legal status of bank customers in such transactions does not have the settled precedents of the older check payments system. In an important case in 1981, an Illinois federal court held that a bank could be liable for consequential damages of $2.1 million for failing to process a $27,000 telex message in a timely manner. While the finding was reversed on appeal, this suggests that banks may be liable for some failures of the system. In addition to risks from failure of a participant in the system before settlement, there are also fraud risks of a generally unknown magnitude in wire transfer systems. It is not clear whether adequate insurance is available for such risks.

AUTOMATED CLEARING HOUSES

The automated clearing house (ACH) is a means of reducing the cost of handling paper checks by putting the information that would normally be found on a paper check in a machine-readable form. A typical ACH transaction would involve a large employer putting payroll information on magnetic tape that would be delivered to the ACH. The ACH would combine the information from that tape with tapes from other employers and sort by payee bank. Each bank that is a member of the clearing house would receive a tape with information on the amounts to be credited to the accounts of its depositors. Actual transfer of funds would be made by the bank of the employer.

ACH volume has been growing rather rapidly, but the principal originator of transactions has been the U.S. Treasury Department. Social Security benefits are paid through ACHs, as are many government salary payments, but private sector use of automated clearing houses has grown slowly. Over thirty automated clearing houses serve most of the country. With the exception of the New York ACH, all of these are operated by the Federal Reserve Banks.

There is no inherent advantage or aesthetic superiority to a computer-based payment system over a paper-based system. The real issue is one of cost, and at the present time the cost of an ACH transaction is far above that of paper checks. The attraction of the ACH is that there appear to be large economies of scale in the process, so that as volume grows, the cost per transaction will fall. The cost of transporting and mounting a reel of magnetic tape is the same regardless of the number of records it contains, and existing volumes are very low in relation to the capability of the system. These decreasing costs with increases in volume contrast with the paper check system, which faces diseconomies of scale.

BANK CARDS

Credit card transactions rank next to the check in the volume of transactions. In 1980 Visa and MasterCard, the two bank card systems, accounted for a total of 1.3 billion transactions. The two systems have about 120 million cardholders, so that for a large segment of the population the bank card has become a familiar vehicle with which to access the payments system.

While credit cards were heralded in their early days as the means to a "checkless society," they do not eliminate paper. Consumers sign credit slips which the merchant deposits in his bank. The paper processing is truncated at that bank, with information transmitted electronically from that point forward. Cardholders receive a monthly statement listing transactions, but without the original sales slips. This "descriptive billing" was controversial when first introduced, but now is routinely adopted. As we have noted, there are great potential savings from truncation of the check payment system if that could be introduced and accepted.

The familiar plastic card has been the key to use of other

payments services. The "debit card" is used to authorize a payment charged to the cardholder's checking account. It is similar to a check payment but with the card issuer, in effect, guaranteeing the merchant will receive payment. This system represents a step toward the use of point-of-sale (POS) terminals to effect instantaneous transfer of funds from the deposit account of the consumer to the account of the merchant. Some experimental POS systems have been developed, and the equipment exists to implement such systems, but operational POS systems are virtually nonexistent. While there are reasons to believe that this may indeed represent the payments system of the future, there are also reasons why it is not the system of the present. These reasons lie in economic considerations, consumer psychology, and government regulation, rather than in technology, and will be discussed in more detail later in this chapter.

The plastic card has also been the method of access to automated teller machines (ATM). The number of ATMs in use has grown dramatically in recent years, and the average usage of each machine has also risen as consumers have become more familiar with the systems. The amount of usage has been enhanced by the development of shared systems so that the consumer's card can be used at many locations. These systems represent a means by which financial institutions can economize on the need for labor and for brick-and-mortar branches, rather than a means of making payments generally. However, with an enhanced ability of consumers to obtain cash with which to make payments, the need for check or credit card transactions may be reduced.

HOME BANKING

In the future, a significant portion of consumer payments may be made through home-based systems. These systems include payments by telephone, computer, or cable television. Pay-by-phone systems are currently in operation, but most of these still involve a heavy labor component. The full potential of such systems will not be achieved until the customer's communication is directly with the bank's computer without human intervention. Volumes have generally not been high enough to make the systems cost-effective for most banks, while users find the systems economic when the benefits of postage savings are taken into account.

Experiments have been launched based on computers and cable television. While there is some long-run potential in such systems, at the present time and for a number of years into the future, too few households will have computers or interactive cable systems to make such systems economically viable (though there are some estimates that over 50 percent of U.S. households will have interactive television by 1990).

This brief review of the various components of our payments system suggests that there is little reason for public concern with its development. The mainstay of the system—the paper check—is functioning smoothly with no danger of an imminent breakdown. Other payments systems reflect technological developments and incorporate new technology when they become economic. The interests of the providers of payments services lie with lowering costs and improving efficiency, and competition is a stimulus to such improvements.

Unfortunately, the sanguine conclusion that the public can ignore the payments system is no longer warranted. Several recent developments threaten some participants in the payments process and may affect the ability of the system to move toward greater efficiency at the optimal pace. These recent developments are described in the following section.

Factors Affecting Payments System Development

The progress of payments system development has been affected in recent years by several important changes in the economy and society. These changes include higher and more volatile interest rates, rapid advances in technology, increased competition, regulatory reform, and increased consumer sophistication. These changes are interrelated—interest rate developments may have stimulated regulatory changes and have increased consumer awareness of rate differentials—but it is not necessary for our purposes to separate cause and effect. What is relevant is that all these changes have had significant impact on the payments system.

The increase in interest rates has made the public—consumers and business firms—reluctant to hold wealth in the form of non-interest-earning financial instruments. Traditionally, the check payment system in the U.S. has been based on transfers of ownership of demand deposits on which, under existing laws, banks cannot pay interest. The earnings on these interest-free funds were sufficient so that banks usually did not charge for the costs of handling transactions. Put another way, since banks were not allowed to compete for deposits on a rate basis, they competed by offering services free or at a low cost.

This system was workable as long as market interest rates were low, but higher interest rates stimulated bank customers to economize on their demand deposit balances. High interest rates, combined with legal interest rate ceilings, led to the development of the money market mutual fund industry. Most of the money market mutual funds combined a going market rate on shares with the ability to write checks on the fund balance (though there were usually restrictions on the check writing privilege).

High interest rates also increase the problem of float. Some float may be inevitable in the check collection process, but high interest rates have led some participants in the payments system to seek an artificial increase in float to their benefit by writing checks on banks in remote locations. Obviously, float is more valuable with high interest rates. On the other hand, it may be wasteful to use additional real resources—labor, computer time, or transportation services—to speed up the transfer of ownership of funds from one holder to another, with no net creation of value.

Technology, particularly in the computer and communications fields, has been changing at a rapid rate. These changes have lowered the cost of information processing and, perhaps more important, have reduced the size and cost of equipment for smaller installations. A variety of means of handling transactions is now technologically feasible. Plastic cards are not merely the means of instituting a paper-based credit transaction, but can, through magnetic-stripe or other technology, contain information that can be used on an on-line basis. Point-of-sales terminals exist, as do home computers and interactive cable television systems that have the capability of use for transactions purposes. The number of alternatives poses problems, because it is difficult to foresee which method will win out, and there are substantial risks in backing the wrong technology.

Changes in regulation have probably been the most significant factor affecting the course of the payments system. The Depository Institutions Deregulation and Monetary Control Act of 1980 (DIDMCA) has several provisions that relate directly or indirectly to the payments process. That legislation authorized negotiable order of withdrawal (NOW) accounts on a national basis for both commercial banks and thrift institutions. NOW accounts represent a checking account that pays interest, and this tends to reduce the incentive for households to economize on checking account balances (corporations are not allowed to have NOW accounts). However, from the time NOW accounts were authorized in January 1981 until January 1983, the Depository Institutions Deregulation Committee set the ceiling rate on such accounts so far below open market rates that the incentive to economize on transaction balances remained strong. NOW accounts, however, did allow for a substantial entry into the transaction business by savings and loan associations, thus providing substantial new competition for commercial banks.

The DIDMCA requires all depository institutions to meet reserve requirements imposed by the Federal Reserve and also gives all these institutions—nonmember banks, mutual savings banks, savings and loan associations, and credit unions, as well as Federal Reserve member banks—access to Federal Reserve services (primarily check collection services). The act also requires the Federal Reserve to charge for these services, which formerly were provided free to member banks. The charges must be sufficient to cover the full costs of providing the services, so as to allow room for competition from the private sector. The Federal Reserve does not pay interest on reserves, and this puts institutions subject to such reserve requirements (primarily commercial banks) at a cost disadvantage as compared with institutions not subject to reserve requirements (such as brokerage firms).

These legal changes disrupted the existing process of check collection. Many member banks had previously used the Federal Reserve for check collection services since they were available at no cost. With pricing, these institutions now have an incentive to seek alternatives in the private sector. Similarly, correspondent banks which made great use of Federal Reserve services are developing alternate check collection paths (such as establishment of new local clearing houses). On the other hand, many nonmember banks had previously relied on correspondent banks for such services since they did not have access to the Federal Reserve.

Moreover, these banks were usually subject to state reserve requirements, which could be met with deposits at correspondent banks. These balances (at zero interest rates) are highly desirable to correspondent banks, which compete for them by providing check collection and other services at low cost. Nonmember banks must now meet Federal Reserve reserve requirements, rather than state requirements, and this allows them to economize on their balances with correspondents. Since they now have access to Federal Reserve services (though at a price), some of their activity will be shifted to the Federal Reserve.

Perhaps as a result of these economic and regulatory developments, consumers have become much more sophisticated and knowledgeable about financial instruments, interest rates, and financial services. While inertia still plays an important role in financial decisions, the general public has become more aware of the difference between rates available on market instruments and the rates on some types of accounts at depository institutions. This has been stimulated, of course, by the very high market interest rates of recent years, but the increased knowledge is permanent. That is, the consumer who shifts funds from a 5 percent passbook account to a money market mutual fund paying 15 percent will probably not shift back to the passbook when the yield on the money market fund drops to, say, 9 percent.

These considerations have led to a substantial decline in the proportion of bank and thrift institution funds accounted for by demand deposits, savings accounts, and other low-yielding consumer time deposits. Both households and business firms have economized on demand deposits at commercial banks, but banks and, more importantly, thrift institutions have held some low cost funds through the growth of NOW accounts—transaction accounts that are interest-bearing. The new Money Market Deposit account and the "Super-NOW" account have accelerated the conversion of funds from low-rate accounts to those paying market rates.

The full effects of the development of NOW accounts have yet to be felt by the financial system. NOW accounts were pioneered in Massachusetts in the early 1970s, and, despite great popularity with customers, their spread was rather slow. While many thrift institutions were anxious to have authority to offer NOW accounts as a means of entering the payments business, commercial banks feared that the need to pay interest on checking accounts (which had been non-interest-bearing) would be devastating to profits. (Massachusetts commercial banks were among the least profitable in the country.) Many savings and loan officials opposed NOW accounts because of their concern that their obtaining checking account powers would be linked to an end to the .25 percent interest ceiling differential which they enjoyed as compared with commercial bank ceilings. In their view, the differential was an important competitive advantage that outweighed the benefits of offering transaction accounts.

The debate over NOW accounts was heated during the late 1970s, but when NOW accounts became legal on a nationwide basis in 1981, market interest rates were so high that NOW accounts, even with a 5.25 percent interest rate, represented a rather cheap source of funds. As market interest rates declined in late 1982, the cost of NOW accounts became a matter of growing concern to commercial banks, a concern that increased as the rate ceiling was removed in early 1983. Banks and thrift institutions face the cost of handling transactions as well as the interest cost of such accounts. Moreover, for many institutions the gathering of household deposits has rested on a system of branch offices (or holding company subsidiaries). The substantial cost of this deposit-gathering infrastructure could be justified when banks were forced to compete on the basis of convenience, but branches may be a burden in competing on a rate basis. The future payments system will reflect the effects of these changes in the financial system. The implications of these developments will be discussed in a later section.

Future Problems of the Payments System

While progress is evident, the developments described in the previous section of this chapter suggest some problems that will eventually face the payments system. Past problems of the payments system have been resolved by a mixture of governmental and private efforts. Private firms have incentives to make improvements in the payments system. They may profit from faster collection of funds or by selling improved service to customers. The government also has a legitimate role in the payments system. The Constitution specifically allocates responsibility for control of money to the federal government. The key question to be addressed in the remainder of this chapter is whether the problems to be faced by the payments system require additional government intervention, or whether we can rely on competitive market forces to shape the payments system in an optimal manner.

THE ROLE OF COMMERCIAL BANKS IN THE PAYMENTS SYSTEM

For nearly all of our history commercial banks have been virtually the only institutions active in the transactions business. In recent years, mutual savings banks, savings and loan associations, and credit unions have provided checking accounts services for households, primarily through the NOW account and share-draft account of the credit unions. Money market mutual funds have provided for access to funds and transfer of funds through wire transfer and checks, though the ability to write checks on most such funds is limited. Some brokerage firms have combined the money market fund with a broader ability to write checks and carry out other financial transactions. The Merrill Lynch Cash Management Account was the first, and it has been most successful in attracting customers—as well as attracting several imitators.

So far, the money market funds (and the cash-management-type accounts) have handled transactions through commercial banks. That is, the money market fund drafts are written on zero-balance accounts at commercial banks, and then are cleared through the traditional paper check mechanism. If this continues, commercial banks will maintain their predominance in the check clearing system, though whether that continued role will be profitable will depend on whether the commercial banks can charge appropriately for their services. But it is by no means clear that that predominance will continue. When thrift institutions entered the transaction business through NOW accounts, the resulting drafts were handled exclusively by commercial banks. The DIDMCA gave thrift institutions direct access to Federal Reserve services, with the opportunity to clear checks without going through commercial banks. The money market funds and brokerage firms do not have direct access to Federal Reserve services, but they can gain such access by establishment or acquisition of a commercial bank. Acquisition by a brokerage firm of a nonmember bank that does not make commercial loans does not violate either the Bank

Holding Company Act or the Glass-Steagall Act. This opportunity for access to the payments system, as well as competitive pressures among commercial banks, suggests that the ability of commercial banks to earn substantial profits from payments services provided to other institutions will be limited in the future. That is, they will be able to maintain a predominant role in the payments process only to the extent that they price their services no higher than the cost of a nonbank firm doing the work itself.

Further, as electronic payment spreads into the consumer sector, nonfinancial firms may assume a major role in that process. Such firms may operate POS or ATM systems, with the banks playing a role only in settlement. Cable television companies may provide basic services which banks will buy. A number of scenarios are possible which involve only a subsidiary role for commercial banks.

The possibility that the future will see a diminished role for commercial banks in the payments system is clearly a matter of concern to the banking industry and to individual commercial banks. But this is not a matter of broader public policy concern. As long as payments services are generally available and are provided at reasonable cost, the public has little need for concern as to which institutions provide those services. The increased competition that will result from nonbank entry into the payments business will benefit consumers.

ELIMINATION OF DEPOSIT INTEREST RATE CEILINGS

A general conclusion of economic analysis is that efficient resource allocation requires that the prices of goods and services equal the marginal costs of producing those goods. The financial services business, like many other regulated industries, has operated with a great deal of *cross-subsidization,* where some services are priced below cost, subsidized by high profits on other services. For several reasons this cross-subsidization is likely to disappear, resulting in severe strains on the traditional means of operating the payments system.

Cross-subsidization has resulted from the prohibition of interest on demand deposits and the regulatory ceiling on interest on time deposits. As we have noted, banks have not been allowed to compete for demand deposits on a rate basis. They have competed by providing services free or at less than full cost, and they have also competed on the basis of convenience by opening multiple offices. Even where banks have charged for checking services, the pricing system generally involves free checking accounts for balances above some amount, with a flat charge for accounts below the minimum. In this case, less active accounts subsidize active accounts. As interest rate ceilings are phased out, and particularly when the prohibition of interest on checking accounts is eliminated completely, the opportunity for cross-subsidization will disappear, as depositors will not hold large idle balances at below market interest rates.

Until the DIDMCA, Federal Reserve membership involved a similar form of cross-subsidization. The Federal Reserve imposed reserve requirements on member banks, paid no interest on these reserve balances, but provided various services (primarily related to check collection) free of charge for member banks. As noted earlier, correspondent banks could recoup some of the cost of reserve requirements by providing services to other banks with much of the cost borne by the Federal Reserve. The DIDMCA changes the ground rules by applying reserve requirements to all depository institutions and requiring the Fed to charge for services (with access to all). The opportunity to repackage Federal Reserve services and resell them at a profit is thereby limited. (Federal Reserve pricing of services involves a significant cross-subsidy in that collection of checks on banks in remote locations is done at below cost, in a manner analogous to the U.S. Postal Service's rural delivery program.)

The current legal framework will put commercial banks at a disadvantage in competing for transactions business with non-depository institutions as these other firms expand in this area—banks will be faced with the burden of reserve requirements with no offsetting advantage in access to Federal Reserve services. This could be resolved if the Federal Reserve paid interest on reserve balances—a change that would have merit for other reasons which will be explored later.

Cross-subsidization affects consumers of financial services in a manner that leads to inefficiency. Under the present situation, most consumers receive payments services—checking accounts—at no explicit cost. Consumers have no incentive to economize on the number of checks. Equally important, consumers have no incentive to seek out lower cost payments methods. The banker who seeks to introduce a cost-saving innovation, say, truncation, faces a very difficult time in persuading his customers of the advantages. The customer cannot be offered a higher interest rate on a demand deposit account (the ceiling is fixed by law), and he cannot be offered a lower cost (the service is already free). It is not easy to persuade the customer to switch from a familiar, satisfactory system to a new one simply to save money for his banker.

We have already noted that the eventual phase-out of interest rate controls will end the opportunities for cross-subsidization. This process is now well under way, particularly with the end of ceilings on NOW accounts in January 1983 (these accounts are available to households but not to business firms at the present time). But the need for explicit pricing in a free market will be very difficult for many banks used to the protection of the regulatory umbrella. It is likely that a number of institutions will make mistakes in their pricing and marketing of services and, in a competitive environment, will fail. While this is a problem for poorly managed banks and their stockholders, it is not a matter of broad social concern. This existing deposit insurance system should be sufficient to preserve the soundness of the financial system despite some increase in the number of bank failures. There is no reason to believe that such an increase in failures would bring about a loss of confidence in the system. Further, the disappearance of a number of banks will have no implications for the efficiency of the payments system itself.

THE FEDERAL RESERVE WILL LOSE MARKET SHARE IN THE PAYMENTS SYSTEM

The response of the Federal Reserve and depository institutions to the DIDMCA has led to a significant decline in the number of checks processed by the Federal Reserve. The Federal Reserve has attempted to retain its role in the check collection system within the constraints of the act (which requires that Federal Reserve prices cover the full cost of providing such services) through marketing efforts aimed at persuading financial institutions to use its services and by improving its processing and transportation schedules.

Despite these efforts, the loss of business by the Federal Reserve appears irreversible. While this is apparently a matter of serious concern to the Federal Reserve, it does not necessarily have important implications for the efficiency of the payments process. This turns on whether there are significant economies of scale in the check processing business and whether the Federal Reserve is more efficient than other providers of such services.

If there are economies of scale, a decline in volume for the Federal Reserve will increase its average costs. Under the DIDMCA, the increase in average costs requires an increase in prices, which will lead to a further loss in volume. This process would ultimately result in the Federal Reserve being forced out of the check clearing business and in higher costs of check collection services.

There is substantial evidence, however, that check processing is not characterized by economies of scale. If that is correct, a loss in volume by the Federal Reserve need not increase average costs (though in the short run, where much of the cost is fixed, a decline in volume can temporarily increase average costs). The Federal Reserve can retain that business which it can handle more efficiently than its private sector competitors. This competition results in an efficient allocation of resources and lower costs for users of checks.

It is important to consider, however, whether there are other public policy implications of a changed role for the Federal Reserve in check processing. Bankers competing with the Federal Reserve argue that there is a conflict of interest in the Fed's dual role as a supervisor of the banking system and as a competitor. In their view, the Federal Reserve has taken advantage of its position as holder of the banks' reserve accounts to offer processing schedules that cannot be matched by private competitors. Moreover, the Federal Reserve's regulatory decisions reflect concern for preserving of its role in check processing rather than for the interests of users of checking accounts. Competing bankers contend that the public interest would best be served by total Federal Reserve exit from check processing, or by its taking a role solely as a "clearer-of-last-resort." In any case, they oppose any effort by the Federal Reserve to set its prices below full costs.

The Federal Reserve believes that it must maintain a major role in check processing to assure that banks throughout the country, even those in relatively remote areas, have access to service on an economical basis. They argue that profit-oriented correspondent banks will have little incentive to provide such services, which are necessary to maintain a unified, national financial system in which checks are accepted at par. The argument is similar to that over the subsidization of rural postal service. Critics argue that while Americans may choose to live in remote areas that generate inefficiently low volumes of checks to process, they cannot expect the general public to subsidize that choice.

It appears that a major factor in the Federal Reserve determination to hold processing volume is a concern about personnel. The Federal Reserve employs thousands in the check processing function and is understandably reluctant, on both humanitarian and efficiency grounds, to see this trained work force disbanded. But there are other good reasons for the Federal Reserve to maintain some operational role in the payments system. It has an essential role to play in settlement. The most convenient means for net settlement, even of payments systems in which the Federal Reserve plays no other operational role (such as credit card drafts or CHIPS) is on the books of the Federal Reserve where all banks maintain accounts. Further, the Fed Wire is the only payments system on which transfers are immediate and final, with no risk of default. It is desirable that such a system exist, and no private party is in a position to make the same guarantees as the Federal Reserve.

A broader operational role for the Federal Reserve may be appropriate in ACH systems. The evidence indicates that ACH operations are subject to economies of scale (Humphrey, 1981), and, until a private operator is willing to take on this function (as has been done by the New York Clearing House Association, for example), there are benefits to the Federal Reserve assuming this responsibility. None of these considerations, however, indicates that a major role for the Federal Reserve in check processing is necessary or even desirable. If the competitive forces that result from the DIDMCA, with its pricing and access provisions, result in a reduced role for the Federal Reserve, or eliminate it entirely, that is consistent with efficiency in the payments system.

It is important to make sure that the Federal Reserve does not take advantage of its unique monetary and regulatory powers to preserve a role in check processing beyond what is necessary for efficiency.

RISK IN THE PAYMENTS SYSTEM

As a result of the economic and technological developments discussed earlier, the rate of turnover of bank assets has increased greatly. In 1970, the annual turnover rate of demand deposits of New York City banks was 155 times. By 1981 that figure increased to 1,326 times. That is, every day more funds flow into and out of the bank than the total assets of the bank. This very high volume of transactions per dollar of transactions balances means an increased degree of risk. Over a great many years banks have developed means of dealing with risk in the payments system. The risks are greater now in the wire transfer systems, and we have less certainty as to our ability to deal with this risk.

Loss in payments transactions can arise from mistake, fraud, delay, or credit risk. The frequency and seriousness of these problems differ from one type of payments mechanism to another. Fraud is a common problem in credit card transactions but is very rare in wire transfer systems. However, while the amount at risk in an individual fraudulent credit card transaction is relatively small, a single wire transfer fraud may involve millions of dollars. Failure of an institution can involve losses to other institutions receiving messages (checks, wire transfers) from the failed institution for which good funds have not yet been received. Bank A may receive a wire from Bank B indicating a transfer of funds to a customer of Bank A. If A allows the customer to draw on those funds before settlement is made by B and if B fails before payment is made, A faces a potential loss. CHIPS has reduced the length of exposure by moving to same-day settlement rather than waiting until the following day for settlement. Checks, on the other hand, are in the collection pipeline for a longer period during which failure could occur. But individual checks are for smaller amounts, and banks have rather well-established rules that prevent most customers from drawing on deposited checks until they are determined to be good.

An Arthur D. Little (1982) study of the payments system done for the Association of Reserve City Bankers noted several serious issues relating to risk in wire transfer systems.

> The banking industry has no comprehensive industry data on the frequency and size of fraud losses relating to wire transfers. . . . Many wire system risks are generally not covered by contract, statute or insurance. . . . Prices for wire transfer do not now reflect a full allowance for risk and cannot until responsibility for losses is resolved. . . . If losses from failing institutions are to be limited, participation in payments systems may have to be restricted to credit worthy institutions (p. 43).

These problems are related—it is difficult for an insurer to offer insurance protection in the absence of information on risk and without clear understanding of the allocation of responsibilities of the various parties in case of failure or loss. In the case of checks, credit card transactions, and ACH operations, risks tend to be fully allocated among the participants by contract, statutory law, or years of experience in which virtually every possible eventuality has been litigated and resolved. With some wire transfer transactions, it is not clear for which fraud a given bank is responsible, as opposed to those that are the responsibility of its customers or the other banks which participated in the transaction.

It is an appropriate governmental responsibility to establish the legal framework necessary to protect consumers as they participate in payments transactions. The Uniform Commercial Code does this fully with respect to the check system, and existing law spells out consumer rights with respect to a variety of EFT systems. The relationships among the financial and communications firms involved in wire transfers or other electronic payments systems can be resolved by contract among the parties, but there may be need for additional law. Work is currently being done to develop a "Payments Code" for all types of payment (except cash) to supplement or replace the Uniform Commercial Code and other state and federal laws.

IMPLICATIONS FOR COMPETITION

The paper check system is a highly competitive business, albeit one laced with a heavy dose of regulation and governmental involvement. Bank and thrift institutions offer their own checking accounts at prices they determine (though restricted as to the payment of interest on business accounts) and with services and conditions they specify. Various vendors compete to provide services to banks to facilitate the check collection process. These participants include correspondent banks, computer service bureaus, courier services, the Federal Reserve System, and the U.S. Postal Service.

The credit card business is also a competitive one, although the situation in which many banks offered proprietary cards has changed to one in which two credit card systems, Visa and MasterCard, account for nearly all of the bank credit cards issued. Competition exists within those systems, however. Each participating bank decides to whom cards will be issued and sets the terms of payment. Some banks charge an annual fee; others, a transaction charge; some charge interest from date of purchase, while others provide a grace period. Each determines the interest rate charged on credit balances (subject to usury ceilings) and sets the discount rate charged to merchants. Other firms, such as American Express, Sears, and other retailers, compete in the credit card business.

Despite these examples, there has been concern that competition may not work in electronic-based consumer payment systems, particularly ATMs and POS systems. The concern is that costs of developing and operating such systems are so large, and economies of scale so prevalent, that only the largest banks could afford to offer such systems. If that is the case, many analysts seem to prefer the model of a regulated utility (i.e., local telephone or electric power delivery), rather than relying on competitive forces to protect consumers. Where service might be provided by joint ventures of potentially competing institutions, access to the system must be assured to smaller institutions through mandatory sharing rules.

Participants in the market may be too quick to assume that a natural monopoly exists. As Donald Baker (1974) has put it:

> Businessmen are, in the main, fairly cautious with their money. When they are faced with a new and untried system that requires a large capital outlay, they are very much given . . . to assume that anything so large and new and difficult should be handled jointly by all competitors. In effect, they try to turn it into a monopoly in order to minimize their own competitive risks. If the new system works, they are guaranteed a piece of the reward; if it fails they are not hurt very badly; but, above all, no

> one else will be able to take away their share of the business. A joint venture is a form of insurance against risk (p. 50).

With such joint ventures or shared systems there is less incentive to innovate or expand. Several competing banks may have an incentive to establish a new ATM in a location if they see an opportunity to gain new business and enhance their market share. But if that new equipment must be shared with competitors, there is less to be gained and the incentive to expand is reduced. Traditional antitrust considerations hold that those who jointly control an essential facility must grant access to it on reasonable terms to all in the trade. This applies to a local clearing house, for example. But it is a question of fact as to what facilities are essential. Furthermore, the traditional mandatory sharing approach applies to joint venture rather than to individually owned facilities.

The public generally benefits from competition. It may still be too early to judge which electronic systems involve economies of scale that require treatment as natural, shared monopolies. In several cases, state laws have prejudged the situation with mandatory sharing rules that seem more designed to protect small banks and their market share than to stimulate competition so as to provide the best service to consumers. There is an important public policy interest in seeing that competition prevails to the maximum extent feasible, but existing law and oversight by the Justice Department may be adequate. In the past public policy has erred in the direction of not allowing full opportunity for competition in the provision of financial services. Restrictions on competition still exist, and we should avoid additional laws that may work to preserve competitors rather than competition.

PRIVACY

The concept of an ultimate electronic payments system, with all income and expenditures of an individual recorded in the giant computers of a nationwide financial utility, raises the spectre of what civil libertarians have condemned as an "Orwellian horror delight." As Alan F. Westin (1979) has put it:

> The automated data base of individual accounts would allow managers of the system—and anyone else allowed to use it or able to penetrate it unlawfully—to accomplish unprecedented feats of surveillance: to locate

> individuals at a given moment, to track their movements over time, develop profiles of their spending and saving habits, monitor whether their use of government or private funds met various regulatory or program requirements, identify their money-based political, religious, civic, or sexual affairs, and impose various controls over access to funds that could have enormous regulatory consequences for various economic and social groups in the population (p. 300).

This image of tracing the private life of an individual through the trail of payments permanently emblazoned on the memory of a huge computer is a vivid one, and one that will be technologically feasible eventually (if not now). It is less clear that there will ever be economic incentives to create and maintain a permanent payments record. As Westin notes: "One of the most important findings of the National Academy of Sciences' Project on Computer Data Banks was that there are enormous organizational, legal, competitive, social, and cost-effective constraints on the adoption of technologically possible computer and communications systems" (p. 301).

Of course, a paper trail of payments has long existed with checks, but retrieval of these without the cooperation of the subject is difficult. Analogous issues of privacy and control of records have arisen with respect to credit bureaus, an area in which there were documented cases of serious abuse. These problems were dealt with in the Fair Credit Reporting Act, which, among other provisions, guarantees consumers access to their own records and the opportunity to correct erroneous information.

Appropriate public policy must walk a fine line in this area. Nearly everyone, and not just devoted civil libertarians, supports the concept of a right to privacy. Yet most would not want to shield the records of illegal activities from appropriate law enforcement officials. Construction of appropriate safeguards is not easy, but the issue must be resolved before the system can be developed in an optimal manner. It is possible that concern over privacy will affect the public's willingness to use electronic payments techniques.

MONETARY POLICY

A basic assumption of monetary policy is that there is some set of assets in the economy, which we designated as "money," whose volume can be controlled by the monetary authority.

Monetary policy rests on the existence of a fairly stable relationship between that volume of money and total spending in the economy. There are different views as to the best definition of money, the best means of controlling its supply, and the mechanism by which changes in supply affect spending.

The developments we have discussed that affect the payments system also have important implications for monetary policy. The introduction of NOW accounts has given savings deposits a transaction capability. Money market mutual funds are not only highly liquid assets; they can be used, within limits, for transactions. Products similar to the Merrill Lynch Cash Management Account have full payments capability, with the power to draw on securities as collateral for credit card transactions. While it was possible at one time to define the money supply meaningfully as consisting solely of currency and demand deposits, that concept is no longer useful. This problem has been greatly exacerbated by the removal of interest rate ceilings on NOW accounts. With these accounts paying market rates, consumers have an incentive to combine transactions balances and investment or savings funds in one account. The relationship between various measures of the money supply becomes permanently altered.

More important than the definitional problem, however, is the dramatic increase in the turnover of deposits, particularly at large banks. This suggests the possibility of a substantial change in the relationship between money supply and spending in the economy. Statistical studies seem to indicate that the velocity of M1 (the relationship between gross national product and the narrowly defined money supply) has been increasing at about its historical rate, while the velocity of M2 (a broader definition of the money supply) has been relatively stable. If this finding is valid, then monetary policy can continue to operate as it has. Other analysts argue, however, that the changes in the payments system, such as the development of the "Super-NOW" account, will require the Federal Reserve to abandon its efforts to focus on something called "money," and emphasize rather some other variables in the economy, such as interest rates or aggregate credit. There are shortcomings to either of these variables as the basis of monetary policy.

This problem should not be confused with the matter of the Federal Reserve's operating role in the payments system. As we have noted, continuation of the Federal Reserve's operating role is not important for efficiency in the payments system if there are cheaper alternatives, while maintenance of its monetary policy powers is an important social need. There is no evidence that the likely changes in the payments system over time will interfere with the Federal Reserve's ability to conduct monetary policy. In particular, there is no evidence that a continued role for the Federal Reserve in the payments business is essential for monetary policy.

Conclusions

This chapter has described the present status of the payments system and has discussed some potentially serious problems that the payments system faces in the years ahead. These problems arise now because of economic, technological, sociological, and regulatory developments that have changed the pace of the normal evolution of payments systems. The key question raised by these developments is simply whether we can continue to rely primarily on competitive market forces and the development of technology to result in the optimal payments system, or whether some additional governmental/regulatory shaping of the system is necessary.

If we could determine today what the optimal payments system of the future should look like, it would be appropriate public policy to adopt policies that would steer the financial system toward the optimal structure. We cannot, however, have sufficient confidence in any such forecast. There are a number of promising avenues that are being explored simultaneously in a competitive system. The Federal Reserve has attempted to spur the growth of the automated clearing house by subsidizing its processing of such transactions, but that has correctly been criticized by private market participants. Such subsidy tends to promote not only ACH development, but also Federal Reserve monopoly operation of the ACH. Even if the ACH is the correct way to go, there is no assurance that a dominant Federal Reserve role in the ACH is optimal. The odds are that any attempt to steer the payments system in a particular direction will turn out to have been the wrong choice.

The preceding section has discussed a number of specific problems. For the most part, these problems are serious from the point of view of particular participants in the payments system: the Federal Reserve may lose its role in the payments system operations; the role of commercial banks may shrink; various participants face significant risks in the newer electronic payments techniques. These problems should be faced by the participants, with government providing only the necessary legal framework and background for private contracts and for protection of competitive forces. Legislation should make clear the responsibilities of various parties to payments transactions and should protect consumers' rights, including rights of privacy. The competitive process should be assured through antitrust standards that are appropriate to the nature of the problem and that do not prematurely assume that electronic funds transfer systems are natural monopolies. Competition is enhanced by the existing rules that prevent the Federal Reserve from competing with the private sector with below-cost pricing. Efficiency would also be enhanced by eliminating the prohibition of interest on checking accounts of businesses.

The one major public policy issue posed by payments system development is the threat to the ability of the Federal Reserve to conduct monetary policy in its traditional manner. Resolving this issue may require some change in the ground rules. An example might be the payment of interest on reserves held by depository institutions with the Federal Reserve. The requirement to hold such reserves at zero interest forces banks to economize on such balances, but still puts them at a competitive disadvantage with respect to institutions not facing such requirements. That cost advantage can lead to the development of payments systems outside the banking system, not because the outside provider of services is more efficient, but simply because it is not subject to the costly requirement. While this issue cannot be resolved in this chapter, it is possible that payment of interest on reserves combined with the payment of interest on demand deposits may reverse the increase in the rate of turnover of deposit accounts that poses a threat to the operations of monetary policy.

There is no guarantee that the payments system will develop smoothly and without problems in the years ahead. There is reason to believe, however, that a competitive system will provide benefits to users of the payments system, with greater efficiency and lower cost. There is little justification for increased governmental intervention into the evolution of the system. Government intervention to protect individual institutions, particular types of institutions, or particular means of payment seems unnecessary and undesirable.

George G. Kaufman, Larry R. Mote, and Harvey Rosenblum

4

The Future of Commercial Banks in the Financial Services Industry

Introduction

This chapter is concerned with the future of commercial banking. It is legitimate to ask why this is an important subject. Most of the population could care less what happens to commercial banks—or savings and loans or stockbrokers, for that matter—as long as their deposits are safe. They view the ongoing battle over turf between these institutions much as they view an unfriendly corporate takeover—an interesting conflict having little or no significance for anyone outside the companies involved. Many, if not most, of the legislative skirmishes now being fought concern parochial, intramural issues having little to do with any

---

GEORGE G. KAUFMAN *is the John F. Smith, Jr. Professor of Economics and Finance at Loyola University of Chicago. From 1970 to 1980 he was the John B. Rogers Professor of Banking and Finance, as well as director, of the Center for Capital Market Research at the University of Oregon. Before entering academia, Dr. Kaufman was senior economist at the Federal Reserve Bank of Chicago. He has served as a consultant for the Federal Reserve Bank of Chicago, the U.S. Treasury Department, the Federal Home Loan Bank Board, and the Securities Industry Association. In addition to publishing extensively in several professional journals, and being on the board of three,*

broader public interest. Nevertheless, we will argue that the customers of financial institutions, as well as the general public, have a major stake in the nature of the financial system that eventually emerges from the current period of flux, if not in the specific identities of the winners and losers.

WHY THE FUTURE OF BANKING MATTERS

Clearly, owners, managers, and employees of commercial banks have important and well-defined interests in the future success of their particular banks. But there is no reason why, in the long run, even they could not make the transition to other banks or even other types of financial business. Thus, it is not the particular institutions that we call commercial banks whose future concerns us, but the terms on which the vital services now provided primarily by commercial banks are made available in the future.

Customers stand to gain if these services are offered efficiently, on competitive terms, and at convenient locations, regardless of who provides them. They will lose if regulations evolve in such a way as to maintain arbitrary pricing restrictions and entry barriers that protect existing banks from competition, prevent banks and other institutions from taking full advantage of the most efficient organizational options, and discourage full use of available financial technology.

---

he is the author of two books; the most recent is The U.S. Financial System: Money, Markets, and Institutions.

LARRY R. MOTE *is economic adviser and vice president of the Federal Reserve Bank of Chicago. He also serves as an instructor of finance at the College of Commerce at De Paul University. Mr. Mote was a visiting associate professor of finance at the University of Oregon. He has written numerous articles on aspects of bank financial structure, interest rate regulation, and other regulatory topics.*

HARVEY ROSENBLUM *is economic adviser and vice president at the Federal Reserve Bank of Chicago and adjunct professor in the Department of Finance at De Paul University. He was previously a visiting associate professor of finance at the University of Oregon. Dr. Rosenblum has also served as a consultant to a number of financial institutions. In addition, he has published articles on a wide range of topics in academic and professional business journals.* *The authors wish to acknowledge George J. Benston and Robert A. Eisenbeis for their perceptive and useful comments reflected in this chapter.*

Recent Developments in Banking

For many years banks were unique among financial institutions because of their power both to issue demand deposits and to make commercial loans. Many other lenders, such as independent or captive commercial finance companies, could and did make a wide variety of commercial loans, but only banks issued demand deposits. Furthermore, banks could make a number of other types of loans such as home mortgages, consumer loans, farm loans, and loans to other financial institutions (including securities brokers and dealers). Banks competed in their lending against (1) other depository institutions such as credit unions, savings and loan associations, and mutual savings banks, none of which could issue demand deposits, and (2) nondepository institutions like insurance companies, finance companies, cooperative lenders, and government and quasi-government agencies. Each of the nonbank lenders tended to specialize, primarily by law, in a single type of lending or a narrow range of lending products.

WHAT BANKS CAN DO NOW

The business of banking today still centers around the lending function. Banks can make loans to just about any individual, partnership, corporation, government entity, or group of individuals for virtually any purpose. The only regulatory restrictions are those of prudence; banks must limit their exposure to individual borrowers (loans to any single borrower may not exceed some legally set proportion of a bank's capital, now 15 percent for national banks) and are under subtle regulatory pressure through the bank examination process to lend to creditworthy customers.

Sources of Funds—To fund the wide variety of loans that they make, banks rely on an equally wide variety of sources of funds. Non-interest-bearing demand deposits no longer constitute the dominant or even leading source of funding. In 1950, the ratio of demand deposits to assets stood at 70 percent; at year-end 1981 it had fallen to 19 percent; and it may be expected to fall even further with the growth of money market deposit accounts and "Super-NOW" accounts. Presently the most important source of funding for banks is time deposits, including those available for third-party transactions purposes. As of year-end 1981 they were equal to 52 percent of assets. Within this broad category are several dissimilar instruments differing in denomination, maturity, negotiability, transactions capability, interest sensitivity, holder, and issuer. In addition to deposits, banks utilize other sources of funds. These include federal funds, repurchase agreements, commercial paper downstreamed from the parent bank holding company, capital notes, and equity. The most noticeable feature about the sources of bank funds today versus, say, 1950, is the substantially higher proportion of interest-sensitive funds—i.e., liabilities offering market-related rates of return.

This last point is worthy of additional emphasis because it marks a fundamental turning point in the underlying nature and economics of the banking business. Banks' established position as the most important and diversified lenders in the United States was fortified in the 1930s by the monopoly power created by federal deposit insurance and interest rate ceilings on deposits, which, when combined with banks' exclusive franchise to offer demand deposits, gave them advantages over their competitors. However, no monopoly lasts forever, and banks' local monopolies in the provision of demand deposits were no exception. They were eroded eventually by the incentive they created for customers and potential competitors to develop substitute products, by technological developments that reduced customers' dependence on the monopolized product, and by the natural inefficiency that eventually afflicts any monopoly not subject to direct competitive pressures.

The erosion of their monopoly positions has forced banks to change. Although they still have a large clientele for loans, banks have to be more innovative in the new environment than they were and work harder to find sources to fund the loans. Wholesale banks have been faced with this reality for a long time; retail-oriented banks have only begun to face this situation in the last few years. Large money center banks were the first to make this transition because their customers were big enough both to be attractive to the nonbank competition and to raise funds on their own without going through the banks—e.g., by selling commercial paper. Demand deposits have declined sharply in importance at all banks because of reduced transactions costs and a growing number of highly liquid (though imperfect) substitutes that can easily and cheaply be converted into commercial bank demand deposits just long enough to effectuate a transaction. As a consequence of these developments, the deposit relationships between banks and their business customers are less important now than in the past.

Diversification—In part because of increased competition and reduced margins in lending, banks began to diversify into other lines of activity. However, such diversification has not been taken very far, at least as measured by the ratio of noninterest revenue to net interest income, which averaged about 40 percent for the fifteen largest banks in 1981. Nevertheless, this was still a substantial increase over the 28 percent in 1977. Because interest rate ceilings on deposits encouraged bundling of services and payment for services with deposit balances, rather than explicit fees, noninterest income relative to interest income may understate the importance of nonlending output. But even after allowing for this factor, it is clear that intermediation between borrowers and ultimate lenders is still the banks' primary activity. Diversification by banks and bank holding companies into nonlending activities is constrained by various laws and regulations to such bank-related activities as trust services, data processing, money orders and travelers checks, management consulting to depository institutions, and providing courier services, among other things. (For a complete list of permissible activities see chapter 5, Table 2.) The extent to which banks and bank holding companies have taken advantage of individual diversification possibilities is difficult to quantify because they are not required to report income by product line.

RECENT LEGAL AND ECONOMIC CHANGES

In recent years banks have begun to offer both new and old services over greatly expanded geographic areas. They have accomplished this expansion by taking advantage of "loopholes" in the existing legal structure. Much of this structure was outmoded by changes that have taken place in technology and in the level of interest rates relative to the interest rate structure that had been in effect at the time the statutes, regulations, and interpretations were written.

Product Market Expansion—Banks, either themselves or through their holding companies, have entered a number of new product lines in recent years. Since 1975 these have included management consulting for unaffiliated banks, retail sales of money orders, real estate appraisal, issuance of small-denomination debt instruments, and check verification. Recently, the Federal Reserve Board added four new activities: acting as a futures commission merchant; performing an expanded range of data processing services; purchasing a financially troubled savings and loan association; and discount brokerage—which was previously approved by the Office of the Comptroller of the Currency (OCC) for national banks and the Federal Deposit Insurance Corporation (FDIC) for nonmember insured banks. Each of these was permitted by order to particular individual institutions rather than by regulation to all institutions.

Geographical Expansion—On the surface, the barriers to geographic expansion in banking seem to be quite severe, particularly in comparison with the freedom enjoyed by nondepository financial institutions and nonfinancial firms. Nevertheless, very large banks appear hardly constrained. (For example, according to its 1981 *Annual Report,* Citicorp had 2,265 offices worldwide. In the United States alone it operated 848 offices in forty states and the District of Columbia.) Yet, roughly half the banks in the U.S. operated either a single office or one head office and at most two or three additional limited facilities, usually within a mile or two of the main office. This paradox results from the interaction of several types of legal restrictions: (1) state laws that limit the freedom of state chartered banks to expand geographically; (2) the McFadden Act of 1927, as amended by the Banking Act of 1933, which subjects national banks to the branching laws of the states in which they are domiciled; (3) the Douglas Amendment to the Bank Holding Company Act, which prevents bank holding companies from acquiring out-of-state banks except with the express authorization of state law; and (4) the absence of geographic restrictions on nonbank subsidiaries of bank holding companies. A bank in Illinois, for example, can establish one branch within a mile of its head office and another within two miles. Until as recently as 1967, Illinois banks were only allowed the head office. Yet Illinois bank holding companies can—and do—establish nonbank offices throughout the country. Numerous other states, such as Texas, Nebraska, and Oklahoma, also have unit banking laws. In these states a large number of independently chartered banks are needed to meet the population's banking needs. Thus, in 1980 Illinois had 1,286 banks for a population of 11.4 million, but only 16 banking offices per 100,000 population. By contrast, in 1980 California, which allows statewide branching, had only 283 banks to meet the banking needs of 23.7 million people; however, these banks operated 4,563 banking offices (including head offices), or 19.3 offices per 100,000 population.

The really binding rules with respect to geographic expansion have to do primarily with deposit-taking; a bank cannot establish an out-of-state office for the purpose of accepting deposits. A bank can, however, accept and solicit out-of-state deposits from offices within its home state, either through brokers or by placing ads in out-of-state newspapers and other media, and banks do so at both the wholesale and retail level. As the technology of transferring funds has improved and as transaction costs have been reduced by improvements in the means for disseminating information, the importance of out-of-state offices for generating deposits has greatly declined. Large denomination or wholesale sources of funds, such as federal funds and large negotiable certificates of deposit (C/Ds), have long been purchased in national money markets. More recently, banks have been able to sell fully insured deposits in smaller denominations through offices of brokerage firms throughout the country.

Bank lending is much less restricted geographically. Banks may establish loan production offices wherever they please, and most larger banks have taken advantage of this leeway to service loan customers concentrated in particular geographic areas. Loans can be solicited anywhere; it is merely the location of the office that issues the loan that may be restricted.

Because nonbank subsidiaries of bank holding companies do not accept deposits, they are afforded more geographic freedom than bank subsidiaries. Permissible nonbank activities may be carried on anywhere in the U.S. unless restricted by state law.

TABLE 1. OUT-OF-STATE OFFICES OF LARGE BANK HOLDING COMPANIES

	Nonbank Subsidiary Offices	*Banking Offices*	*Total Offices*	*Total States*
Citicorp	422	25	447	40 & D.C.
BankAmerica Corp.	360	38	398	40 & D.C.
Chase Manhattan	42	4	46	15 & D.C.
Manufacturers Hanover	471	28	499	32
Continental Illinois	20	28	48	14
Chemical New York Corp.	135	6	141	23
J.P. Morgan & Co.	7	5	12	6
First Interstate Bancorp.	19	24	43	13
Security Pacific Corp.	427	7	434	39
Bankers Trust	2	8	10	4
First Chicago	23	14	37	27
Wells Fargo & Co.	52	6	58	16
Crocker National Corp.	15	5	20	6
Marine Midland Banks	14	N.A.	14	5
Mellon National Corp.	151	11	162	13 & D.C.

Source: Rosenblum and Siegel, 1983, Table 15.

Many of the nation's larger banks have achieved a near nationwide geographic presence by expanding into permissible nonbank activities like consumer finance, mortgage banking, and numerous other lending and nonlending activities under Section 4(c) 8 of the Bank Holding Company Act. Table 1 shows the geographic dispersion of some of the larger bank holding companies. In general, the only current limitations on geographic expansion, other than the establishment of deposit-gathering offices, seem to be a banker's imagination, capital resources, and perceived profitable opportunities.

CAUSES OF CHANGE

The primary reason for the present regulatory reform is that the existing structure was becoming increasingly ineffective. As documented above, such dramatic changes had occurred that the reality bore little resemblance to the legal structure. But this did not happen overnight. Signs of the growing ineffectiveness of regulation had been noticeable for many years. A number of banking reform commissions had been established, starting with the Commission on Money and Credit in 1958, to examine the reasons for the deterioration and to make recommendations for changes to improve the effectiveness of the laws governing the financial system. (The work and recommendations of these commissions are reviewed in chapter 9.) But the recommendations were, for the most part, left lying on the table (Jones, 1979). Until the enactment of the Depository Institutions Deregulation and Monetary Control Act of 1980 and the Garn–St Germain Depository Institutions Act of 1982, only piecemeal changes had been made. These changes served to delay more serious deterioration but did not make the fundamental changes that could have prevented the decay.

Much of the existing regulatory structure was put in place in response to the crisis of the 1930s. Bank safety and the preservation of the country's financial system were the overriding considerations (see chapter 1). Economic efficiency, equitable treatment of customers, and other desirable objectives were put on the back burner. New regulations reduced competition through restricting entry, limiting branch banking, and curtailing interest rates paid on deposits. They also reduced risk exposure through eliminating the need to seek higher yielding, riskier loans to finance high deposit rates and by restricting the types of activities in which banks could engage. These regulations were grafted onto a structure of specialized financial institutions which were kept out of each others' turf partly by their own conservatism, but primarily by the high costs of transfer, processing, and storage of funds and information.

But few things in life stay fixed, and the economic and technical environments began to change shortly after World War II. In the 1960s, the changes in these environments accelerated and provided both the economic incentive and the technical means to circumvent existing regulations. The acceleration of the rate of inflation in the mid–1960s caused market rates of interest to climb above the ceiling rates commercial banks and other depository institutions were permitted to pay on deposits, bringing about disintermediation on a broad scale. Further acceleration of inflation in the 1970s pushed market rates on some loans, particularly to households and smaller business firms, above usury ceilings in many states.

Immediate raising or removal of the ceilings on deposit rates has not always been viewed as desirable by policy makers, as some institutions, particularly thrifts, were locked in to low fixed-rate mortgages that they had made in earlier periods of slower inflation, and payment of the higher deposit rates would have been a serious drain on their resources. Moreover, policy makers tended to be overly optimistic that inflation would slow in the near future and viewed the ceilings as temporary expedients until interest rates declined again. Thus, depositors searched for alternative securities that had characteristics similar to deposits but paid market rates of return, while thrift institutions searched for new powers that would protect them from similar experiences in the future.

The development of the electronic computer provided the means by which financial institutions were able to offer deposit-like services that made it easy and cheap to by-pass deposit rate ceilings on savings and time deposits and the prohibition of interest payments on demand deposits. This culminated with the introduction by existing depository institutions of interest-bearing transactions balances in the form of negotiable order of withdrawal (NOW) accounts and the introduction by new, unregulated competitors of money market mutual funds. The popularity of these accounts led those institutions hurt most by deposit losses to bring intense pressure on legislators and regulators either to liberalize the regulations or to extend them to competitors. The major successes of the deregulation movement so far have been the Depository Institutions Deregulation and Monetary Control Act of 1980, which enlarged thrift institutions' asset powers and will phase out deposit interest rate ceilings by 1986, and the Garn–St Germain Depository Institutions Act of 1982, which authorized money market deposit accounts effective December 1982. Subsequently, the Depository Institutions Deregulation Committee authorized "Super-NOW" accounts effective January 1983. The interest rates on balances over $2,500 in either of the accounts are not regulated. The new technology also permitted the development of new products, such as generic cash management accounts that bundle into one package a number of services previously marketed separately, including interest-bearing accounts, check writing privileges, credit cards, lines of credit against predetermined collateral, and security trading, combined with complete on-line and hard-copy accounting statements of all transactions.

There is some evidence that the new electronics technology may have eliminated the already small economies of scale in banking, thereby enhancing the ability of smaller institutions to compete and survive (Benston, Hanweck, and Humphrey, 1982; Metzker, 1982). This conclusion contradicts the frequently heard assertion that small institutions will not survive in the age of the computer because of the great economies of scale and utilization associated with electronic processing of transactions. However, the conventional argument confuses economies of scale in data processing with economies of scale in the financial services firm. To the extent that data processing services can be purchased from a service bureau—and small banks not only do this but, in some cases, have organized jointly owned service companies to provide such services—the economies are external to the financial services industry itself and need not imply economies of scale for firms within that industry. Such economies could, of course, result in some degree of concentration in the computer services industry. But the ultimate outcome in banking depends on future developments, both in technology and in the organizational arrangements by which financial institutions obtain data processing services.

How Banks Have Fared in Recent Years

PROBLEMS OF MEASUREMENT

In assessing how well banks have fared in recent years relative to their competitors, one encounters several problems of measurement. One of these is of an organizational nature. In comparing banking with nonbanking competitors, should only the bank's activities be considered or, when the bank belongs to a holding company, those of the entire organization? There would appear to be a strong case for including the activities of all the subsidiaries of the holding company in such comparisons. Clearly, the performance of the holding company, not the bank, is the ultimate concern of stockholders and managers. More importantly for our purposes, the competitive effects of market share and concentration are best measured by combining the shares of all institutions under common control, rather than by looking only at the share accounted for by some selected group of subsidiaries.

Another problem concerns the choice of the unit of measurement. Assets has been a common choice, largely because data have usually been available. However, a total assets measure would greatly understate the importance of a brokerage and investment banking firm like Merrill Lynch relative to the banking industry. On the other hand, total assets inflates the economic contribution of money market mutual funds, since the service offered by such funds is primarily to add an additional layer of intermediation between investor-depositors and banks, thereby enabling smaller investors to overcome the impediments to higher returns imposed by interest rate regulations and reserve requirements.

A possible alternative measure that would avoid these problems is employment, which is not subject to the same distorting effects as total assets and, presumably, is closely related to the firm's economic contribution. However, employment is an input, and its use begs the important question of whether institutions differ in their productivity and/or relative use of labor and capital in generating output. Moreover, employment is itself a function of banking structure, varying directly with the number of banking offices and inversely with the degree to which banks are free to compete on price. A related measure that in some degree accounts for differences in the quality and productivity of employees is employee compensation. Other measures, such as profits and value added, are superior on conceptual grounds, but accurate data on them are simply not available.

BANKS' SHARE OF THE FINANCIAL SERVICES MARKET

There is a widespread impression that banks have continually lost market share to other financial and nonfinancial firms in recent years. After a sharp loss in market share in the years following World War II, banks seem to have held their own since 1960. Data from the Flow of Funds Accounts indicate that, although bank holding companies have gained market share in some product lines and lost share in others, their share of total financial intermediation as measured by assets has varied between 36.5 percent and 39.5 percent in the 1960–81 period. The continued strength of banks' position in the financial sector is also evident in the data on employment and employee compensation shown in Table 2.

TABLE 2. BANKING'S PERCENTAGE OF FINANCIAL SECTOR EMPLOYMENT AND COMPENSATION *

	1950	*1960*	*1970*	*1979*
Full-time employees	32.8	31.8	35.4	37.2
Employee compensation	32.3	31.3	33.2	33.2

* Includes commercial banks and mutual savings banks.

INROADS BY OTHER FINANCIAL AND NONFINANCIAL FIRMS

The stability of banks' overall market share since 1960 contradicts the perceptions of many bankers that nonbanking financial and nonfinancial firms were steadily encroaching on commercial banking's traditional product lines. In large part, that perception was based on the fact that such firms have, indeed, made major inroads in specific financial services. It was also engraved in bankers' consciousness by a study by Cleveland Christophe (1974) which documented the extent of unregulated firms' activities in the extension of consumer credit. Christophe's findings were startling to many bankers, as few had recognized the importance of the competition represented by firms such as Sears and General Electric whose primary activities were nonfinancial. Most bankers were aware of competition from consumer finance companies and depository institutions, but the fact that Sears had more active charge accounts and volume (as of 1972) than either Master Charge or BankAmericard (the predecessors of MasterCard and Visa) was somewhat disquieting to many in the banking industry. Indeed, Sears and its two large national retailer rivals, Montgomery Ward and J.C. Penney, had combined consumer installment credit ($6.9 billion) exceeding by more than 50 percent the amount outstanding at the nation's three largest bank holding companies (Bank America, Citicorp, and Chase Manhattan with $4.3 billion). If that were not bad enough, Sears earned more money after taxes in 1972 on its financial service business than did any bank or bank holding company in the country. That Sears had such a large volume of consumer receivables—its $4.3 billion of credit card receivables at year-end 1972 was roughly 80 percent of the $5.3 billion of installment credit on all bank credit cards—should not have been surprising. Sears began to provide consumer credit to support its retail operations in 1910.

However, by 1981 bank cards had displaced Sears from its preeminent position in the credit card business. Visa is the current leader in charge volume, a very important measure of business activity because the income generated from merchants' discount fees is proportional to charge volume. With domestic charge volume of $29.3 billion in 1981, Visa nearly tripled Sears's volume. In 1972, Sears's volume was 73 percent greater than Visa's. Visa is also the leader in number of active accounts and customer balances. Moreover, MasterCard is only slightly smaller than Visa. Many retailers have begun accepting one or both cards alongside their own proprietary cards. For example, J.C. Penney began accepting Visa in 1980 and MasterCard in 1981. Montgomery Ward now accepts both bank cards.

To analyze the extent to which other changes occurred over the past decade, Rosenblum and Siegel (1983) updated and expanded the Christophe study and compared the bank-like activities of about forty financial and nonfinancial companies with those offered by the largest bank holding companies. The trends cited by Christophe nearly a decade earlier continued unabated through 1981, as most of the industrial and retailing giants identified in his study expanded their financial services further. In 1981, fifteen companies had profits from financial activities that exceeded $200 million. Of these, nine are bank holding companies; the other six are Prudential, American Express, I.T.T., Sears, General Motors, and Merrill Lynch. Furthermore, captive finance companies are no longer strictly "captives." Five of the top companies—General Electric Credit, Borg Warner Credit, Westinghouse Credit, Associates/G&W, and Commercial Credit/Control Data—have evolved in a way that allows them to conduct less than 10 percent (and as little as 1 percent) of their financing in conjunction with the sale of their parents' products.

Table 3 lists twenty-seven of the largest lenders in the United States (each with over $5 billion in receivables). Of the top ten companies shown, seven are bank holding companies, one is an

TABLE 3. TOTAL DOMESTIC FINANCIAL RECEIVABLES OF SELECTED COMPANIES HAVING OVER $5 BILLION IN FINANCIAL RECEIVABLES

Companies	*Receivables (in billions of dollars)*
BankAmerica	$ 52.0
General Motors	45.1
Citicorp	40.6
Continental Illinois	23.7
Manufacturers Hanover	23.1
Prudential/Bache	23.0
First Interstate	21.3
Chase Manhattan	21.2
Chemical	20.3
Ford	19.5
Security Pacific	19.2
Wells Fargo	16.1
First Chicago	14.5
Sears	13.8
Equitable	13.7
Bankers Trust	13.0
J.P. Morgan	12.9
Crocker	12.7
General Electric	12.3
Aetna	10.8
American Express	9.5
Mellon	8.1
Marine Midland	7.8
Gulf and Western	5.9
National Steel	5.9
Merrill Lynch	5.1
Walter Heller	5.1

Source: Rosenblum and Siegel, 1983, Table 4.

insurance company and broker, and two are the finance subsidiaries of automobile manufacturers. Of the other seventeen companies, only eight are bank holding companies.

Perhaps the best way to examine the effect on banks of nonbank entry is to look at what has happened in individual product lines. Turning first to consumer finance, we find that the largest bank holding companies made impressive gains in the last decade vis-à-vis certain of their nonbank competitors. This is shown in Figure 1.

Fig. 1. Worldwide consumer installment credit held by selected large banks, holding companies, retailers, and consumer durable goods manufacturers at year-end

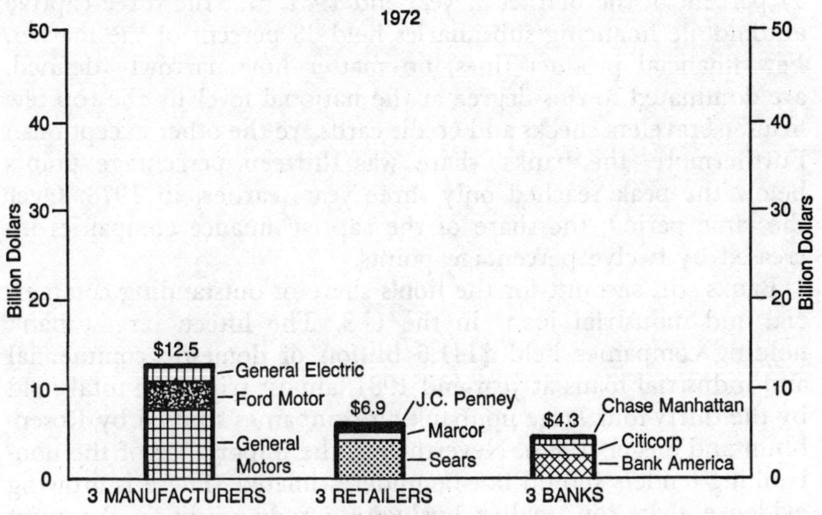

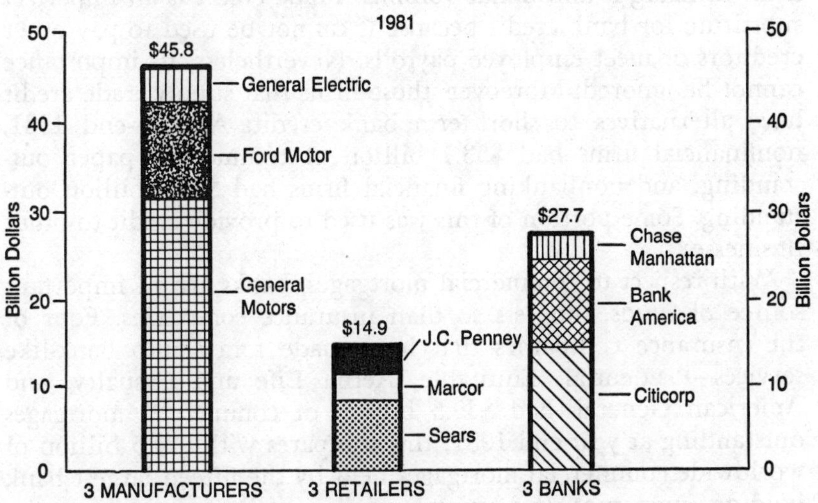

Source: Rosenblum and Siegel, 1983, Chart 1.

Auto lending is dominated by commercial banks, which held 47 percent of the market at year-end 1981. But the three captive automobile financing subsidiaries held 33 percent of the market. Few financial product lines, no matter how narrowly defined, are dominated to this degree at the national level by the top few firms. (Travelers checks and credit cards are the other exceptions.) Furthermore, the banks' share was thirteen percentage points below the peak reached only three years earlier, in 1978. Over the same period, the share of the captive finance companies increased by twelve percentage points.

Banks still account for the lion's share of outstanding commercial and industrial loans in the U.S. The fifteen largest bank holding companies held $141.6 billion of domestic commercial and industrial loans at year-end 1981, almost triple the total held by the thirty-four large nonbanking companies studied by Rosenblum and Siegel (1983). Nevertheless, the importance of the nonbanking lenders should not be underestimated. There is growing evidence that, for smaller businesses, trade credit is the most widely used source of credit, in terms of both the percentage of firms utilizing it and dollar volume. Trade credit is an imperfect substitute for bank credit because it cannot be used to pay other creditors or meet employee payrolls. Nevertheless, its importance cannot be ignored. Moreover, those firms that supply trade credit have alternatives to short-term bank credit. At year-end 1981, nonfinancial firms had $53.7 billion of commercial paper outstanding, and nonbanking financial firms had $77.4 billion outstanding. Some portion of this was used to provide credit to other businesses.

With respect to commercial mortgages, banks are an important source of funds, but less so than insurance companies. Four of the insurance companies that have made forays into bank-like services—Prudential, Equitable, Aetna Life and Casualty, and American General—had $35.5 billion of commercial mortgages outstanding at year-end 1981; this compares with $24.5 billion of worldwide commercial mortgages held by the fifteen largest bank holding companies. If a greater number of insurance companies had been included, the insurance sector would have appeared more dominant in this lending area.

Nor do commercial banks dominate in lease financing. The $17.2 billion of lease receivables of the thirty-four nonbanking companies studied by Rosenblum and Siegel exceeded the total lease receivables of all commercial banks combined.

Of these thirty-four nonbanking firms, ten operated money market funds. These companies accounted for nearly 40 percent of all money market fund assets in September 1982. If money market fund shares are directly competitive with commercial bank deposits, then these ten companies combined rank about halfway between the Bank of America and Citibank, the nation's two largest banks. Merrill Lynch, with money market fund assets of $46.2 billion as of September 29, 1982, was roughly comparable in size to Manufacturers Hanover Bank, which had worldwide deposits of $42.5 billion at year-end 1981. Among the ten companies offering money market funds, only Sears and Ford were among the companies studied by Christophe in 1974.

Despite losing market share in a number of product lines—e.g., automobile lending and the provision of liquid savings instruments—banks have outstripped their rivals in a number of other areas, most dramatically in credit cards. On balance, their gains have roughly offset their losses, leaving their share of the financial services market unchanged, as the aggregate figures suggested. In order to judge how well banks have done in the more fundamental sense of their basic financial strength and their probable ability to compete in the future, it will be necessary to look beyond market share to profitability and riskiness.

BANK PROFITABILITY

In 1982 William Ford, president of the Federal Reserve Bank of Atlanta, startled bankers by arguing that the primary reason so many financial and nonfinancial institutions were encroaching on the traditional turf of commercial banks was that banking has been very profitable (Ford, 1982). In a market characterized by no barriers to entry, entry occurs where the grass is the greenest. And the evidence appears to support Ford. Banking has been highly profitable throughout the post–World War II period and has become even more profitable in recent years. According to data from FDIC *Annual Reports,* net after-tax accounting income of insured commercial banks increased steadily from about .60 percent of assets in the 1950s to almost .90 percent in the early 1970s before sliding down to near .75 percent in the last half of the decade. As a percent of either total capital or only equity capital, bank net income increased through most of this period and reached record levels in recent years. The return on equity was 50 percent greater for banks than the average for all financial and nonfinancial firms, as calculated from Internal Revenue Service data. However, it was slightly less than for some individual nonfinancial industries, such as motor vehicles. Bank return on assets was consistently lower than for nonfinancial firms, but this reflects primarily differences in leverage ratios and in accounting practices, since assets are not stated at market values, and stated net income does not directly reflect changes in the market value of net worth.

In contrast, the accounting earnings of mutual savings banks and savings and loan associations deteriorated sharply from 1960 through 1980. Indeed, considering that the bulk of the thrifts' assets (mortgages) are overstated as a consequence of unexpected increases in interest rates, their earnings during this period are overstated. Thus, their true profitability relative to commercial banks is even worse than the figures indicate.

As noted, accounting data have severe limitations which are compounded by the fact that assets are of different importance in different industries, and book values differ from market values by different amounts in different industries. Thus, the book value of assets or of capital makes a poor base against which to measure profitability. The failure to treat market value equally in all industries also distorts the income data. These problems are generally not present if profitability is measured by the total return to stockholders' investment, as valued in the stock market. But data on returns on commercial bank shares are only fragmentary at this time and require further refinement before they can be used meaningfully. Further, data are available only for the largest banks and bank holding companies, as the shares of smaller banks are not actively traded.

As documented in an earlier section, commercial banks have expanded into a variety of nonbanking financial activities through bank holding companies. But, based on the fragmentary evidence available, they do not seem to have done too well. Two studies found that mortgage banks affiliated with bank holding companies were not only less profitable than independent mortgage banking firms, but grew more slowly (Rhoades, 1975; Talley,

1976). Studies also found that bank affiliated finance companies were less profitable than unaffiliated companies, but did grow faster (Rhoades and Boczar, 1977; Talley, 1976). Lastly, equipment leasing firms affiliated with banks were considerably less profitable and considerably riskier than their unaffiliated counterparts (Rhoades, 1980).

Nevertheless, after allowing for the less-than-resounding success of bank holding companies in these activities, their overall profitability still appears to have been impressive. But profitability is only one side of the coin in evaluating the performance of an industry. The other is risk.

RISKINESS

It is often argued that bank failures have greater adverse impact on the economy than the failures of most other firms, in particular when they accumulate. The original justification for many of today's regulations was that they would reduce the risk of widespread bank failures. Thus, the present and potential risk exposure of banks is important for formulating both private and public policy toward banking.

Risk, though, is even more difficult to measure than profitability. For a firm, risk is often considered as the probability that losses will exceed capital, forcing the firm into bankruptcy. Under certain assumptions regarding the expected distribution of returns, this probability can be measured by the volatility or variability of earnings. The more volatile are earnings, the greater is the probability that cumulative losses may exceed total capital. The standard deviations of banks' annual returns on assets and on total equity between 1960 and 1980 were .1 percent and 1.43 percent, respectively. In contrast, the standard deviations for these two measures for mutual savings banks were .14 percent and 2.33 percent and for savings and loan associations .17 percent and 2.74 percent. For all firms, the standard deviations were .24 percent and 1.12 percent, and they are considerably greater for the nonfinancial sectors examined. Measured on a return per unit of risk basis, commercial banking was by far the most profitable industry relative to assets and was only slightly less profitable relative to equity than the average for all firms.

Because of the shortcomings of accounting data, some analysts prefer to measure profitability by stock market returns. Risk is then measured either as the overall volatility in returns or as the volatility of an individual stock or portfolio relative to the volatility of the stock market as a whole. The latter risk measure is said to reflect "systematic" risk, or the riskiness of a given stock or portfolio relative to the risk inherent in the stock market as a whole, and is quantified by the "Beta" (β) coefficient. A β equal to 1.0 for an individual stock or a portfolio of stocks indicates that it is just as risky as the market as a whole; a β greater than 1.0 indicates above-average risk; and a β of less than 1.0, below-average risk. The average β for a sample of large bank holding companies over the last fifteen years has been close to .90, suggesting that commercial bank holding companies have been slightly less risky than the average firm whose shares are traded on major stock exchanges. In more recent years, β for these holding companies has increased somewhat, possibly suggesting that banking has become more risky as a consequence of deregulation.

Commercial banks, like other firms, are able to control the risks they incur to some degree by managing their asset and liability portfolios. For banks, the two major risks assumed are interest rate risk and default risk. Interest rate risk occurs because the interest paid on deposits does not always change by the same amount and at the same time as the interest received on loans and investments. If the average maturity of deposits is shorter, an unexpected large increase in interest rates causes the interest paid on deposits to exceed that earned on assets; thus, the bank experiences losses. The bank can influence its losses or gains from unexpected interest rate changes by changing the average interest rate sensitivity of its deposits relative to its assets. Rate-sensitive securities are securities whose coupon or contract interest rates change in parallel with changes in market rates of interest on fixed-rate securities with shorter maturities. Moreover, by matching the average interest sensitivity of its assets perfectly with that of its liabilities, a bank can eliminate interest rate risk, as all interest rate shocks are passed through from deposits to assets on a one-to-one basis. Recent studies suggest that, unlike thrift institutions, commercial banks have balanced the interest rate sensitivity of the securities on the two sides of their balance sheets reasonably well and have incurred little interest rate risk (Flannery, 1980A, 1980B). However, some individual banks—for example, the First Pennsylvania Bank, N.A. in 1980—have deliberately mismatched the interest sensitivity of the two sides, often with poor results.

Traditionally, the risk with which bankers have been most concerned has been default risk. For purposes of analysis, actual defaults may be divided into two types—noncrisis defaults and crisis defaults. Noncrisis defaults are defaults that occur randomly at any stage of the national business cycle. Crisis defaults are defaults that are triggered by downturns in national economic activity that reduce the ability of a large number of firms to service their debt fully. The risk of noncrisis defaults may be controlled by the individual institution through diversification and the establishment of adequate loss reserves. To the extent that crisis defaults are more difficult to predict and the losses very large, the risk of their occurrence is much less under the control of the individual bank. But crisis and noncrisis defaults are limiting cases; most defaults are a blend of the two. As the economy weakens, more and more marginal borrowers experience lower than expected revenues and find it more difficult to make timely payments on their debt. Thus, defaults are likely to be clustered.

Default risk is priced by the market as the difference between the expected returns on a security and a comparable default-free security. This difference represents the market's best estimate of the expected loss from default. The available evidence indicates that, at least for marketable securities, actual losses do not differ greatly from default-risk premiums over long periods of time (Hickman, 1958; Atkinson, 1967). It is thus necessary that these premiums be recognized by lenders as reserves to cover future losses and not as earnings. The recent experiences of some major banks with energy loans and loans to less developed countries suggest that, prior to these developments, the banks failed to accord appropriate accounting recognition to this risk.

As is well known, firms may reduce their overall risk by entering, either *de novo* or through acquisition, new activities that have earnings streams either negatively correlated with or independent of their own. This has been one motivation for the use of bank holding companies to expand into nonbanking types of activities. Three recent studies have examined the evidence on the success of this strategy. The first study (Boyd, Hanweck, and Pithyachariyakul, 1980) examines the impact on the probability of bankruptcy of bank holding company expansion into nonbanking activities in the years 1971–77. It concludes that

> the results to date suggest that the potential for risk reduction via nonbank diversification is, at best, limited. The probability of bankruptcy is minimized by very small investments in each nonbank line of business. In fact, the industry has already exceeded the risk-minimizing level of investment in 11 or 19 lines of business. However, the industry has not yet expanded sufficiently into any nonbank area so as to materially increase bankruptcy risk (p. 113).

Indeed, because the variance of returns is much higher in many nonbanking activities than in banking, bank holding company expansion into some permissible activities could significantly increase the likelihood of bankruptcy. These activities include investing in community welfare projects, credit cards, investment advising, and trust services. Bank investments in these lines, however, are currently well below the levels that would threaten solvency. For most bank holding companies, commercial banking is by far the most important activity, accounting, on average, for 97 percent of their assets in 1977.

A later study (Stover, 1982) using similar methodology reports that these results understated the potential risk reductions because the earlier study considered only activities which were permissible to bank holding companies at the time and in which they actually participated. This study also analyzes the implications of diversification into both permissible activities (not all of which the holding companies actually participated in) and nonpermissible financial activities. It concludes that risk could be significantly reduced and performance significantly increased by entering some of these activities. In particular, Stover identifies casualty insurance, investment banking, and savings and loan associations. The last activity was included primarily because its earnings were negatively correlated with those of commercial banking. In light of recent events, the value of the negative correlation would have been offset by the negative earnings of savings and loan associations.

This finding is indirectly supported by another study (Eisenbeis, Harris, and Lakonishok, 1982) that examines the stock performance of banks after they formed bank holding companies. It finds that stock prices of large banks that established one-bank holding companies in the late 1960s increased on the announcement date of the formation by more than would have been predicted on the basis of past relationships. This suggests that investors believed that the new organizations would be more profitable, less risky, or both. Announcements of holding company formations after 1970 were not accompanied by unpredicted jumps in stock prices. The authors of the study attribute this to the Bank Holding Company Act Amendments of 1970, which subjected one-bank holding companies to the same restrictions on activities as multibank companies, thereby limiting the possible diversification and risk reduction.

Probable Future Developments

What banks have done in the past and how well they are doing now has been amply documented. But what does the future hold? What role will commercial banks play? In part, this will be determined by legislation and regulation, but it will largely depend on the banks themselves and, in particular, the decisions they make over the next several years.

GOALS AND STRATEGIC PLANNING

In a deregulated environment, banks will have to decide which services to emphasize, which customers to pursue, and how best to meet the competition of others. No longer will their product lines and geographical market areas be determined for them by the government. They will have to survey the market, identify potential opportunities, specify their goals, and determine how best to achieve them. This process is what is meant by strategic planning. In a world of choices, planning becomes an increasingly important function. Deregulation increases the risks and the work load.

Banks may want to examine the market structure of the investment banking industry, their perceived major rival. The structure of this mostly unregulated industry resembles that of the grocery store industry: a few large supermarkets operating retail and wholesale offices nationally, a few large wholesale firms operating nationally out of a limited number of offices in major cities, a greater number of regional supermarkets and specialty retail firms, and numerous local specialty firms. The industry even has its counterpart of the "7-11 stores" and "warehouse" bare-shelf markets. Edward Jones, a regional firm out of St. Louis, operates 377 basically one-person shops. This is the second largest number of offices of any firm in the industry, even though Jones ranks only 102nd in capital and 27th in number of employees. Bare-shelf, no-advice discount brokers developed after the deregulation of commission rates in 1975. As would be expected from the industry's dynamism of recent years, most investment banking firms are profitable. While there is an ongoing consolidation of larger firms, primarily as a result of continuing deregulation, there has been substantial entry by smaller firms.

A study by Bleeke and Goodrich (1981) examines the characteristics of industries that underwent deregulation. Among the effects observed were increased variability in profits, severe price pressures, unbundling of products, introduction of new products, cost cutting, and increased need for capital. In large measure this was brought about by the entry of new low-cost specialized producers, who aimed at particular segments of the market previously overlooked, and by mergers among existing firms, particularly the absorption of weaker firms that had not prepared for the changeover. The study concludes that the winning firms fell into three broad categories: (1) national, full-line firms; (2) low-cost producers; and (3) specialty firms. Each group followed different and distinct marketing strategies. The study suggests that planning is particularly important for firms in industries undergoing deregulation. They have to learn how to operate under different ground rules.

The importance of this may be seen by noting that brick-and-mortar branches were a necessity under Regulation Q to compete for consumer deposits, but they are less necessary under a free market where competition is largely on the basis of price. In addition, deregulation tends to reduce bank employment, because many more personnel are required to compete when service competition is the only kind allowed. The recent speed-up in deregulation caught many banks and, in particular, thrift institutions with excessive numbers of branch offices. Planning might have prevented at least some of this overinvestment, which will be costly for some years to come. Unlike gifts, branches cannot be readily disposed of when conditions change.

Commercial banks can ease the process of deregulation and

succeed in the new environment by taking advantage of all the flexibility and options that are now available to them. On the lending side, for example, many banks have shaken off their product and geographic shackles by using the bank holding company device. Deregulation of deposit interest rate ceilings will likely improve the penetration by nationally oriented bank holding companies into the markets of self-chosen locally limited banks.

In the last year or so competition for deposits has taken some new forms. Alliances that would have been termed "unholy" not long ago are commonplace now. Merrill Lynch, the same company that has $46.2 billion of money market fund assets that purportedly compete with bank and thrift deposits, acts as a broker in the placement of retail C/Ds issued by many banks and thrifts, thus giving them a nationwide reach. Nor is Merrill Lynch alone in this regard; it is joined by many other investment banking firms, including Sears/Dean Witter, Shearson/American Express, and E.F. Hutton. Together, these four companies operate about 1,325 offices nationwide. Collaboration with national brokerage houses enables comparatively small institutions such as City Federal Savings and Loan of Elizabeth, N.J., to compete toe-to-toe with Bank of America for retail C/Ds.

The market for funds in denominations greater than $1 million has been national ever since Citibank invented the negotiable certificate of deposit in 1961. The same is true of the market for large repurchase agreements. Bank-related commercial paper, also sold in a national market, amounted to some $31.9 billion at year-end 1981. What was true a decade ago for wholesale deposit markets is now becoming true at the retail level—the geographic scope of retail deposit markets is broadening. Some banks have begun to compete for retail deposits nationally, particularly since deposit interest rate ceilings have been eliminated on most time and savings deposits, and these accounts are fully insured so that the identity of the banks is not of great interest to most depositors using brokers.

BANKERS' COMPLAINTS: JUSTIFIED OR GRATUITOUS?

In recent years, commercial banks have increasingly complained about the inroads other financial and nonfinancial firms have made into their traditional banking turf and about regulations that hamstring them from counterattacking and invading their opponents' home turf. This attitude is reflected vividly in a booklet entitled *The Old Bank Robbers' Guide to Where the New Money Is* published by Citicorp. The booklet counsels Willie Sutton, the well-known bank robber of yesteryear who guaranteed his immortality by explaining that he robbed banks because "that's where the money is," to "try the brokerage houses that run the money market funds. But that's not all. Try the insurance companies, the retailers, bus lines, manufacturers, travel agents, movie makers, utilities, data processors, publishers and anyone else who's gone into the financial services business. That's where the money is!" The extent of the inroads of nonbanks into commercial banking has already been documented in the previous section.

Are the commercial banks justified in their complaints? Are they constrained by regulatory, legal, or other external barriers from offering the same services as their new-found competitors? We shall examine the ability of banks to offer each of the eighteen services cited in the Citicorp booklet, only the first five of which Citicorp acknowledged banks could offer (Table 4).

Perhaps the service offered by nonbank competitors that bankers have complained about most is the generic cash management account (CMA). This account usually combines five separate services, all of which are included on Citibank's list—a consumer credit line, a credit card, security trading, a money market account, and check writing—wrapped together by a single accounting statement. It was first introduced by Merrill Lynch in 1977, but did not take off immediately. Indeed, for some years it was viewed as a "dog," generating much paperwork, but little income for brokers (Smith, 1982).

Commercial banks were always able to offer consumer credit lines and credit cards, to trade and take positions in federal government and most municipal government securities, and to serve as agents for the remaining municipal and all corporate security transactions. However, only recently did banks attempt to expand their activities in the corporate security area. In 1983, BankAmerica Corporation received permission from the Board of Governors of the Federal Reserve System under the Bank Holding Company Act to acquire all the shares of Schwab and Company, the nation's largest discount broker. A year earlier, the Security

TABLE 4. FINANCIAL SERVICES OFFERED BY BANKS AND OTHER FINANCIAL FIRMS: WHO DOES WHAT

Activities	*Banks*	*Other Financial Firms*
1. Take Money/Pay Interest	x	x
2. Check Writing	x	x
3. Loan	x	x
4. Mortgage	x	x
5. Credit Card	x	x
6. Interstate Branches		x
7. Money Market		x
8. Securities		x
9. Life Insurance		x
10. Property Insurance		x
11. Casualty Insurance		x
12. Mortgage Insurance		x
13. Buy/Rent Real Estate		x
14. Cash Management Account		x
15. Travel Agency/Service		x
16. Car Rental		x
17. Data Processing (General)		x
18. Telecommunications		x

Source: Adapted from data in Citicorp, *The Old Bank Robbers' Guide to Where the New Money Is* (Sept. 1981), p. 22–23.

Pacific National Bank entered into a cooperative arrangement with Fidelity Brokerage to provide brokerage services to its customers on a fee basis and also received permission from the OCC to operate a discount broker service as a subsidiary of the bank. Although commercial banks are prohibited by the Glass-Steagall Act of 1933 from giving investment advice and taking positions in some municipal revenue and all corporate securities—that is, from being full-service investment bankers—as agents they can directly execute trading orders on all securities generally included in cash management accounts. In contrast, savings and loan associations may invest in full-service investment banking firms.

Paying market rates of interest on deposits has been a more severe problem for the commercial banks when market interest rates climbed above Regulation Q ceilings. Selling money market funds not subject to interest rate ceilings has been considered a sale of securities and therefore not permissible under the Glass-Steagall Act. However, it is clear that the problem is due to Regulation Q, not to the Glass-Steagall Act, insofar as it prevents banks from offering small investors a deposit account paying market interest rates. Yet, until recently, few banks, other than the largest, actively lobbied for the repeal of Regulation Q. In addition, banks could have provided customers with repurchase agreements. Although these are not insured, neither are money market fund accounts.

Check writing facilities are no problem, of course. Indeed, money market funds use commercial banks for this service. It would have been technically possible for banks to tie check writing with repurchase agreements through some form of overdraft provision. Although such arrangements were likely to have encountered resistance from the Federal Reserve, the important point is that they were not tried. If they had been combined with earlier lobbying against Regulation Q, changes might have occurred before December 1982.

Continuing down the list, commercial banks always were able to extend loans and mortgages. Thus, any losses of market share in these services could not be blamed totally on regulation. As discussed earlier, historically banks were Johnnies-come-lately in both services.

The other services on the list are either not flourishing or not strictly financial and have not been the target of major inroads. Life, property, and casualty insurance have not been exceptionally profitable in recent years, although insurance brokerage probably would complement nicely the activities of larger banks. Real estate trading may complement mortgage banking, but is not strictly financial. Nor are travel agencies and car rentals. This is also true of data processing and telecommunications, which banks can do for themselves and, on a limited basis, for others.

Thus, with the possible exception of full-line securities activities, it would appear that commercial banks have been inhibited in their expansion into other financial services in recent years as much by internal, self-imposed constraints as by external constraints. They were simply out-imagined and out-competed. Because banking has been relatively profitable during these years, bank management may not have felt the drive to seek additional profits in new, unchartered waters. Belatedly, commercial banks have begun to realize this and have taken the first steps to break their cultural bonds and do battle with the invaders.

Public Policy Concerns

As far as regulatory reform has already gone, and despite the effective nullification of some restrictions by the workings of the marketplace, further legal and regulatory changes are necessary if the goal of an optimal financial structure is to be achieved. To the extent that it is deemed desirable for banks and other financial institutions to offer broader ranges of services or compete in broader geographic markets, they should not be forced to resort to clumsy organizational expedients to do so.

GEOGRAPHICAL RESTRICTIONS

Among the most obviously outdated and undesirable restrictions remaining are geographical limitations on holding company and branch bank expansion, including home office protection. Although geographic expansion through nonbanking subsidiaries of bank holding companies, loan production offices, banking by mail, and toll-free phone numbers has negated some of the barriers to competition erected by state branching laws, protected pockets of privilege still prevail in some local markets, particularly in deposit-taking and small business lending. There are no obvious economic reasons why even these isolated sanctuaries from competition should be allowed to survive.

Branch banking has been severely restricted in most states, for reasons ranging from fear of monopoly to outright protectionism designed to maintain the small bank as a local institution. The latter reason for restricting branching has often been buttressed by the argument that branch banks have not been convincingly demonstrated to be superior to unit banks in terms of operating efficiency—although a study by Weisbrod (1980) indicates that when account is taken of the benefits to consumers of the greater convenience offered by branching, branch banks do much better in comparison with unit banks. In any event, this argument is irrelevant. Enlightened public policy does not consist in outlawing all those forms of business enterprise which have not been shown unquestionably to be efficient, but in allowing all forms to compete for the consumer's favor in a free marketplace.

The states' rights arguments against a federal override of existing state branching restrictions, at least for national banks, are similarly misguided. The fact is that there appears to be little popular opposition to branch banking. In practice, the branching issue has been decided in most states by the small-bank lobby. More importantly, the arbitrary restrictions placed on banking by state branching laws should no more be tolerated than state taxes designed to eliminate chain stores or the sale of yellow-colored margarine. All are impediments to commerce imposed for the benefit of competitors, not competition.

On the other hand, in phasing out these geographical restrictions, certain safeguards would seem desirable. The frequent proposal to move first to reciprocal interstate branching on a regional basis is not as innocuous as it may seem. In fact, it would enable existing institutions within each region to merge, increasing local concentration and reducing the opportunity for heightened competition that would result if each such institution were acquired by, or acquired, a banking organization headquartered in another region of the country.

MERGERS AND ACQUISITIONS

Similarly, though some liberalization of merger and acquisition policy might be a natural and desirable result of eliminating geographic restrictions, care should be taken to prevent anti-competitive acquisitions. Existing antitrust laws may be adequate to the task, but greater assurance might be achieved through new legislation. One option that might be considered would be an upper limit on the number of offices a banking organization could operate in any local market, perhaps taking account of area and population. While allowing banks to expand essentially wherever they wished, such a provision would prevent concentration in local banking markets and impose an upper limit on concentration nationwide.

The arguments for eliminating existing restrictions on product offerings of various institutions are similar, although some of the side issues are quite different. A continuation of the trend in the

Depository Institutions Deregulation and Monetary Control Act and the Garn–St Germain Depository Institutions Act would eventually result in a financial system consisting of firms with all-purpose charters and no price constraints in which specialization would simply be the result of a business decision, rather than of law or regulation. In such an environment, a congressional decision to subsidize housing would be an aboveboard choice to override the marketplace, rather than to grant special benefits to a specialized financial institution. The result, one may surmise, would be a reduced level of subsidization of housing, but a more efficient subsidy.

Among the few serious issues that might reasonably be invoked to block the complete abolition of functional restrictions is the fear of conflicts of interest. Despite assurances that such conflicts could easily be policed, and despite the skepticism regarding conflicts of interest by some academic economists, this fear remains strong, and little concrete evidence has been adduced to assuage it. Consequently, the Glass-Steagall restrictions on security underwriting and dealer activities by banks may be among the last to go—if, in fact, they do go. In this context, it is also of some importance to remember that the Glass-Steagall restrictions on bank securities activities are not barriers to entry in the usual sense, but only barriers to entry by only one type of institution representing only 15,000 of the more than 70,000 financial services firms and the nearly 3 million nonfinancial firms in the country.

The Future

The future of the banking industry will be exciting, both for the public and, in particular, for the industry itself. More changes are likely to occur in the next five years than in the last fifty in terms of both products and structure. Deregulation has displaced the structure from its previous equilibrium. There will be considerable, and at times rather wild, churning until a new equilibrium is reached. As the old ground rules disappear, uncertainty will increase. Conditions may appear chaotic for a period, particularly to outsiders. In such a situation, not everyone will react the same way or as effectively. Thus, there will be winners and losers before everyone settles down to the new ground rules. Market shares will change, and, either through absorption or through liquidation, the losers will depart from the industry. There will even be some new entrants. How many firms will survive when the churning stops is anyone's guess. What is obvious is that they will be fewer than the 15,000 commercial banks, 4,000 savings and loan associations, 500 mutual savings banks, 20,000 credit unions, 2,000 life insurance companies, 250 money market funds, 500 other mutual funds, 3,000 property liability insurance firms, 3,000 security dealers, 3,000 finance companies, 800 mortgage bankers, and many more self-managed pension funds and other financial institutions that we have now.

Although the departure of a goodly number of firms will produce a considerable uproar about the plight of the industry, it should be of no more concern to the public than the failure of a number of brokerage firms after the demise of fixed commissions in 1975 or, more recently, the actual and threatened departures of some older firms in the airline industry. (Actually, there are almost twice as many airlines today as there were before deregulation, albeit many are small and specialized.) The institutions that we call commercial banks today are likely to be heavily represented among the survivors of deregulation in the broader financial services industry, but that result is by no means guaranteed, nor is it a matter of great concern from society's standpoint. As we argued at the beginning of this chapter, the public is interested in the quality and prices of the services offered, not in the identity or health of any particular suppliers.

Robert A. Eisenbeis

5

Bank Holding Companies and Public Policy

Introduction

The decade of the 1970s saw the emergence of bank holding companies (BHCs) as the dominant form of organization in the U.S. banking system, culminating an evolutionary process begun before the turn of the century. Almost all of the nation's top fifty banks have converted to the bank holding company form, and these companies presently control about 75 percent of U.S. banking resources and about 33 percent of its banks. This proportion and number of banks has more than doubled since pas-

---

ROBERT A. EISENBEIS *is the Wachovia Professor of Banking at the University of North Carolina at Chapel Hill. Prior to this appointment, Dr. Eisenbeis was the senior deputy associate director in the Division of Research and Statistics of the Federal Reserve Board. Previously he had been assistant director of research and chief of the Financial and Economic Research Section of the Federal Deposit Insurance Corporation. In addition to serving on the editorial advisory boards of five professional journals, Dr. Eisenbeis has written over thirty articles and is coauthor of two books; the most recent is* Application of Classification Techniques in Business, Banking, and Finance.
Dr. Eisenbeis would like to thank Richard C. Aspinwall, George Benston, Thomas Huartas, Edward J. Kane, and George Kaufman for helpful insights and comments reflected in this chapter. This chapter draws heavily on work presented previously in Eisenbeis (1980, 1983).

sage of the 1970 Amendments to the Bank Holding Company Act of 1956. Not only have bank holding companies come to control a majority of banking resources, but also they have begun to provide an expanded array of intermediary and other bank-related services.

Many of these services are close substitutes for those provided by insured banks and thrifts and by less regulated suppliers. Consequently, the future role and function of bank holding companies in the U.S. financial system and how they should be supervised and regulated have become important public policy issues. These issues have been elevated to a high profile as the result of Treasury Department proposals in 1982 to expand the permissible nonbanking activities of bank holding companies and to restructure holding company regulation. These issues have been further complicated by passage of the Garn–St Germain Depository Institutions Act of 1982, which expanded bank authority to establish service corporations and to engage in activities generally permissible to bank holding companies.

This chapter discusses the issues raised by the changing role of bank holding companies in the U.S. financial system and explores their implications for future regulatory policies toward these organizations. The chapter begins with a discussion of the historical evolution of bank holding companies and why banks have been induced to adopt the holding company form of organization.

The Evolution of Bank Holding Companies

The explanation for why bank holding companies evolved lies in understanding how regulation affects banking organizations and how they respond to binding regulatory constraints. Early U.S. financial history proved that our economy could not function smoothly with a rapidly expanding money supply followed by financial panics. Therefore, because of the unique role banks and their deposit liabilities play in our economy, they traditionally have been heavily regulated. Restrictions have been placed on the scope of their assets and liabilities, on the geographic locations at which business may be conducted, and on their capital structure to ensure that banks are operated in a safe and sound manner (see chapter 2). In addition, deposit rate and usury ceilings have been imposed to redirect credit flows.

Finally, Federal Reserve member bank reserve requirements and related regulations have been imposed, first, to maintain the liquidity and safety of the banking system, and then to facilitate the conduct of monetary policy.

Kane (1981) and others (see Eisenbeis, 1980) have convincingly argued that regulation imposes costs and limits profit-making alternatives and, therefore, has provided powerful economic incentives for banks to innovate to avoid as many of the costs of regulation as they can. The consequences of these regulatory-induced financial innovations have been numerous and far reaching; they have radically affected the structure and functioning of financial markets. For example, these innovations have altered the array of financial services provided to the public and have substantially increased the number of close money substitutes. An unintended consequence has been to complicate the measurement of the monetary aggregates and the implementation of monetary policy. Avoidance efforts have also increased banks' reliance on shorter term, more interest sensitive sources of funds. This in turn implies greater earnings variability over interest rate cycles and hence greater risk over business cycles, which appear to have increased in both frequency and amplitude. The process of financial innovation has also broken down traditional barriers to competition between banks and thrifts and has opened the door to new unregulated purveyors of financial services.

Most important, however, from the perspective of this chapter, are the effects of financial innovation and regulation on the organization, structure, and operations of banking firms. In particular, banks were induced to form bank holding companies because of that form's advantages in facilitating regulatory avoidance. As such, the evolution of bank holding companies may be viewed as part of the broader process of financial innovation designed to avoid regulation. The early history of the bank holding company movement, discussed in the next section, suggests that the ability to avoid state and federal limitations on branching was the primary reason for the expansion of bank holding companies until 1956 (see Savage, 1978, and Fischer and Golembe, 1976). Thereafter, restrictions on geographic and product expansion were but two of several important stimuli accelerating bank holding company formation. These included deposit rate ceilings, reserve requirements, tax considerations, and capital adequacy requirements (see Eisenbeis, 1980).

BANK HOLDING COMPANIES BEFORE 1956

The pre–1956 growth of bank holding companies is closely rooted in federal and state policies toward bank branching and geographic expansion. In particular, the National Banking Act of 1864, while apparently silent on the issue of branching, was interpreted by the Office of the Comptroller of the Currency (OCC) as prohibiting nationally chartered banks from operating branches. This interpretation, coupled with generally restrictive state branching laws, meant that unit banking dominated the scene well into the 1920s. (By 1920, for example, only 530 of the 30,291 banks in existence operated branches, of which 60 percent were located in the same city as the head office.)

Multioffice banking, however, existed in other forms besides branching. In particular, even before 1900, individuals began acquiring interests in more than one bank and linking them together in chain relationships. Similarly, once several states began relaxing prohibitions on corporate ownership of stock in the late 1800s, bank holding companies came into existence. But significant growth in bank holding companies did not occur until the 1910–30 period which coincided with heightened economic pressures stimulating the expansion of branch banks.

As urbanization, income growth, and customer mobility increased, the inability to branch on the part of national banks and state banks in states with restrictive branching laws inhibited banks from serving customers within their natural markets. The resulting loss of profit alternatives increased pressures to relax restrictions on branching and stimulated the growth of group and chain banking. In the face of these forces, individual states began to relax their limits on branching for state banks. This placed national banks at a competitive disadvantage because of the restrictive interpretation of the National Banking Act of 1864, which stimulated conversions of national banks to state bank status. The competitive inequity and concern for the viability of the national banking system resulted in compromise federal legislation in the form of both the McFadden Act of 1927, permitting national banks to branch within their head office city, and the Banking Act of 1933, allowing national banks to branch intrastate on the same basis as state banks.

Despite this liberalizing trend of state and federal policies toward branching, however, more than half of the states still prohibited any form of branch banking as late as 1929. And it was especially in those states (such as Texas, Illinois, Colorado, and Wisconsin) that chain and group banking flourished.

In addition to the ability to expand in states with restrictive branching laws, several other factors have been cited by Savage (1978) as being important in explaining bank holding company expansion. For example, the series of bank failures in the 1920s made geographical diversification desirable and affiliation with bank holding companies attractive. Second, the general wave of business mergers during the period undoubtedly carried over to banking as well, probably motivated in part by the desire of banks to achieve greater size to serve larger businesses. Also, the upward surge of the stock market in the 1920s probably enhanced bank holding company access to capital markets and made further expansion possible. Although data are not generally available on the extent of banking company and chain banking relationships, it is known that by the end of the decade there were nearly 300 group and chain organizations controlling more than 2,000 banks.

During the 1930s, many group and chain banking organizations failed; however, the failure rate was about half that of commercial banks in general. Savage has indicated that between 1930 and 1934, the failures included 201 banks in 40 bank groups having resources of about $1.5 billion. However, about half of the total resources of these failed banks were accounted for by only two companies in Detroit. In some instances, bank groups actually expanded during the thirties due to their generally sounder condition which led to supervisory and other mergers and acquisitions.

The growth of bank holding companies during the thirties was also accompanied by legislative attempts at both the state and federal level to expand supervision and regulation of bank holding companies and to limit the concentration of economic power. The Banking Act of 1933 extended, for the first time, federal regulation to bank holding companies; those companies with a majority interest in a member bank were required to obtain Federal Reserve approval to vote their stock. In granting voting approval, the Federal Reserve usually required such companies to be subject to examination, to publish financial reports, to divest themselves of their securities activities, and to adhere to several other restrictions as well.

Passage of this act did not eliminate concern over bank holding companies for several reasons. Holding company formation and expansion were not subject to regulation. Moreover, since the restrictions in the act applied only to companies with a majority interest in Federal Reserve member banks, it was easy for companies to avoid regulation by reducing their ownership and by acquiring nonmember banks. As a result several legislative initiatives were undertaken that were designed to increase bank holding company regulation and to eliminate many of the deficiencies of the Banking Act of 1933, including the definition of control.

Although numerous efforts were undertaken between 1935 and 1956, no further legislation was enacted until passage of the Bank Holding Company Act of 1956. The failure of the Supreme Court to sustain the Federal Reserve Board's charges that Transamerica Corporation violated Section 7 of the Clayton Act by acquiring banks in five western states finally crystallized congressional concern that bank holding company expansion should be regulated. Among the more significant of the 1956 act's provisions were those prohibiting interstate expansion unless the host state explicitly permitted entry by out-of-state holding companies (the Douglas Amendment), extending regulation to include those companies controlling 25 percent of the stock of two or more insured banks, limiting expansion without regulatory approval, and prohibiting ownership in nonbanking firms engaged in other than Federal Reserve approved bank-related activities. The act did not apply. however, to companies owning only one bank.

BANK HOLDING COMPANY FORMATION FOLLOWING THE BANK HOLDING ACT OF 1956 AND THE ROLE OF DEPOSIT RATE CEILINGS AND RESERVE REQUIREMENTS

The credit crunch of 1959–60 ushered in a new set of stimuli, in addition to the desire to avoid restrictions on geographic and product diversification, which contributed to bank holding company growth. More specifically, accelerating inflation coupled with binding deposit rate ceilings increased the opportunity costs to large corporations and individual depositors of holding temporarily idle cash balances in demand deposits. The more sophisticated of these depositors sought higher returns in the open market from less regulated competitors. The resulting disintermediation placed commercial banks in a liquidity squeeze. In response, banks began to create new instruments in attempts to reclaim existing deposits and attract new funds by offering market rates to their most interest-sensitive customers.

Successful innovation, however, did not go unnoticed by the Federal Reserve, other regulators, and Congress. Often, out of concern for housing and the stability of financial markets, one or more of these groups stepped in and either attempted to shut down the innovation or ratified it by raising interest rate ceilings on close substitutes offered by banks and thrifts. The general process being described, then, is a continuous evolutionary cycle involving banks, thrifts, unregulated suppliers of financial services, money markets, and the regulators, all interacting in response to market pressures. And the principal economic force sustaining these pressures was inflation, accompanied by rising interest rates.

The persistence of the pressures stimulating financial innovation during the late 1960s and early 1970s and the variety of institutional responses is quite striking. For example, the development of the Eurodollar, federal funds and repurchase agreements (R/P), and large certificate of deposit (C/D) markets are all examples of innovations that expanded as the result of disintermediation pressures. It was also during this period that the first of the financial innovations having significant implications for the growth and expansion of bank holding companies developed.

Shut out of the Eurodollar and other markets and pressed for funds in late 1969 and early 1970, as interest rate ceilings again became a significant constraint, banks began to exploit the holding company organizational form by issuing nonreservable commercial paper as a liability of the holding company and downstreaming funds to subsidiary banks. (Commercial paper sales by banks were already reservable.)

There is little, if any, direct evidence to suggest that banks had perceived the financing advantage of bank holding companies when the first wave of formations occurred following Citicorp's announcement of its intention to form a one-bank holding company in July of 1968. It is interesting to note, however, that the great bulge in interest in the one-bank holding company organizational form occurred over the last half of 1968 when the gap between Regulation Q (savings and time deposit interest rate) ceilings and commercial paper rates widened by over 250 basis points. Between September 1 and December 31, 1968, seven banks with $14.1 billion in deposits formed one-bank holding companies, and another seventy-six banks with deposits of $71.8 billion—including thirty-four of the nation's one hundred largest banks—announced their intentions to form one-bank holding companies (see U.S. Congress, 1969). This compares with the $17.8 billion in deposits in the 684 companies existing prior to September 1, 1968 (Table 1).

Over the last two and one-half quarters of 1969 and the first half of 1970, commercial paper issued by bank holding companies became a major source of funds to banks. Sales of bank-related commercial paper increased from about $1.9 billion in July of 1969 to a high of $7.8 billion a year later in late July of 1970. The significance of this source of funds is placed in better perspective when it is recognized that banks lost over $13 billion in C/Ds between November of 1968 and September of 1969 but were able to recover nearly 20 percent through commercial paper sales over that period.

Bank holding companies' sales of commercial paper remained

TABLE 1. EXISTING ONE-BANK HOLDING COMPANIES 1955–70 AND PROPOSED FORMATIONS SEPTEMBER-DECEMBER 1968

Year	*Number of One-Bank Holding Companies*	*Bank Deposits ($ Billions)*
1955	117	$ 11.6
1965	550	$ 15.1
1968 (September 1)	684	$ 17.8
1968 (December 31)	691	$ 31.9
Banks announcing plans to formulate one-bank holding companies (September 1-December 31, 1968)	76	$ 71.8
1970	1,318	$191.0

Source: U.S. Congress (1969).

high over the summer of 1970 until they began a slight downward trend in late August. On September 18, 1970, following a Federal Reserve Board proposal made a year earlier, Regulation D (member bank reserve requirements) and Regulation Q were amended to cover commercial paper sales by bank holding companies and their subsidiaries whenever the proceeds were used to supply funds to bank affiliates; a 10 percent marginal reserve requirement applied. The effect of this regulatory change was to price banking organizations out of the commercial paper market.

Commercial paper sales were not the only vehicle for bank holding companies to finance their activities free from Regulations D and Q. Beginning in July of 1974 Citicorp and other holding companies began issuing a series of small denomination floating rate notes. Congress acted by promptly passing Senate Bill 3838 in October of 1974 giving the Federal Reserve Board authority to regulate nearly all bank holding company note issues and to subject them to Regulations D and Q. At first, these regulations were not applied by the Federal Reserve to bank holding company note issues. But finally to shut down a series of note issues designed to be just outside existing Regulation Q ceilings, all bank holding company note issues were gradually brought under Regulations D and Q (the last being in 1979 during the Credit Restraint Program) regardless of whether the funds were used to fund banking subsidiaries or nonbanking affiliates.

1970 AMENDMENTS TO THE BANK HOLDING COMPANY ACT OF 1956 AND THE ROLE OF GEOGRAPHIC AND PRODUCT DIVERSIFICATION

Although avoidance of Regulations D and Q was an important consideration in bank holding company funding and formations during the late 1960s and early 1970s, the desire to achieve greater product and geographic diversity continued to play an important role in bank holding company growth. It will be remembered that the Bank Holding Company Act of 1956 and related regulatory restrictions applied only to companies owning two or more banks. In early 1968 North Carolina National Bank and Wachovia Bank and Trust, N.C. announced their intentions to form one-bank holding companies. The full potential of the one-bank holding company form did not attract public attention, however, until July of 1968 when Citicorp announced its intention to become a one-bank holding company. The principal reasons Citicorp cited for becoming a one-bank holding company related to the additional flexibility to expand geographically and to offer new services. The proxy statement notes that:

> Some of the Bank's present departments or activities such as leasing, factoring, or travel services could have greater growth potential if operated by First National City Corporation directly or through subsidiaries, because geographic expansion would be easier. . . .
>
> It is also expected that the new corporate structure can be used advantageously to move into other financially oriented activities either directly or through newly formed subsidiaries, or by acquiring companies already established in such fields.

Almost immediately it was argued in the financial press (Strachan, 1968) that the virtually unlimited geographical and product diversification potential of this new conglomerate form had sparked the broad rally that occurred in the market for bank equities following Citicorp's announcement; as discussed in the previous section, a host of other major banks also announced their intention to form one-bank holding companies (Table 1).

Congress responded almost immediately to this end run around the McFadden Act and Douglas Amendment restricting interstate banking, the Glass-Steagall Act provisions separating banking and investment banking, and the general threat to the historical separation between banking and commerce. The U.S. Congress published a study in 1969 of the one-bank holding company movement and its potential problems, and legislation was introduced in both the House and Senate in mid-February of 1969. This legislative activity culminated in passage of the 1970 Amendments to the Bank Holding Company Act of 1956. (For a detailed chronology see Eisenbeis, Harris, and Lakonishok, 1982.)

These amendments subjected one-bank holding companies to the same rules and regulations as multibank holding companies and modified the criteria contained in the act for bank holding company expansion into permissible nonbanking activities. On balance, these amendments significantly narrowed the diversification possibilities for one-bank holding companies and slightly expanded those for multibank companies by allowing expansion only into those activities that were so closely related to banking to be a proper incident thereto. (See Aharony and Swary, 1981; Martin and Keown, 1981; and Eisenbeis, Harris, and Lakonishok, 1982, for analyses of the effects of these changes on BHC share values.)

Since no geographic restrictions were imposed on the locations of permissible nonbanking activities, an opportunity was provided for banking organizations to avoid the limitations of the McFadden Act and Douglas Amendment, at least with respect to certain functional banking activities. It is not surprising, therefore, that many large bank holding companies have actively used nonbanking expansion to establish a physical presence throughout the country.

More recently, several states have taken more direct steps, as permitted by the Douglas Amendment to the Bank Holding Company Act of 1956, to allow out-of-state holding companies to enter their states. New York State, Massachusetts, and Maine, for example, have passed reciprocal legislation. Alaska now permits entry by out-of-state organizations, while South Dakota and Delaware have permitted acquisitions of newly chartered banks, provided certain minimum capital and other operational, employment, and locational restrictions are met. (Hawke, 1982, argues that many of these restrictions may be unconstitutional.) Many large banking organizations have already established banking subsidiaries in at least South Dakota and Delaware in order to take advantage of less restrictive usury ceilings.

A second wedge was driven in the restrictions on interstate banking with passage of the Garn–St Germain Depository Institutions Act of 1982. This act permits the interstate acquisition of a thrift institution or a failing bank with assets in excess of $500 million. Many restrictions are placed, however, on the order of preference to be given to bidders for such failed banks based on their geographic location.

With respect to product diversification, the requirement of the 1970 amendments that the nonbanking activities be "closely related to banking or managing or controlling banks as to be a proper incident thereto," has resulted in only twenty-five activities (seventeen by rule making and eight by order) being approved by the Federal Reserve Board as of May 1982 (Table 2). All but four were essentially permissible for national banks at the time the activity was approved. Only two denied activities,

TABLE 2. PERMISSIBLE NONBANKING ACTIVITIES FOR BANK HOLDING COMPANIES—UNDER SECTION 4(c)8 OF REGULATION Y (MAY 1, 1982)

Activities Permitted by Regulation	*Activities Permitted by Order*	*Activities Denied by the Board*
1. Extension of credit [2] Mortgage banking Finance companies, consumer sales, and commercial Credit cards Factoring	1. Issuance and sale of travelers checks [2, 6]	1. Insurance premium funding (combined sales of mutual funds and insurance)
2. Industrial bank, Morris Plan Bank, industrial loan company	2. Buying and selling gold and silver bullion and silver coin [2, 4]	2. Underwriting life insurance not related to credit extension
3. Servicing loans and other extensions of credit [2]	3. Issuing money orders and general purpose variable denominated payment instruments [1, 2, 4]	3. Real estate brokerage [2]
4. Trust company [2]	4. Futures commission merchant to cover gold and silver bullion and coins [1, 2]	4. Land development
5. Investment and financial advising [2]	5. Underwriting certain federal, state, and municipal securities [1, 2]	5. Real estate syndication
6. Full-payout leasing of personal or real property [2]	6. Check verification [1, 2, 4]	6. General management consulting
7. Investment in community welfare projects [2]	7. Financial advice to consumers [1, 2]	7. Property management
8. Providing bookkeeping or data processing services [2]	8. Issuance of small denomination debt instruments [1]	8. Computer output microfilm services
9. Acting as insurance agent or broker primarily in connection with credit extensions [2]	9. Arranging for equity financing of real estate	9. Underwriting mortgage guaranty insurance [3]
10. Underwriting credit life, accident, and health insurance	10. Acting as futures commissions merchant	10. Operating a savings and loan association [1, 5]
11. Providing courier services [2]	11. Discount brokerage	11. Operating a travel agency [1, 2]
12. Management consulting for unaffiliated banks [1, 2]	12. Operating a distressed savings and loan association	12. Underwriting property and casualty insurance [1]
		13. Underwriting home loan life mortgage insurance
		14. Orbanco: Investment note issue with transactional characteristics
		15. Real estate advisory services

13. Sale at retail of money orders with a face value of not more than $1,000, travelers checks and savings bonds [1, 2]	13. Operating an Article XII investment company
14. Performing appraisals of real estate [1]	14. Executing foreign banking unsolicited purchases and sales of securities
15. Audit services for unaffiliated banks	15. Engaging in commercial banking activities abroad through a limited purpose Delaware bank
16. Issuance and sale of travelers checks	16. Performing appraisal of real estate and real estate advisor and real estate brokerage on nonresidential properties
17. Management consulting to nonbanking depository institutions	17. Operating a Pool Reserve Plan for loss reserves of banks for loans to small businesses
	18. Operating a thrift institution in Rhode Island
	19. Operating a guarantee savings bank in New Hampshire
	20. Offering informational advice and transactional services for foreign exchange services

Source: Economic Review, Federal Reserve Bank of Atlanta, April 1983.

[1] Added to list since January 1, 1975.

[2] Activities permissible to national banks.

[3] Board orders found these activities closely related to banking and denied proposed acquisitions as part of its "go slow" policy.

[4] To be decided on a case-by-case basis.

[5] Operating a thrift institution has been permitted by order in Rhode Island, California, and New Hampshire only.

[6] Subsequently permitted by regulation.

real estate brokerage and travel agencies, were approved activities for national banks. (The latter has since been ruled impermissible for national banks by the courts.) Thus, because of legislative and regulatory restrictions, it appears that the bank holding company movement has not resulted in significant additional product diversification potential. In fact, it is probably a misnomer to call such activities "nonbanking" activities. They are really *banking activities* being carried out in separately financed departments or subsidiaries, often outside of Regulations D and Q and McFadden Act restrictions. That is, they permit the banking organization to conduct lending and other services outside of subsidiary banks that could just as well, except for certain regulatory constraints, be done by the banks directly.

A recent series of events is raising once again the issues Congress considered in passing the 1970 amendments to close the loophole in the Bank Holding Company Act of 1956 exposed by the one-bank holding company movement. To qualify as a bank under the definition in the 1970 amendments, an organization must both make commercial loans and accept demand deposits. By divesting of either activity (or spinning it off into a separate affiliation), it has proved possible for nonbanking companies to acquire chartered commercial banks and avoid the nonbanking activity restrictions of the 1956 act. Such a device has enabled Dreyfus to acquire a national bank in New Jersey and several other firms, including Shearson/American Express, to acquire commercial banks. The extent to which this loophole will be exploited or that the agencies will permit nonbanking and securities firms to acquire commercial banks remains to be seen. Even more interesting, however, is the possibility that major U.S. bank holding companies will subdivide their demand deposit business into one particular bank subsidiary and their commercial loan business into another bank subsidiary and suddenly no longer be a bank holding company for purposes of the act.

THE ROLE OF TAX CONSIDERATIONS IN BANK HOLDING COMPANY FORMATIONS

Of all the incentives to bank holding company formation, tax considerations have probably been the single most important catalyst to the formation of the majority of the nation's bank holding companies. For example, of the more than 2,300 bank holding companies in existence, more than 80 percent are one-bank holding companies. Of these, about 55 percent are single-subsidiary companies (see Strover, 1978). Thus, diversification, in terms of either the product or geographic markets to be served, cannot account for the existence of these single-subsidiary holding companies.

There are several reasons why the bank holding company form might be preferable for tax purposes. These advantages stem from the fact that, if the bank holding company is properly structured, dividends received from subsidiaries are tax deductible, and a consolidated tax return may be filed for the entire organization. The tax deductibility of dividends especially benefits those who purchase control of a bank through the use of debt, and it facilitates capital injections into subsidiary banks as compared with nonsubsidiary banks. In the former case, the typical procedure is for an individual or group of individuals to borrow money to purchase a bank. They then form a bank holding company which is given the bank stock and assumes the debt in return for stock in the bank holding company. Since dividends received from a bank by the bank holding company are tax deductible, the principal on the debt can be repaid out of dividend income. Dividend income is taxed only at the bank level. In addition the bank holding company interest payments are a deductible expense (as they are for individuals). In the case of individual ownership, dividends received would first be taxed before the principal on the acquisition debt could be paid.

Since the only source of bank holding company income is typically tax-deductible dividends from subsidiaries, the bank holding company usually starts with a zero taxable income base from which interest and other expenses are subtracted. (This assumes, of course, that the parent company is not an operating company, in which case it would have other sources of income.) This results in negative taxable income for the parent. Filing a consolidated return allows the organization to offset positive taxable income in the rest of the organization. In addition, consolidation also permits operating losses in some subsidiaries to offset operating gains in others for tax purposes.

There are two other dimensions of taxation which tend to provide significant incentives for banks to form holding companies and also to spin off permissible banking activities into subsidiaries. The first relates to the ability to avoid local taxes. Income generated within a bank is taxed by the state and perhaps municipalities in which the institution is headquartered or operates. Performing the same activity in a subsidiary of a bank holding company permits the organization, in some instances, to charter the subsidiary in a state with lower taxes which then subjects the subsidiary to "doing business" taxes only in the original state. A vivid example of this type of tax avoidance is provided by the method Citicorp chose to market the rising-rate thrift notes it announced in July of 1977. The prospectus indicates that the notes were to be offered through a specially chartered, wholly-owned subsidiary of Nationwide Financial Services Corporation (Citicorp's consumer finance company subsidiary). This subsidiary was organized to avoid subjecting the parent company to taxation in the states in which the notes were to be sold and to avoid the necessity of qualifying Citicorp to do business in those states. Additionally, it also simplified meeting the technical Securities and Exchange Commission net capital rules to qualify as a broker-dealer.

Federal tax law also provides an incentive for a holding company (and/or bank) to conduct foreign business through separately chartered subsidiaries rather than through foreign branches. The incentive stems from a provision in the present tax law permitting a subsidiary of a U.S. corporation also holding a foreign charter to retain abroad indefinitely any portion of its net income rather than upstreaming it in the form of dividends. Since only repatriated income is subject to U.S. tax, there is an incentive to conduct foreign business through separately chartered subsidiaries in low-tax countries. In contrast, income earned abroad through a foreign branch is treated as if it were earned domestically and is subject to U.S. tax (and perhaps foreign tax as well). This feature of the tax law helps to explain the growth of foreign subsidiary activities of the large U.S. money center banks in Bermuda and the Cayman Islands, both of which are low-tax countries. It may also stimulate the proliferation of foreign operations in countries that would not be profitable except for the tax advantages that result. For example, until March 16, 1978, banks were able to claim full foreign tax credits for a 25 percent tax that Brazil imposed on interest that banks earned in the country. Brazilian authorities typically rebated 85 percent of the tax to the borrowers, but the bank still received a full tax credit on the paper transaction. The intent of the tax and rebate system was to stimulate investment in Brazil by reducing the interest cost on foreign loans; the borrower benefited because of the rebate, and the lender got a tax savings from its home country.

CAPITAL ADEQUACY REQUIREMENTS AND OTHER SUPERVISORY INCENTIVES TO BANK HOLDING COMPANY FORMATION

It has already been argued that deposit rate ceilings and reserve requirements provided a significant inducement to bank holding company formations. More importantly, these regulations also provided incentives for a holding company to spin off banking activities into other parts of the organization and for a parent holding company to fund both banking and nonbanking expansion, especially during tight money periods and when interest rates are rising. As a consequence, one of the main implications of the bank holding company form of organization is that it has facilitated increased leverage of the banking entity as a whole.

Interestingly, the thrust of early bank holding company regulatory and supervisory policy has reinforced and unintentionally tended to encourage the conduct of financing and certain activities in other parts of the organization rather than within banking subsidiaries. Following the 1970 Amendments to the Bank Holding Company Act of 1956, regulatory policy was designed to compartmentalize bank holding companies into two segments—a regulated component consisting of the banking subsidiaries and the parent holding company with its nonbanking subsidiaries. The objective was to isolate and protect banks from risk and abuse and, thus, to limit deposit insurance risks flowing from the rest of the organization which was permitted to complete and operate in a less regulated and relatively unsupervised manner (see Chase, 1978). At the same time bank holding companies were expected to be "sources of strength" to their banking affiliates, and there was an attempt to permit any benefit from bank holding company affiliation to be downstreamed to banking subsidiaries. In particular, the issuing of debt at the parent company level and use of the proceeds to purchase equity of subsidiary banks—a practice known as double leveraging—was not only condoned but often encouraged as a means to improve the capital positioning of a bank holding company's banking subsidiaries. This double leveraging was permitted since the financing capabilities of the parent were presumably being relied upon to inject equity into subsidiary banks. As long as banking affiliates were effectively isolated by laws and regulations, such as Section 23A of the Federal Reserve Act which limits permissible transactions among affiliates and subsidiaries, it was believed that the corporate veil would not be pierced in the event of bankruptcy or other legal action and no harm would befall subsidiary banks.

Such a policy would be appropriate if it were truly possible to isolate totally bank holding company banking subsidiaries from the rest of the organization. Separation would clearly be feasible if a holding company functioned as a mutual fund and was only a passive investor, exercising no management, operational, or financial influence over independently operated firms. The available evidence, however, indicates that bank holding companies tend to operate more as integrated firms with the parent company dictating the key aspects of their banking subsidiaries' operations, such as organizational structure, financial and managerial philosophy, as well as specific functions, such as funds management, correspondent relationships, asset and liability management, capitalization, and budgets. Moreover, bank holding company nonbanking subsidiaries appear to be even more integrated and tightly controlled than their banking subsidiaries. (See Whalen, 1982A, 1982B; Rose, 1978; and Murray, 1978.)

The implication is that when bank holding companies operate as integrated firms, rather than as a collective of truly independent companies sharing only a common mutual fund–type owner, regulatory policies designed to force compartmentalization are likely in the long run to be self-defeating. The very attempt to isolate the more heavily regulated subsidiary banks from the rest of the holding company only creates further economic incentives for the organization to attempt to circumvent banking regulations and to spin off more and more activities of the banking subsidiaries into the less heavily regulated segments of the organization. The reason, of course, is that to a firm, total profits of the organization are maximized and not necessarily the profits of individual subsidiaries. Thus, it matters little to the firm where a particular function is being conducted within the organization as long as its contribution to total firm profits is optimized.

There are likely to be two major consequences of bank holding company regulatory policies designed to force compartmentalization. First, there will be a shrinking of the regulated components relative to the nonregulated components as more and more activities are shifted from regulated to less regulated segments of the organization. Second, the operational and other interdependencies within the firm are likely to increase. This is particularly the case if customer relationships are served by coordinating the products offered by a number of different subsidiaries. Moreover, the entire holding company is likely to become more of an integrated firm with respect to risk-taking than it was before because of the integration of operations and provision of services. Integration also increases the potential for regulatory conflicts when different federal and state agencies are responsible for supervising only portions of the entity.

This shifting of activities from banking to nonbanking subsidiaries poses special public policy problems when a parent company or its nonbanking affiliates issue uninsured liabilities that are close substitutes for the insured liabilities of subsidiary banks. As a greater and greater proportion of financial liabilities shift from insured to uninsured status, then the stabilizing benefits of deposit insurance will be lost unless the government chooses implicitly to extend guarantees to such claims. This, in fact, appears to be what has occurred, at least where larger troubled or failed banking organizations have been involved. With this extension of implicit guarantees to more than insured liabilities, however, also goes the legitimate concern on the part of banking regulators and the Federal Deposit Insurance Corporation for monitoring and limiting undue risk-taking in the nonbanking segments of a holding company.

To date, the regulators have responded quite predictably to the shifting of certain funding and other activities to the nonbanking components of a holding company and to the realization that a banking subsidiary cannot be isolated from what goes on in the rest of the organization. In particular, they have begun to extend banking-type supervision and regulation, on a selective basis, to formerly unregulated segments of holding companies. The objective is both to monitor and limit risk-taking and to facilitate monetary control. The application of Regulations D and Q to bank holding company commercial paper and short-term debt and the newly revised capital adequacy standards are clear examples. For larger banking organizations, capital adequacy will now be assessed on a consolidated basis, and account will be taken for the proportion of bank equity funded with subsidy debt at the parent company level.

Implications of Financial Innovation for Regulation and Supervision of Bank Holding Companies

There are several general observations and conclusions that flow, either explicitly or implicitly, from the analysis of the effects of regulation and innovation that have important implications for public policy and the future structure of the supervision and regulation of banking organizations. They highlight the need to develop a consistent framework for the supervision and regulation of financial institutions and, in particular, for bank holding companies. These implications warrant restating.

First, the evolution of bank holding companies is an integral and natural part of this broader process of regulation-induced financial innovation. Banks were moved to adopt the bank holding company form as one means to escape certain regulatory constraints, namely Regulations D and Q, restrictions on geographic and product market expansion, capital regulation, and taxation.

Second, it appears that an increasing proportion of banking activities is being conducted at the holding company level in an attempt to avoid regulation. As mentioned earlier, parent holding companies have begun to play an increasing role in the financing of both banking and nonbanking activities through commercial paper, small note sales, and debt issues. This is presumably due to attempts to avoid Regulations D and Q, and to the accommodating capital policies of the regulators. In addition, there are increasing incentives to spin off operations of subsidiary banks, both to avoid federal and local taxes as well as the prohibition on geographic expansion in restrictive state banking laws and the McFadden Act.

Third, both banks and bank holding companies have become more highly leveraged and have also tended to rely more and more on short-term, interest-sensitive sources of funds. To this extent regulation has indirectly induced more risk-taking.

Fourth, in the 1970s, the combination of higher yielding investment alternatives, accommodating tax laws, and Regulation Q ceilings has resulted in significant expansion of U.S. banks' foreign operations. Indeed, many of the major U.S. money center banks have recently been generating more of their earnings abroad than they have domestically.

Fifth, the process of financial innovation has resulted in a blurring of the distinctions among the liabilities of not only different types of depository financial institutions but also nondepository institutions. Consequently, competition has been increased.

Sixth, financial innovation has resulted in increased competition from merchants, brokerage firms, money market mutual funds, and other financial and nondepository institutions creating competitive inequities resulting from the fact that these institutions are not subject to the same regulatory costs as banking organizations. To meet this competition and to operate profitably during periods of rapidly rising rates, banking organizations have powerful incentives to conduct as many as possible of their activities in an unregulated, or less regulated, environment. Hence, they are under constant pressure to spin off activities and functions of subsidiary banks and operate through bank holding companies and nonbanking and foreign subsidiaries.

Seventh, attempts to regulate a firm such as a bank holding company, operating under a single-objective function, by dividing it into regulated and unregulated segments, will tend to induce a reshuffling of activities into the nonregulated portions of the organization whenever a regulation becomes a binding and costly constraint. The implication is that it is not practical or possible to segment risk-taking or to separate the financial health of parts of the organization from the whole. Thus, it is also not realistic to act as if significant subsidiaries of such an organization would, in most instances, be permitted by the parent to fail. The only way to truly isolate subsidiaries would be to impose regulations to make them totally independent except for the passive ownership of shares by the parent. The problem with such a policy, however, is that it would negate the basic rationale for establishing a holding company so as to take advantage of a beneficial synergistic or other relationship that might result from financial conglomeration.

Finally, so long as it is public policy to attempt to minimize the likelihood of financial crisis by insuring deposit-type liabilities, either explicitly or implicitly, then the efficacy of such insurance can only be maintained by minimizing inducements to shift funds from insured to uninsured status. Moreover, the need to monitor and control the insurer's exposure to risk suggests that any changes in the asset and liability powers of such institutions should take place within the insured entity.

Alternative Policies and Bank Holding Company Supervision and Regulation

In view of the effects of financial innovation and the risk-inducing nature of current regulatory policies on bank holding companies, it is both appropriate and necessary to explore feasible alternatives and/or reforms. In that process it is important that any new system address or consider several factors.

1. Attempts to maintain Regulations D (member bank reserve requirements) and Q (savings and time deposit interest rate) have been the root cause of many of the restrictions placed on banking organizations affecting the terms under which financial services can be provided. In addition to inducing banking organizations to form BHCs and to take on more risk, they have provided economic incentives for nonfinancial and nonregulated firms to begin to provide financial services.
2. The entry by nonregulated firms into many financial markets suggests that bank holding companies will continue to be at a competitive disadvantage unless given increased flexibility to meet that competition.
3. The financial system has had to deal over the past few years with a series of movements in which interest rates have fluctuated widely in response to changes in the rate of inflation, the level of economic activity, and government economic policy. Such cycles are potentially destabilizing unless financial institutions are free to adjust and adapt to changing conditions. There is nothing to suggest that these cycles are dampening or will occur with less frequency in the future. Added to this domestic source of financial instability is the increased vulnerability of our financial institutions to changes in world economic conditions resulting from rapid expansion abroad. The expansion of foreign banks into the U.S. as a result of the recently passed International Banking

Act will only serve to integrate further both our real sectors and financial systems with those of the rest of the world.

4. Regulation which is designed to force banking organizations to operate as a collection of single, independent entities, when the organization's incentive is to operate as an integrated entity, that also does not regulate each and every part of the entity, will only result in attempts to circumvent that effort.

There are two sets of regulatory policies which, when coupled with actions to phase out and to reduce significantly the costs of reserve requirements and Regulation Q, would achieve the long-run safety and soundness goals and be responsive to the continuing destabilizing pressures affecting banking organizations. The first is to reorient supervisory attention away from primary emphasis on subsidiary banks to focus on the consolidated bank holding company as a single, regulated entity. Some steps have already been taken with the agencies' new consolidated capital adequacy standards for large banks. The second is to create a set of regulatory incentives to encourage bank holding companies to fold activities and functions back into a consolidated subsidiary bank. Each of these alternatives raises separate sets of issues with respect to regulatory and structural reform together with political issues which may affect the practical implementation of the alternatives, and these are discussed in the next section. On the other hand, both of the proposals share certain desirable common features. For example, they both imply that substantial deregulation is justifiable on equity and economic grounds. Second, they increase institutions' flexibility to adapt to changing economic conditions. Finally, they simplify the process of supervision.

DISCUSSION OF POLICY ALTERNATIVES

Consolidated Bank Holding Company Focus—The first alternative would reorient regulatory and supervisory policy away from primary emphasis on subsidiary banks and focus on the consolidated bank holding company as the single, decision-making entity. Taking this policy to its logical conclusion, there would be no need to be concerned, for safety and soundness reasons, with the financial relationships among subsidiaries or with maintaining their independence. Under this alternative the holding company organizations could be regulated, examined, and supervised analogous to a branch system, with the structure of the parent and its subsidiaries simply representing ways for the firm to organize its internal accounting and control procedures. If regulated in this manner, and when accompanied with general deregulation, bank holding companies could evolve into the functional equivalent of banks.

For the purpose of regulation relevant for monetary control, a bank holding company could be treated as a single entity with its consolidated liabilities subject to the same limits and reserve requirements as banks. This policy approach also would avoid the problems of attempting to sort out and reserve certain intracompany transfers and to trace the sources and uses of intrafirm transactions to determine their regulatory status. It would have the additional benefits of (1) eliminating incentives to innovate different types of intrainstitutional fund transfers and investments to avoid reserve requirement–related constraints and (2) reducing associated reporting burdens.

This single-entity approach also holds the possibility to deregulate further the industry since regulations that have been instituted to force separation or to limit transactions between and among subsidiaries would no longer be necessary. For example, Section 23A of the Federal Reserve Act could be dropped, as could regulations, supervisory conventions, rules, and reporting requirements pertaining to intercompany transfers of funds and tax liabilities. Moreover, reporting burdens for supervisory purposes could be drastically reduced, since only consolidated entity data would need to be collected.

A principal argument that would no doubt be raised against this single-entity approach is that it would require an extension of banking-type regulation to the nonbanking activities of bank holding companies. This might place the organization at a competitive disadvantage to the extent it competed with nonregulated firms. It should be remembered, however, that with only a couple of minor exceptions, the nonbanking activities of bank holding companies are really banking activities that could legally be conducted within a bank. Therefore, the single-entity approach would not really be extending regulation, but simply closing the ability of the organization to avoid regulation by use of the bank holding company form. But still the valid point does remain that regulated firms are at a competitive disadvantage relative to less regulated firms. Therefore the long-run goal should be to reduce and limit the extent that bank holding companies are constrained by regulation, to eliminate the regulatory-induced incentives for nonbanking firms to enter financial markets, and to provide banking organizations with the needed flexibility to meet changing economic conditions.

Despite the potential appeal of this approach, substantial transitional and legal problems would exist. For example, although subsidiaries might be operated as a part of a single entity, they remain legally separate in that the minority shareholders and debt holders may have claims on the resources of subsidiaries. Ownership of assets and settlement of claims might greatly complicate the resolution of failures. Also, state and local regulatory and tax policies might conflict with federal regulatory policy. There could also be the need to reevaluate federal policy toward insurance of bank holding company liabilities. Despite these problems, the general single-entity regulatory policy could shape and provide guidance to needed legislative and regulatory changes that ultimately would lead to a parent bank holding company having all the powers permitted to its subsidiaries.

The present trend in bank holding company supervision seems already to be evolving in the direction of treating a bank holding company as a consolidated entity. The Federal Reserve recently instituted a bank holding company surveillance and computer-based monitoring system that focuses almost exclusively on the holding company as a consolidated organization. Also, the chairman of the Federal Deposit Insurance Corporation and past comptroller of the currency have argued that it is not possible, because of the interrelated nature of the holding company and its subsidiaries, for them to assess the risk and financial condition of the nonmember and national bank subsidiaries of bank holding companies without also having information on the entire organization. This raises the question of the feasibility and the desirability of maintaining the present regulatory structure giving different federal agencies supervisory responsibility for only a portion of the consolidated entity. Finally, consolidated capital standards for large bank holding companies have been put in place.

Consolidated Bank Subsidiary Focus—To avoid some of the problems—especially the legal ones—that might be associated with consolidation and regulation of bank holding companies as single entities, the second alternative policy is to provide the necessary inducements for a bank holding company to consolidate its operations into a single-bank subsidiary, which would then be regulated as a single firm. The principal areas affected for most of the nation's bank holding companies could be the financing and operations of nonbanking subsidiaries, especially those extending across state lines. The simplest way to accomplish this would be to provide banks with all the powers of their nonbanking subsidiaries. This approach has several advantages. First, as mentioned previously, the nonbanking activities involved are—with only minor exceptions—really banking activities that banks are able to engage in directly. Thus, consolidation would not be disruptive to the financial operation of a bank or to the traditional concept of what banking really is. Furthermore, nonbanking activities account for only a small proportion of banking organizations' resources (about 3 to 5 percent in the aggregate). Therefore, consolidation would be technically feasible in most cases without disrupting the organizational structure or portfolio composition of the resulting bank. Second, for the most part, inducing consolidation would involve removal or reduction of regulation. In most instances, bank holding company activities, especially financing activities, could likely be accomplished more efficiently within a bank subsidiary except for the existence of Regulation Q and other constraints making it uneconomical to do so. Third, reduction in regulation has the beneficial side effect of increasing banking organizations' flexibility, which, as was argued earlier, would be necessary if they were to meet the competition of nonbanking firms and to adjust to the stress of economic cycles. Fourth, relaxation of regulation would tend to break down the barriers that provide the incentives for nonregulated firms to offer financial services. Fifth, consolidation of a bank holding company into a bank subsidiary simplifies and reduces the burden of supervision since only a single entity would need to be examined. Under the present regulatory structure this would eliminate, or reduce substantially, the jurisdictional problems that presently exist because several banking agencies have authority over parts of existing holding companies. Finally, consolidation would focus public debate on the proper scope of banking functions, both in terms of permissible activities and also with respect to the McFadden Act, Douglas Amendment, and Glass-Steagall Act.

Interestingly, the Garn–St Germain Depository Institutions Act of 1982 has already taken a significant, though interim, step toward this second policy option by expanding the powers of bank service corporations. Under this act, banks are now permitted to establish wholly-owned bank service corporations and (1) to engage in clerical activities previously authorized by the Bank Service Corporation Act of 1962; (2) to offer any service, except deposit-taking, permitted to the parent bank; and (3) to engage in any nonbanking activity, except deposit-taking, authorized by Federal Reserve Regulation (Table 2) to bank holding companies. The Garn–St Germain Act "McFaddenizes" those bank service corporation activities offered under authority granted to parent banks but does not similarly limit the geographic scope of other bank service corporation activities (see Hawke, Sweet, and Mierzewski, 1982).

The 1962 act, as amended by the Garn–St Germain Act, both simplifies and complicates some of the regulatory problems for the banking agencies. For example, banks may organize bank services corporations as joint ventures with other banks and nonbanks as well. The risk issues and supervisory implications of such joint ventures are not totally clear, especially since transactions with bank services corporations less than 25 percent owned by individual banks are not subject to Section 23A of the Federal Reserve Act. The agencies do have authority, however, to supervise and regulate these joint ventures. For majority-owned bank service corporations, banking transactions with these subsidiaries are also not subject to Section 23A, so presumably the activities of such subsidiaries will be consolidated with the parent bank for supervisory purposes. Finally, the act reduces the incentives for banks not presently part of bank holding companies to form such a company and engage in permissible nonbanking activities.

Summary and Conclusions

This chapter reviews the forces stimulating the growth of bank holding companies. It is shown that their expansion is an integral part of the broader process of financial innovation.

High and variable interest rates, inflation, and binding regulatory constraints not only have stimulated the entry of less regulated competitors (such as merchants, brokerage house and money market mutual funds) into the financial service industry, but also have induced changes in the organization of banking firms. To avoid the costs of regulation and to compete more effectively with unregulated competitors, banking organizations have exploited the potential of the bank holding company device. Traditional functions and activities have been shifted from bank subsidiaries to less regulated nonbank subsidiaries.

This trend has complicated the supervisory and regulatory process. Bank holding companies are becoming more integrated, making it more and more difficult to insulate insured bank subsidiaries from risk-taking in the rest of the organization. Furthermore, attempts to protect the insured subsidiaries by dividing a banking organization into regulated and unregulated segments, as has been proposed by the Treasury Department, are bound to be self-defeating. Whenever regulation becomes a binding and costly constraint, banking organizations will simply shift even more activities to their less regulated subsidiaries, and because it is not realistic to believe that a highly integrated firm would let a significant affiliate fail, the risk exposure of the insurance fund becomes more difficult to manage. Thus, the efficacy of deposit insurance depends upon reducing regulatory incentives to shift funding activities from insured to uninsured subsidiaries.

Two policy proposals are put forth to deal with this problem. Both involve the combination of deregulation (basically the elimination of deposits rate ceilings and the payment of interest on reserves) and treatment of banking organizations as consolidated entities for risk assessment purposes.

The ultimate conclusion is that so long as bank holding companies—and financial institutions more generally—are regulated in ways that impose costs and induce regulatory-avoidance activities by both regulated and unregulated firms, the organizational structure of financial firms and the financial system will continue to be under dynamic pressure and continue to change. This suggests that the regulatory-induced evolution of the financial system and all the regulatory, supervisory, deposit insurance, and macro monetary policy formulation problems that are attendant with that process will continue into the future unless the necessary reforms are undertaken.

Edward J. Kane

6

The Role of Government in the Thrift Industry's Net-worth Crisis

For the purposes of this volume (which assigns credit unions to the consumer finance industry), it is possible to claim that thrift institutions are known by categorical names that feature the word *savings* as either the first or second word in their titles. The genus, thrift institution, includes two species: savings and loan associations (S&Ls) and mutual savings banks (MSBs). (Rule-proving exceptions occur in several states, where S&Ls go by

---

EDWARD J. KANE *is the Everett D. Reese Professor of Banking and Monetary Economics at Ohio State University and a research associate of the National Bureau of Economic Research. Dr. Kane is also a trustee and member of the finance committee of the Teachers Insurance and Annuity Association. A past president of the American Finance Association, he taught previously at Boston College, Princeton University, and Iowa State University. He has consulted for the Federal Deposit Insurance Corporation, the Federal Home Loan Bank Board, the Department of Housing and Urban Development, several components of the Federal Reserve System, and the Joint Economic Committee of the U.S. Congress. He has published widely and serves on the editorial boards of seven professional journals.* *For helpful comments on an earlier draft, he wishes to thank George Benston, Robert Eisenbeis, and Harvey Rosenblum.*

such pattern-breaking names as "cooperative banks" and "building-and-loan societies." The word *savings* accurately portrays the specialized focus of the liability side of both institutions' business. The archetypal thrift institution finances its lending activities by selling depository savings vehicles to household customers. Until the 1970s, thrift institutions' predominant financing vehicle was the passbook savings account. But competitive pressure generated by the interaction of accelerating inflation with unrealistically low ceilings on passbook interest rates encouraged the proliferation of savings certificates and the development of negotiable order of withdrawal (NOW) accounts. Along with expanded opportunities for advantageous S&L borrowing from the Federal Home Loan Bank System, by the 1980s this process had remade the liability side of thrift balance sheets. Because thrift institutions are highly levered and continue to hold assets whose average life substantially exceeds the average life of even these reconstituted liabilities, unanticipated run-ups in interest rates (such as occurred in the thirty-four months that ended in July 1982) place them in precarious condition.

As interest rates and servicing costs on savings vehicles soared above the contract yields on thrift assets, newspaper articles on thrift institutions morbidly began to count down the months of life expectancy left to the weakest of them. Reporters depicted firms in the thrift industry as though fate had involuntarily enrolled them in a financial dance marathon. Like the contestants featured in the movie *They Shoot Horses, Don't They?,* thrift institutions were expected to keep dancing until their individual resources were exhausted.

Most observers of the thrift institution dance contest conjectured that an institution was no stronger than its net-worth account, where net worth was calculated as the difference between the market values of the assets and liabilities that generally accepted accounting principles recognize as bookable. The level of interest rates was seen as setting the tempo at which the contest orchestra played. The faster the beat and the longer an up-tempo rhythm was maintained, the more rapidly the market value of the bookable net worth of individual thrift institutions would be used up.

This countdown perspective on thrift institution net worth had several things wrong and only one thing right. What was right was the assertion that jumps in interest rates and in interest rate volatility associated with the Federal Reserve's announced efforts to hold down monetary growth from October 6, 1979, through mid-1982 required savings institutions to reposition themselves to survive. But the perspective fails in three important ways.

First, it neglects the impact of technological change on the outlook for savings institutions. We can liken technology to the instruments available to members of the contest orchestra. Improvements in computer and communications technology are progressively robotizing and "remotizing" the nature of financial services competition and expanding thrift institution product lines. Systems of strategically located branch offices are no longer the only feasible ways to provide customers convenient access to their savings funds. Electronic terminals and toll-free telephone numbers are steadily shrinking the costs of monitoring an individually tailored combination of savings vehicles and of overcoming physical distances between customers and financial services offices. At the same time, contractual linkages between depository and nondepository firms are increasing rapidly. These linkages allow thrifts to offer their customers an extensive menu of services (such as discount brokerage) without necessarily producing them in-house.

Second, it distracts attention from other participants in the contest. To concentrate only on the weakest savings institutions—those that are near to closing down—ignores the great stamina exhibited by the large number of thrifts that everyone expects to keep on going and misses the important role played by the contest promoters. We need to ask ourselves how the dance contest became an industry event in the first place and what forces keep it going year after year, decade after decade. Nobody *makes* S&Ls and MSBs keep taking interest-volatility risk.

Third, reporters' concept of net worth neglects sources of institutional capital that generally accepted accounting principles do not allow thrift institution managers to book. Foremost among these is the market value of federal guarantees of their deposit debt.

This chapter contends that the root cause both of current thrift institution problems and of the industry's ability to keep dancing is one and the same—the mispricing of federal deposit insurance. For savings institutions, deposit insurance acts simultaneously as a blessing and a curse. Like the standard caricature of the Jewish mother, it pushes its offspring up with one hand and holds them down with the other. In effect, federal deposit insurance agencies encourage thrift institution clients to make securities market bets on the future course of interest rates because deposit insurance premiums permit them to lay off these bets at favorable odds. Federal insurance agencies insure clients' earnings against interest-volatility risk (i.e., truncate downward fluctuations in an institution's future net rate of return) for less than the compensation that loan and securities markets provide an investor for exposing his or her income to this risk. When deposit insurance agencies charge less than the market price for providing contingent guarantees of thrift institution deposit debt, managers are encouraged to reach out for interest-volatility risk, i.e., to position their firm's balance sheets on the edge of financial ruin.

The major forms of risk taken by thrift institutions come from leverage and from mismatching the lives of assets and liabilities. On average, liabilities of the thrifts turn over much faster than their assets do. This exposes their incomes and capital to interest-volatility risk. Since October 6, 1979, swings in interest rates have been extraordinarily severe. Unanticipated increases in interest rates narrow spreads between accounting yields on assets and the overall cost of funds. On the other hand, unanticipated decreases in interest rates widen these spreads.

Thrift institution managers are by no means forced to operate with mismatched assets and liability positions. Long-term lenders can control the gap between the average life of their asset and liability position in several ways. They can issue more long-term liabilities, stress variable interest rate loans, package the loans they originate for resale in secondary markets, or hedge their net exposure to interest-volatility risk by transactions in interest rate futures, forward contracts, or options contracts. However, although variable-rate lending has increased dramatically, few thrifts have held hedged positions in recent years. For example, surveys conducted by the Commodities Futures Trading Commission (Jaffe and Hobson, 1979) and subsequent reports from futures traders indicate that less than 10 percent of the nation's S&Ls trade in futures and forward contracts at all. Moreover, approximately one-third of those who do trade take what appear to be unhedged positions that perversely compound their risk exposure.

Differences in Governmental Restrictions Applicable to S&Ls and MSBs

Thrift institutions are becoming more and more like commercial banks. New financial functions and servicing systems are steadily being grafted onto these firms' traditional specializations. Historically, only commercial banks were authorized to make commercial loans and offer checking accounts. But 1980 and 1982 federal legislation allows thrifts to offer these services today, subject to percentage limitations that are unlikely to prove binding, given competitive efforts by other institutions to attract these same customers.

Both MSBs and S&Ls share a similar client base, deposit structure, and exposure to interest-volatility risk. However, patterns of governmental oversight for MSBs and S&Ls have differed in three important ways. First, MSBs have been granted a wider range of asset and liability powers. Second, until very recently, savings banks were forbidden to operate as stockholder-owned corporations. Third, MSBs face a different set of chartering and deposit insurance authorities.

The typical S&L has functioned predominantly as a real estate lender. Through the 1970s, about 85 percent of consolidated S&L assets consisted of mortgage loans. The rest of these firms' consolidated portfolio consisted of liquid assets and net worth, held in amounts sufficient to service its depositors' liquidity needs and to conform with governmental restrictions on balance sheet composition. As the effective rate of federal income tax on mutual savings institutions rose in the late 1960s, tax-exempt securities introduced another dimension to S&Ls' portfolio strategy.

MSBs have traditionally been less specialized than S&Ls, though over half of their assets are also in real estate loans. They have regularly been permitted to offer consumer loans (except in New York), to sell life insurance, and to invest in corporate bonds and stock. On the other hand, while S&Ls operate throughout the nation, MSBs function in only seventeen states. Ranked by the amount of deposits held in MSBs, these states are: New York and Massachusetts (where 66 percent of aggregate MSB deposits are located), Connecticut, Pennsylvania, New Jersey, Washington, Maine, New Hampshire, Maryland, Rhode Island, Minnesota,

Delaware, Vermont, Oregon, Indiana, Alaska, and Wisconsin. Until 1980, savings banks had to operate as mutual organizations under a charter issued by the banking department of one of these seventeen states. So far, only a handful of MSBs have converted to a federal mutual or stock charter.

In 1981, deposits at all 499 MSBs were governmentally insured. For 159 banks (48 of whom were also insured by a federal agency), the guarantor was a state operated insurance fund. For nine federally chartered savings banks (an organizational form that did not exist until 1979), the guarantor was the Federal Savings and Loan Insurance Corporation (FSLIC). However, the bulk of MSB deposits (331 institutions) was guaranteed by the Federal Deposit Insurance Corporation (FDIC), which also is the federal guarantor for deposits at commercial banks.

Unlike state chartered MSBs, S&Ls and a few federal MSBs have their own federal deposit insurance fund, the FSLIC. At year-end 1981, the deposits of all but 93 S&Ls were insured: 3,779 by the FSLIC and 475 by insurance funds operated by five states (Massachusetts, Maryland, North Carolina, Ohio, and Pennsylvania).

S&Ls have long been eligible to operate under either state or federal charters. In 1981, 49.2 percent of S&Ls held federal charters issued by the Federal Home Loan Bank Board (FHLBB). Most S&Ls (77.3 percent) were mutuals and most of the stockholder-owned S&Ls were state chartered. The FHLBB has permitted over a hundred federal S&Ls to convert from a mutual to a stock charter, beginning with an "experimental" program that operated officially during 1974–76 and since 1980, and unofficially in the years in-between. Applications for stock charters have accelerated during the 1980s; in 1982 alone, the FHLBB approved thirty-one mutual-to-stock conversions, a figure that represents 22 percent of the conversions approved since 1974.

As they moved into the 1980s, managers of S&Ls and MSBs increasingly began to investigate whether some kind of charter conversion (perhaps leading ultimately to affiliation with a holding company) would be advantageous—either for the institution or for themselves. Among the conspicuous benefits of charter conversion is the possibility that it could increase a firm's access to the deposit insurance subsidies. This issue is analyzed later.

Regulatory Competition for Charter Conversions

Regulators act as agents and shields for elected politicians in the legislative and executive branches of state and federal governments. Political pressure for regulatory changes takes the form of competitive public relations and lobbying activity by industry and customer interests. Political pressure is transmitted to regulators by proposals to realign an agency's budget and statutory domain. Politicians reinforce interest-group demands for regulatory change by altering the bureaucratic costs and benefits of alternative regulatory strategies. Contending interests aim at building a coalition among incumbent politicians and regulators for what they deem to be favorable adjustments in the framework of governmental supervision.

Of course, regulatees bring economic as well as political pressure to bear. Just as individual thrifts compete against each other for customer loans and deposits, the FHLBB, state supervisory agencies, and (in a back-up capacity) the FDIC compete for regulatory jurisdiction over individual thrifts. Regulators compete by making strategic reductions in the burdensomeness of the regulations they enforce.

Binding regulations impose legal restrictions on a subject institution's ability to pursue profitable business opportunities. This means that regulations act as a tax on an institution and/or its customers. The effective implicit tax rates levied by governmental supervision vary with the specific requirements and privileges applicable to alternative organizational forms. When a thrift shifts its organizational form, it selects a different structure of implicit and explicit taxation and changes the division of associated tax revenues between state and federal coffers. By switching (and threatening to switch) regulators in response to differences in implicit tax rates, depository institutions keep constant pressure on politicians and regulators to think about adopting a less onerous regulatory framework.

As thrifts' economic prospects deteriorated in the late 1970s, political support for the inherited system of deposit institution regulation began to unravel. The governing strategy of regulation had been to foster specialized financial institutions and to segment and constrain interinstitutional competition by restricting deposit institution office locations, product lines, takeover activity, and deposit prices. Traditional patterns of regulation sought to contain competition on four frontiers: (1) between deposit institutions in different states, (2) between bank and nonbank deposit institutions, (3) between securities firms and deposit institutions, and (4) between financial and nonfinancial firms. During the 1970s, technological innovation supported product line and geographic market expansion and made it relatively easy to design and to deliver service packages that helped account holders circumvent ceilings on deposit interest rates. At the same time, evolution in organizational forms (particularly in activities undertaken by subsidiary service corporations or holding company affiliates) opened gaping loopholes in restrictions against interinstitutional competition.

Because unregulated interinstitutional competition undermined the bureaucratic prospects of specialized regulatory agencies, regulators eventually found it in their self-interest to espouse rather than to oppose fundamental regulatory reform. They proposed a regulatory strategy of discretionary deregulation of deposit interest rates and desegmentation of thrift institution product lines as a way for their regulatees to stabilize their share of the financial services market, and they championed this strategy in congressional hearings and other political forums.

CONVERSIONS FROM STATE TO FEDERAL CHARTERS

Growing pressure on FDIC and FSLIC insurance reserves made federal legislators and regulators especially anxious to carry these reforms through. As this new strategy was embodied in regulatory reforms mandated by the Depository Institutions Deregulation and Monetary Control Act of 1980 and the Garn–St Germain Depository Institutions Act of 1982, federally chartered institutions found themselves surrounded by sympathetic regulators and in possession of significant borrowing opportunities and of a wide range of new powers. New portfolio opportunities included alternative mortgage instruments, greater enforceability of due-on-sale clauses, second-mortgage lending, corporate loans and deposits, personal loans, credit cards, more liberal branching, and trust services. In turn, thrift institution regulators and legislators in states that had not granted similar powers (e.g., in California, New York, and Minnesota) faced political demands for parity backed up by a rising tide of conversions by state chartered thrifts to federal charters. Albeit at differing speeds, state legislatures have attempted to redress the balance.

Even without adaptation by state legislatures, improved borrowing and portfolio powers do not make federal charters better for every thrift. In most states, state chartered thrifts would surrender significant freedoms on other dimensions. In particular, a federally chartered thrift is required to buy Federal Home Loan Bank stock and is subject to FHLBB–administered net-worth requirements and percentage-of-asset limitations on its holdings of corporate bonds and stock, consumer loans, and commercial paper. Converting MSBs face special problems: the possible switch of their federal deposit insurance from the FDIC to the FSLIC; requirements that all trustees stand for election by depositors within six years of the conversion date; fear of potential pressure from the housing-oriented FHLBB to increase their mortgage holdings; and questions about their right to sustain their life insurance activities.

The Garn–St Germain Depository Institutions Act of 1982 removes the need for FDIC–insured MSBs to transfer their coverage to the FSLIC. Difficulties in negotiating appropriate interagency indemnification for an MSB's insurance transfer had previously deterred MSB conversions to federal charters. Switching from FDIC to FSLIC guarantees may well increase the institution's deposit insurance expense. Although both agencies have used the same assessment formulas in the past, the FSLIC has proposed raising its assessment percentage by 150 percent and rebating all or part of the additional premium according to *ex ante* risk criteria. Whether or not this scheme is adopted, the FDIC's effective rate has been lower than the base assessment percentage in recent years because (unlike the FSLIC) it has rebated about 45 percent of its premium income to insured institutions. On the other hand, claims experienced by the FDIC in 1982 and additional claims that threaten to emerge in future years may greatly reduce the FDIC's future rebate rate. Also, because a joint congressional resolution (H. Con. Res. 290) passed in March 1982 put the full faith and credit of the U.S. government behind federally insured deposits, institutions may regard FSLIC guarantees as every bit as secure as those of the FDIC.

CONVERSIONS FROM MUTUAL TO STOCK CHARTERS

A quite different reason for converting from a state to a federal charter relates to subsequent opportunities to incorporate. Although state chartered stockholder-owned S&Ls exist in many states, state chartered MSBs are necessarily chartered as mutual institutions. The FHLBB is empowered to allow federal savings banks and federal S&Ls to incorporate. In addition, emergency incorporation powers apply in the case of FDIC–insured MSBs and FSLIC–insured state chartered S&Ls whose "stability" is threatened.

Conversion from a mutual to a stock charter makes a firm's management more vulnerable to unfriendly takeovers and imposes a burden of disclosing more information about firm operations. It also raises the question of how to resolve equitably the quasi-ownership interests of the institution's existing depositors and managers. Consumerists argue that a financially sound mutual institution is a community asset whose incorporation can, unless carefully explained to depositors, deteriorate into an expropriation of less sophisticated depositors by managers and eventual stockholders. When a mutual institution is incorporated, the funds raised through stock subscriptions become proportionate claims not only against newly paid-in capital of equal value but also against the total of bookable and unbookable forms of net worth accumulated from past operation. This means that the new stockholders have claims against the funds they paid in (net of incorporation expense) and the preexisting economic value of the institution. Because the value of FSLIC and FDIC guarantees is not bookable under generally accepted accounting principles, conventional accounting measurements of a thrift institution's accumulated capital understate the value of the windfall involved.

On the plus side of the social ledger, managerial incentives are likely to be strengthened by shareholder pressure and by opportunities for managers to share in the capital gains generated by the decisions they make. In addition, the inflow of shareholder capital should make the institution stronger by temporarily shoring up its net-worth account. Empirical evidence (summarized in Hadaway and Hadaway, 1981, p. 205) suggests that converted S&Ls "exhibit more aggressive operating behavior and better growth potential than mutual associations."

CHARTER CONVERSIONS ACROSS INSTITUTIONAL TYPE

Odds are that all types of deposit institutions will eventually exercise much the same powers. To improve their ability to confront such a future, many thrift institutions are investigating the costs and benefits of converting currently to a bank charter. In 1982, two California S&Ls (the Point Loma S&L in San Diego and the Regency S&L in Fresno) rechartered themselves as national banks. In 1981, the managers of a Phoenix, Arizona S&L effectively converted their institution into a commercial bank by merging it into a smaller bank, which they renamed and now operate. Managers of the converting institutions cited a desire to offer a broader range of services (e.g., commercial lending and lines of credit) and marketing advantages from being able to label their operation a *bank*. In 1982, improved tax status (relaxed requirements for eligibility for favorable tax treatment of deductions for additions to bad-debt reserves), and marketing advantages encouraged at least one S&L (United Federal in Des Moines, Iowa) to apply for conversion to a federal savings bank.

Interestingly, some commercial banks whose portfolios are heavy in real estate loans see potential advantages from rechartering themselves as stock S&Ls. Such a conversion would lower effective reserve and capital requirements. It would also move the institution's deposit insurance to the FSLIC from the FDIC. This may be advantageous because the FDIC has begun to reduce insurance subsidies to mortgage-lending banks by requiring them to reduce the extent of their maturity mismatching.

TAKEOVER OPPORTUNITIES

A different class of organizational adjustment consists of participation in mergers and holding company acquisitions. As Table 1 indicates, the thrift industry has experienced a continuing decline in the number of independent institutions and a steady growth in average firm size.

During the 1970s, the rate of voluntary mergers among S&Ls averaged roughly a hundred per year. Since 1980, the rate of voluntary mergers has roughly doubled, while over seventy supervisory mergers (combinations in which troubled institutions are merged into stronger ones) have occurred. A few of these post–1980 mergers have even absorbed thrifts into commercial banks and banks into thrifts.

When the thrift crisis deepened in the early 1980s, federal banking regulators' reluctance to approve interstate and interinstitutional mergers of distressed thrifts unnecessarily limited the pool of potential bidders for the franchises of failing institutions. Because the resulting restrictions tended to reduce the average value of winning bids, they increased the pressure on FDIC and FSLIC insurance reserves. To relieve this pressure, federal authorities pragmatically began to relax these restrictions in supervisory mergers and acquisitions, especially (under the leadership of the FSLIC) the policy against interstate acquisitions. Now, the Garn–St Germain Depository Institutions Act of 1982 specifically authorizes federal regulators to consider takeover bids for failing institutions according to the following schedule of priorities:

1. from depository institutions of the same type within the same state;
2. from depository institutions of the same type in *different* states;
3. from depository institutions of *different* types in the same state;
4. from depository institutions of *different* types in *different* states.

In considering offers from different states, the law requires federal regulators to give priority to offers from adjoining states. Congress's continuing refusal to authorize interstate banking in nonemergency situations contrasts unfavorably with state legislatures' burgeoning pursuit of affiliate, subsidiary, and branch operations of out-of-state deposit institutions.

Holding company affiliation can occur only for a stockholder-owned institution. At year-end 1982, the FHLBB regulated 165 S&L holding companies (SLHCs). Federal regulations classify SLHCs along two dimensions: (1) the number of S&Ls owned and (2) the diversity of the other kinds of businesses it operates.

TABLE 1. NUMBER AND AVERAGE SIZE OF THRIFT INSTITUTIONS, 1960–81

	S&Ls			*MSBs*		
		Average Total Assets ($ Millions)			*Average Total Assets ($ Millions)*	
Year-end	*Number*	*Current Dollars*	*1981 Dollars*	*Number*	*Current Dollars*	*1981 Dollars*
1960	6,320	11.3	32.2	515	78.8	224.5
1965	6,185	21.0	55.1	—	—	—
1970	5,669	31.1	66.5	494	159.9	341.7
1975	4,931	68.6	106.7	476	254.3	395.5
1980	4,592	137.4	150.3	463	370.5	405.4
1981	4,347	152.7	152.7	448	392.3	392.3

Sources: National Association of Mutual Savings Banks, *1982 National Fact Book* and United States League of Savings Associations, *'82 Savings and Loan Sourcebook.* (The inflation adjustment employs the implicit price deflator for GNP.)

Unitary SLHCs (those that own only one S&L) may be as diversified as they wish, but multiple SLHCs are restricted to a list of approved activities that is administered by the FHLBB. Unitary SLHCs include firms as diversified as Sears, Roebuck & Company, National Steel Corporation, and MCA, Inc.

Differences between regulation of commercial bank holding companies (BHCs) and SLHCs make a unitary SLHC an attractive vehicle for brokerage firms and other nondepository providers of financial services. All BHCs—even unitary ones—are restricted to a list of approved activities administered by the Board of Governors of the Federal Reserve System. By acquiring a single S&L, a nondepository financial or data processing firm can develop a full line of depository products, extend the blessing of federal deposit insurance over some of its current operations, and avoid restrictions imposed by the Federal Reserve Board.

Behind the scenes, an intense political struggle is going on over the Federal Reserve Board's policy of not including the operation of a subsidiary thrift institution on its approved list of activities for BHCs. Expansion-minded bankers see such acquisitions as a way to resolve the thrift institution crisis, to reduce their taxes, and to expand at low cost into new geographic markets. The

Garn–St Germain Depository Institutions Act of 1982 specifically authorizes interinstitutional takeovers of failing institutions, and just before this act was passed the Federal Reserve Board allowed Citicorp to take over a failing California S&L. Whatever further decisions Congress and the Federal Reserve Board make on this issue, strong reasons exist for anticipating a boom in unitary acquisitions of S&Ls by diversified holding companies. First, the FSLIC and FDIC are anxious to see the nation's weakest thrifts absorbed by well-capitalized firms, but want this to occur at minimal cost to the insurance funds with minimal compression in the number of thrift institutions in operation. Second, managers of nondepository holding companies can use such acquisitions as tax shelters and at least potentially as a means of extending the implicit blessing from deposit insurance guarantees to some of the debt issued by nondepository affiliates.

Evolution of Thrift Institution Prospects

This portrayal of the roots of the thrift institution crisis contrasts sharply with conventional analysis. Popular opinion traces the industry's current predicament to the threatened removal of deposit rate ceilings under the Depository Institutions Deregulation and Monetary Control Act of 1980 (DIDMCA). While the threat of adverse regulation may have increased customer pressure on savings institutions in the short run, financial innovation (symbolized by money market mutual funds and brokerage cash management accounts) made these ceilings increasingly ineffective. Irrespective of regulatory action or inaction, long-run technological and competitive forces steadily squeezed savings institution profit margins.

Recurrent thrift institution crises arise from their seeming addiction to taking substantial portfolio risks. The industry's balance sheet is risky in two ways. First, it is highly levered. This means that the value of assets held is a high multiple of industry net worth. Second, the average savings institution finances itself with liabilities that are, on balance, much shorter in their average life than the assets it holds. This practice is called "short-funding," to emphasize the gap that emerges between the average life of the future cash flows generated on the asset side and on the liability side of an institution's balance sheet.

S&Ls and MSBs have continued to engage in leveraging and short-funding despite being burned in one financial crunch after another. In the face of secularly rising and increasingly volatile interest rates, it is implausible to claim that an industry's learning curve could be so flat. Why does risk-taking predominate among thrifts? Analysis indicates that deposit insurance pricing is the dominant contributory factor. The FDIC and FSLIC subsidize risk-bearing by thrift institutions. Thrifts have been allowed to arbitrage the price of risk-bearing. Thrifts that have not been merged out of existence have lost on only one side (the bookable side) of their interest rate bets. As long as federal insurance agencies choose not to exercise their option to take over the charters of weakened members of the industry, these firms hold unbookable FDIC and FSLIC guarantees that largely offset the cumulative value of their bookable losses.

The temporary delay in public recognition of the decline in thrift institution prospects can be illuminated by recounting a parable. In 1966, a small saver and an S&L manager decided to visit the Washington, D.C. zoo. They reached the grizzly bear cage at feeding time. When the keepers opened the cage, a particularly large and hungry bear pushed them aside and headed directly for the saver and the S&L manager. It was obvious from the bear's demeanor that he thought the visitors would make a pleasant change from his usual bill of fare. In a state of near panic, the small saver asked the manager how they might protect themselves. The manager instantly advised that they should run for it. Dumbfounded, the small saver shouted, "Are you crazy? We can't outrun a hungry bear." With a sly smile, the S&L manager replied, "Maybe not, but if I kick you in the shins hard enough, I am sure that I can outrun *you*."

Most readers can interpret this story for themselves. The grizzly bear is inflation and the keepers are the federal government's chief economic policy makers. The sneaky kick in the small saver's shins is the Regulation Q system of differential ceilings on deposit institution interest rates. Congress first extended deposit rate ceilings to thrift institutions in 1966. Their purpose was to promote construction activity and to protect thrift industry profit margins and capital positions from being undermined by inflation-induced increases in interest rates. But this protection was obtained at the expense of denying the average household a fair market rate of return on savings held in deposit institutions.

For people who are sympathetic to small savers, the good news has been innovation by financial industry bystanders, who helped the saver to escape from the bear. After being mauled briefly, the small saver was able to shake off the effect of the manager's kick in the shins. For the thrift industry and for ordinary taxpayers likely to bear ultimately the burden of industry bailout efforts, the bad news is that the bear now has a firm hold on the thrift institution manager.

Locked in the arms of this bear, the thrift industry is simultaneously dying and being reborn. In the early 1980s, the Phoenix became the operative symbol of the future facing thrift institutions. The industry's flaming metamorphosis is painful for regulators as well as for managers. At the FDIC and FSLIC, bureaucrats need to accept the permanence of the emerging robotized and less segmented competitive environment and go on to develop new regulatory approaches, particularly a system of implicitly or explicitly risk-rated deposit insurance premiums. Managers of individual S&Ls and MSBs must recognize that their firm's rebirth requires conversion (if not *sub*mersion) into a more diversified financial services operation and possibly into a much larger institution. Anyone who has suffered through a bout of cognitive dissonance knows how hard it is to accept the need for putting aside established and previously profitable ways of doing things. As yet, too few thrift institution managers have reconciled themselves to the practical necessity of operating in a volatile and robotized environment.

Can the Next Turn of the Interest Rate Cycle Straighten Things Out?

Some observers expect a downturn in interest rates to put everything right again. However, even if long rates move several points lower, four forces will prevent the industry's recovery from being a permanent one: (1) managerial myopia, (2) the overhang of low-rate mortgages on thrift institution books, (3) deposit insurance mispricing, and (4) the difficulty of keeping FDIC and FSLIC guarantees credible.

MANAGERIAL MYOPIA

Myopia may be the central force in our "live-for-the-moment" culture. Over time, inroads of unregulated competition into thrift institutions' traditional markets have cost the industry more in accumulated profits than it could realistically have gained in the short run from deposit rate ceilings. Nevertheless, into the early 1980s, S&L trade associations chose to squander their lobbying effort on maintaining these leaky ceilings and winning hard-to-hold tax breaks.

This point of view can be illustrated with a riddle. How many S&L executives did it take to open the first All-Savers account? The answer is 536: one to book customer funds and another 535 to lobby every member of Congress for the privilege. The industry's 1981 political effort to win the right to offer the All-Savers instrument for one year represents a tragic waste of its planning resources and political clout.

From the moment that a tax or regulatory subsidy is enacted, market forces go to work to destroy its intended value to beneficiaries. Authorities can control various of the *explicit* terms on deposits, but they cannot fully close off creative schemes for compensating customers in implicit ways. In competitive markets, it was inevitable that institutions would be driven to make gimmicky offers that, until regulators stepped in to halt them, promised to hand over most of the intended subsidy to All-Savers account holders. Even then, brokerage firms developed secondary offerings of All-Savers certificates that shifted away a good portion of the intended subsidy.

As long as industry spokespersons blame their troubles on mistakes in regulation and legislation, the prospects for thrift institutions' secular recovery remain poor. During a decade and a half of well-intended legislative and regulatory action, less regulated competitors such as money market funds and brokerage cash management accounts caused considerable cumulative hurt to thrifts. While thrifts tried to hide themselves behind regulatory walls, substitute institutions and instruments developed to take advantage of emerging electronic funds technologies. Even if securities brokers and money market funds had been far more tightly regulated, these more efficient technologies would have been embodied in different institutional forms that would still have outcompeted traditional deposit institutions for interest-sensitive funds.

OVERHANG OF UNDERWATER MORTGAGES

Holdings of low-interest mortgage instruments are the apparent source of ongoing weakness in S&L and MSB balance sheets. One can only wonder how different thrift prospects would be if antiquated mortgage documents had shared in the nostalgia boom that has driven the price of old comic books and bubblegum cards to stratospheric prices. Across the industry as a whole, however, the value of deposit insurance guarantees largely offsets unbooked losses on S&L and MSB mortgages. Hence, the consequences of mortgage losses are far greater for the FSLIC and FDIC than for their clients.

Even though conceptual weaknesses in accounting principles make it hard to value deposit insurance guarantees directly, the economic effects of FDIC and FSLIC guarantees show up in market phenomena. We can see this by contemplating five rhetorical questions. The answer to each question turns on the value of federal agencies' explicit and implicit deposit insurance guarantees to client institutions.

– Why don't we observe a panicked flight of thrift institution executives into other jobs? Aside from an interest in exploring resort areas, why do they continue to attend trade association meetings, rather than flock out in search of another, less threatened occupation?
– Why have stock S&Ls continued to sell at positive prices?
– Why are voluntary mergers of S&Ls typically consummated at a premium over conventionally booked values?
– Why, during the years 1966–79, did S&Ls and MSBs pay substantial federal taxes, when most of these firms could have written off enough mortgage losses to drive their tax bills down to zero? (These tax payments functioned as implicit premiums for receiving federal deposit insurance. During these years, individual thrifts couldn't realize more than a fraction of their mortgage losses without failing net-worth tests that were then enforced for retaining eligibility for deposit insurance.)
– How long could the average S&L or MSB stay open today if the law allowed its right to display the FSLIC or FDIC seal of approval to be revoked without prior notice? (Customers would start lining up the

instant a window washer began to scrape the deposit insurance seal off; its removal would signal the start of a mammoth deposit run.)

Consistent with this analysis, during 1981 and 1982 the insured liabilities of thrifts typically sold at explicit interest rates equal or below those on U.S. Treasury securities. In contrast, rates on *uninsured* liabilities, such as jumbo C/Ds (certificates of deposit issued in denominations of $100,000 or more) and retail repurchase agreements, offered premiums over yields on Treasury debt of comparable maturity that ranged as high as 250 basis points.

DEPOSIT-INSURANCE PRICING

Premium schedules at deposit insurance agencies violate the "law-of-one-price." Thrifts can secure in private asset and liability markets a higher price for embracing interest-volatility risk than the insurance agencies charge them for underwriting this selfsame risk. This subsidizes thrift institution risk-bearing, establishing arbitrage incentives for thrift managers to reach out for risk—to lever their capital positions and to fund their asset holdings with short-term liabilities. Consequently, the bulk of the industry balances itself precariously on the edge of financial disaster.

The value of deposit insurance guarantees belongs on the asset side of the balance sheets of clients and on the liability side of the deposit insurance agencies' balance sheets. The FSLIC and FDIC cannot escape their liability for losses accrued by S&Ls and MSBs. But, by closing deposit institutions, they could at least limit their exposure to further losses. However, to forestall the possibility of a wave of deposit institution failures, each agency has decided to leave a troubled client in operation whenever this is feasible. As a result of these policies, over the last fifteen years the FSLIC and the FDIC have made the federal government the dominant equity investor in the S&L and MSB industries. What keeps these agencies from exercising their options to take over more than a few at a time of their weakest clients (as in the so-called Phoenix consolidations) is *not* their financial self-interest. What holds them back is political pressure to minimize recorded failures and bureaucratic inertia with respect to seizing the opportunity to expand managerial resources in proportion to their surging equity stake.

Why did FSLIC and FDIC bureaucrats permit thrift institution risk-taking to surge out of control? By law, the FDIC and FSLIC must charge the same explicit price for their insurance services. This premium (which is rebatable if agency expenses and payout experience permit) is .08 percent of a client's assessable deposits. Because this price is insensitive to variation in the riskiness of client portfolios, both agencies must monitor client portfolios to protect themselves against adverse selection. They impose regulatory penalties (i.e., *implicit* premiums) on any client they perceive to be carrying too much of the particular kinds of risks they fear. Whenever a client is discovered to have let its loan quality deteriorate or its net worth fall below a minimum value set by the insurance agency, agency personnel begin to intervene in its operations. If reported net worth approaches zero, the insurance agency can negotiate a capital infusion, offer financial assistance, arrange a takeover, or petition the chartering authority to close the institution.

It is instructive to contrast the FDIC's grim determination to discipline commercial banks that make what it recognizes as risky loans or that become undercapitalized with the indulgent attitude that it and the FSLIC take toward the interest-volatility risk assumed by thrift institutions. Originally for political reasons (Congress wished to promote housing activity) and now for economic reasons (to forestall an assumed financial panic), interest-volatility risk at S&Ls and MSBs has not yet been subjected to adequate regulatory sanctions. Similarly, in the face of financial strain, the net-worth level used to trigger tight agency oversight and regulatory discipline has been relaxed progressively. Since the middle 1970s, the FSLIC trigger level for the book value of net worth has declined roughly from about 5 percent to less than 2 percent of an S&L's assets. At the same time that this relaxation in regulatory standards occurred, the market value of bookable capital at thrift institutions fell completely out of bed. Apart from the technically unbookable value of deposit insurance guarantees, few S&Ls and MSBs have assets that exceed liabilities in market value.

The magnitude of the problem is illustrated by the calculations reported in Tables 2 and 3. The figures presented in the first column report the percentage by which the average yield on mortgages held by each type of institution falls short of the yield on new mortgages. I call this the "pseudo-default rate" on thrift institution mortgages. It serves as a rough proxy for unrecorded capital losses on these institutions' mortgage assets. Other columns serve to estimate the dollar value of unbooked losses on mortgages and to subtract these from the value of net-worth accounts. The last column provides an order-of-magnitude measure of the losses that need to be allocated between uninsured creditors and federal deposit insurance agencies.

These estimates are subject to several biases (Kane, 1983). Most importantly, they neglect the maturity distribution of thrift portfolios of mortgage loans and the possibility of borrower prepayments. For the single date of December 31, 1980, Balderston (1981) prepared estimates of unbooked losses on S&Ls' mortgage holdings that incorporate these elements. Assuming a 14 percent discount rate and that borrowers prepay their loans when half of their contractual life has expired, he calculates unbooked losses for S&Ls of $99.9 billion. This figure is roughly 66 percent of this chapter's estimate for 1980, which employs a lower 12.65 percent discount rate and a $21 billion larger base of mortgage loans at insured S&Ls. Even if conservatively scaled down by a factor of 60 percent, these estimates of unbooked losses on thrift institution mortgage loans dwarf federal deposit insurance reserves, especially at the FSLIC.

DIFFICULTY OF MAINTAINING THE CREDIBILITY OF FSLIC AND FDIC GUARANTEES

The book value of the thrift industry's explicit reserves is the sum of about $36 billion in private capital, about $20 billion in FSLIC and FDIC reserves, and $3.75 billion in combined insurance agency lines of credit from the U.S. Treasury. Of course, because of interest-induced capital losses, the market value of these resources is well below the sum of these figures. Even if we suppose that in 1982 the market value of FSLIC and FDIC assets ran about 90 cents on the dollar, their explicit resources amounted to less than $18 billion. The figures developed in Tables 2 and 3 show that at year-end 1981, the negative market value of industry capital was many times this amount.

What kept the system afloat was depositors' confidence that thrift institutions and their insurers have an unlimited implicit claim on the U.S. Treasury, which is to say, on taxpayers at large. What saved the industry is popular recognition of political incentives for government officials to make good on insured deposits. Almost no one believes that, if a panic were to develop, the President or Congress could fail to back up every dollar of *insured* deposits. This confidence in incumbent politicians' interest in protecting their chances for reelection makes federal deposit insurance an in-place industry bailout scheme.

During 1982, Congress energetically confirmed its susceptibility to these political incentives. A bill to set up an emergency relief fund was proposed in February 1982 by Representative St Germain, chairman of the House Committee on Banking, Housing, and Urban Affairs. In March, Congress passed a resolution declaring that federal deposit insurance "is backed by the full faith and credit of the United States." Finally, in the Garn–St Germain Depository Institutions Act of 1982 (passed on September 30, 1982), Congress gave each insurance agency the authority to issue

TABLE 2. CALCULATED VALUE OF UNBOOKED LOSSES ON AGGREGATE MORTGAGE HOLDINGS OF INSURED S&Ls AND OF POTENTIAL EQUITY CLAIM ON FSLIC, 1971–81

Year	*Pseudo-Default Rate on S&L Mortgage Loans (In Percent)*	*Total Assets (In Millions)*	*Total Mortgage Loans (In Millions)*	*Estimated Value of Unrealized Losses on Mortgages (In Millions)*	*Book Value of S&L Net Worth (In Millions)*	*Net Worth After Deducting Unrealized Mortgage Losses (In Millions)*
1971	19.90	$199,984	$169,568	$ 33,797	$13,096	($20,701)
1972	16.97	236,349	200,876	34,082	14,707	(19,374)
1973	15.47	264,797	226,155	34,980	16,509	(18,471)
1974	20.74	288,223	243,554	50,525	17,868	(32,657)
1975	21.20	330,259	272,456	57,762	19,175	(38,587)
1976	19.91	383,172	316,332	62,993	21,372	(41,621)
1977	18.42	449,998	374,089	68,895	24,525	(44,370)
1978	19.08	513,310	424,969	81,103	28,281	(52,822)
1979	23.77	568,107	462,262	111,065	31,769	(79,296)
1980	30.51	618,466	494,179	150,782	32,436	(118,346)
1981	35.01	651,068	509,133	178,262	27,572	(150,690)

Sources: Kane (1983) for pseudo-default rates; balance-sheet information is taken from U.S. Federal Home Loan Bank Board, *Combined Financial Statements: FSLIC–Insured Savings and Loan Associations* (Annual).

TABLE 3. CALCULATED VALUE OF UNBOOKED LOSSES ON AGGREGATE MORTGAGE HOLDINGS OF INSURED MUTUAL SAVINGS BANKS, 1965–81

Year	*Pseudo-Default Rate (In Percent)*	*Average Mortgage Loans (Book Value) (In Millions)*	*Average Total Assets (Book Value) (In Millions)*	*Estimated Value of Unrealized Losses on Mortgages (In Millions)*	*Average Book Value of MSB Net Worth (In Millions)*	*Net Worth After Deducting Unrealized Mortgage Losses (In Millions)*
1965	9.23	$36,992	$ 48,467	$ 3,412	$ 3,827	$ 415
1966	14.56	40,095	51,400	5,837	4,045	(1,792)
1967	15.85	42,794	55,173	6,784	4,194	(2,590)
1968	19.86	45,566	58,872	9,049	4,346	(4,703)
1969	26.12	48,091	63,519	12,564	4,592	(7,972)
1970	29.47	49,745	65,986	14,661	4,961	(9,700)
1971	19.12	52,365	73,662	10,011	5,236	(4,775)
1972	14.08	56,554	82,996	7,959	5,695	(2,264)
1973	14.84	61,600	90,851	9,140	6,257	(2,883)
1974	21.96	64,696	94,427	14,208	6,668	(7,540)
1975	19.83	66,698	101,715	13,232	7,060	(6,172)
1976	17.34	70,315	114,045	12,182	7,641	(4,541)
1977	15.42	75,524	126,744	11,650	8,391	(3,259)
1978	16.77	81,195	137,597	13,731	8,901	(4,830)
1979	23.12	86,683	145,331	20,026	9,559	(10,467)
1980	32.09	88,883	150,259	28,504	9,756	(18,748)
1981	38.81	89,115	159,210	34,583	9,001	(25,582)

Sources: Kane (1983) for pseudo-default rates; average mortgage loans, total assets, and net worth reported in FDIC *Annual Report* (various issues). Averages for pre-1971 items based on four consecutive call dates beginning with the end of the previous year ending with the fall call for the current year; from 1971 on, the figures reported average the end of the previous year with the middle and end of the current year. Average effective yield is calculated as the ratio of mortgage income net of deductions for service fees to average holdings of mortgages.

net-worth certificates "on such terms and conditions as it may prescribe" to client institutions whose net-worth accounts amount to less than 3 percent of their assets. Because these certificates provide no liquid funds, they will serve principally to document the federal government's equity stake in distressed deposit institutions.

Market confidence in the effectiveness of the incentives facing politicians was indicated by participants' ready acceptance in early 1982 of creative forms of FSLIC financing. From mid–1981 on, merger assistance tended to be promised rather than paid. The FSLIC engaged in creating pseudo-reserves, rather than liquidating and spending assets from its potentially inadequate insurance fund. FSLIC "promissory notes" were accepted as equity capital only because the public trusted in the efficacy of political incentives. (In eighteen cases, FSLIC resources were further conserved by selling regulatory exemptions from traditional limitations on interstate operations, particularly by facilitating out-of-state entry into deposit-rich Florida.)

It is ironic that, to keep from recording a higher value for the published federal deficit, the President and Congress refused to increase the size of the Treasury's formal commitment to the insurance agencies. This refusal to acknowledge the accounting consequences of the Treasury's de facto commitment to back up insured deposits unnecessarily increased investor uncertainty about the future of individual S&Ls and savings banks. It forced FSLIC and FDIC personnel to work under the threat of an embarrassing and potentially dangerous accounting bankruptcy. It is socially wasteful as well as hypocritical to keep the economic impact of the thrift institution problem off the federal government's balance sheet.

FSLIC Pricing and New Regulatory Paradigms

In 1980, DIDMCA purported to establish for thrift institutions a new regulatory strategy of diversification and deregulation (D&D). This strategy is reinforced in the Garn–St Germain Depository Institutions Act of 1982. Implementation of diversification decisions is assigned to the Federal Home Loan Bank Board. The two acts authorize this agency to develop new asset and liability powers for federal S&Ls and savings banks. The deregulation part of the 1980 act consisted of a reversible federal override of state ceilings on mortgage loans and the creation of an interagency Depository Institutions Deregulation Committee (DIDC) to oversee a phase-out of differential interest rate ceilings on deposits. The 1982 legislation provides capital assistance in the form of net-worth certificates for troubled depository institutions and pushes the deregulation component further, requiring the DIDC to create a federally insured money market deposit account "directly equivalent to and competitive with money market mutual funds" and sets January 1, 1984 as the deadline for phasing out differential ceilings on thrift institutions' other deposits. The goal of the D&D regulatory approach is to make it easier for S&Ls to match the time profiles of cash flows generated by their assets and liabilities.

Unfortunately, the D&D program is undermined by counter-incentives growing out of continuing asset specialization requirements for favorable tax treatment of additions to bad-debt reserves and deposit insurance agencies' inadvertent continued subsidization of interest-volatility risk. At the margin, these incentives make it more profitable for thrift managers to reach out for additional portfolio risk than to diversify existing risk away. These incentives limit the exercise of asset diversification powers and slow the pace of deposit rate deregulation by keeping thrift institutions in a state of government dependency.

At the same time, competition among insured institutions tends to shift deposit insurance subsidies through to suppliers of unregulated risks. In competitive markets, subsidies ultimately flow through to the owners of the scarcest resource. This principle explains why yields offered on insured money market accounts (which are nearly equivalent to Treasury securities) are settling at yields twenty-five to fifty points above those paid on substitute instruments available in the open market or on money market funds. It also explains why the deposit insurance subsidy has not done very much for the earnings performance of deposit institution stocks.

Thrift institutions' unprofitability retarded DIDC efforts to relax deposit rate ceilings. Ironically, until net-worth certificates and insured money market accounts debuted in December 1982, the continued existence of these ceilings increased S&Ls' need to issue uninsured liabilities—such as jumbo C/Ds, external borrowings, and retail repurchase agreements—precisely because these instruments were exempt from the protective ceilings. This put larger and larger percentages of S&L liabilities into what were formally uninsured funds, funds whose cost was heightened by uncertainty about the extent of the FSLIC's and the Treasury Department's de facto willingness to backstop these instruments.

What Changes in Public Policy Could Improve the Industry Outlook?

Currently, federal efforts to help thrift institutions focus on two fronts. The idea is to combine a series of quick fix subsidies designed to help thrifts to recover from the 1979–82 storm with structural expansions in the portfolio powers of federal S&Ls and savings banks designed to enable them ride out future storms on their own. Although these new powers are not automatically conferred on MSBs or state chartered S&Ls, economic and political pressures tend to compel state regulators to authorize new powers for their regulatees also. The list of quick fixes is long and growing: progressively lower capital requirements, expanded capabilities for taking tax write-offs, preferential borrowing arrangements, favorable merger and acquisition regulation, the opportunity to issue All-Savers certificates, and access to FDIC and FSLIC net-worth certificates.

Structural reforms aimed at making thrifts more competitive in the long run relax, in the first instance, traditional restrictions on the powers of insured S&Ls and federal savings banks. These structural reforms allow these institutions to operate more and more like commercial banks. Since 1980, insured S&Ls have been empowered to transact more freely in futures markets, repurchase agreements (including arrangements for sweeping funds from transactions accounts into repurchase agreements), consumer leasing, external borrowing, commercial lending, correspondent banking, mortgage swapping, real estate brokering, and data processing. Additional flexibility has been allowed in writing mortgage terms, including freedom to set higher loan-value ratios, higher up-front fees for prepayment options, broader rate-escalation options, and more enforceable due-on-sale provisions. Finally, regulators have made it easier for S&Ls and MSBs to convert from mutual to stock charters and authorized them to offer insured deposit accounts designed to outperform the average money market mutual fund.

Unfortunately, none of these reforms does anything to eliminate the disincentives to thrift institution diversification inherent in the current structure of FSLIC and FDIC pricing and oversight. Establishing a risk-rated system of FSLIC and FDIC premiums is on these agencies' research agendas, but it is not yet a high priority item. Political pressure from troubled clients and agency personnel makes deposit insurance pricing a touchy issue. Examiners dislike the prospect of having their jobs made more complex. They particularly resist the suggestion that in the future their activities should have pricing implications. Industry spokespersons portray proposals to restructure insurance fees as kicking their industry when it is down.

Still, for society as a whole, current pricing policies inefficiently subsidize portfolio risk and inequitably throw the costs of the subsidy onto conservatively managed deposit institutions and the general taxpayer. I believe that widespread pressure to price deposit insurance rationally would develop quickly if the market value of FDIC and FSLIC commitments were fully grasped by the taxpaying public, who is ultimately responsible for backing up these guarantees.

The principal business of any insurer is risk management. Before an insurer can control its risk exposure, it must set up an information system that measures all relevant forms of risk. So far, deposit insurance agencies have focused their examinations only on risks of management incompetence and fraud, robbery, losses at related firms, credit losses, and asset quality. Their underlying view of the causes of bank failure is rooted in past rather than emerging policy problems. Neither the FDIC nor the FSLIC is able to calculate adequately the market value of its ongoing exposure to interest-volatility risk. Neither agency has working procedures to measure the extent of short-funding, or long-funding by its clients either over short periods or over long ones. Both agencies are slowly "developing" appropriate reporting forms and computer software. An important source of delay in Federal Financial Institutions Examination Council negotiations to adapt the quarterly call report to monitor commercial bank exposure to interest-volatility risk is that Federal Reserve officials and the Office of the Comptroller of the Currency have a sharply different bureaucratic stake in this issue. Their interest is to minimize reporting burdens levied on the banks they supervise.

Because their clients' exposure to interest-volatility risk can change suddenly with customer or management initiatives, agency exposure should be monitored more frequently than the four times a year that reports of condition are filed. Federal insurance agencies need to develop weekly or monthly sample surveys of their client population to generate more frequent estimates of aggregate imbalances in the dollar amounts of rate-sensitive assets and liabilities at different maturities. Such data would greatly assist these agencies to manage their risk exposure.

In principle, insurance services associated with measured interest-risk exposures could be priced either by taking appropriate positions on both sides of the interest rate options market or by reinsuring portions of an agency's risk exposure with private insurance companies. However, federal agencies also need to redesign their insurance coverages. If deposit insurance agencies were to introduce substantial differentiation in available contracts, they could encourage high-risk and low-risk clients to sort themselves out. By offering at different prices an array of coverages, each of which incorporates a different degree of self-protection, deposit insurers could generate information on the relative values that clients and their deposit customers place on different types of guarantees. By opting for low coverages, conservatively managed institutions could reduce expenses or increase returns offered to depositors, while aggressive institutions (who would no longer be automatically subsidized) would be subject to increased depositor discipline. Even if this discipline operated to increase the recorded rate of deposit institution failures, federal deposit insurance would continue to protect insured institutions against runs by small depositors. The Garn–St Germain Depository Institutions Act of 1982 takes a first step in the direction of differential coverages by requiring the FDIC and the FSLIC to study the feasibility of offering expanded coverage as an option and of allowing private insurance or reinsurance of this particular coverage.

For a world in which interest rates are highly volatile, the present insurance system is unworkable. It should be clear that naive agency attempts to solicit private bids for reinsuring or coinsuring existing guarantee arrangements are bound to generate tenders that will seem outrageously high. Until the risks to be underwritten can be specified within known stochastic limits, every potential private insurer must incorporate into its bid a sizable allowance for uncertainty about the ultimate extent of the relevant commitments. Only legislators and bureaucrats (who can pass the costs of surprises through to future taxpayers) can afford to make commitments without stopping to price the informational uncertainty involved.

The Current Impasse

The current impasse can be illustrated by recounting a parable about financial re-regulation. While enjoying a deep-sea fishing trip in the company of a congressman, an academic economist, and a government regulator, a thrift institution executive was caught on a small boat during a storm. A huge wave broke over the boat and swept the executive into the choppy sea. Naturally, all three of his fellow passengers rushed to help him. The congressman threw him some money. (What else would a congressman do?) The academic economist gave him a lecture on how to swim. (What else could an academic economist do?) The regulator threw him a fishing net in which to gather the congressman's money. (Need we ask why?) However, each passenger found it too innovative a form of behavior to locate and to throw out the craft's life preserver. In the meantime, the thrift institution executive was too busy to find the time to ask for it himself. Following a survival strategy that seemed to serve him well enough in the past, he was thrashing around, trying to grab the stacks of currency before they stopped floating–striving with all his might to avoid entangling himself in either the economist's lecture or the regulator's net.

Richard L. Peterson

7

Consumer Finance

History of Consumer Credit in the United States

CREDIT REGULATION

The history of consumer credit in the United States is intrinsically linked to the history of credit regulation and particularly to usury laws. These laws have a long history. Homer (1963) traces them back to India in 2400 B.C. In western civilization, they are closely linked to biblical injunctions against profiting on loans to one's "brother" (Leviticus 25:35-37 and Deuteronomy 23:19-20). Because of these injunctions, it wasn't until the nineteenth century that the taking of interest was approved by the Holy Office of the Catholic Church and the mid-twentieth century that the Pope declared that "bankers earn their livelihood honestly."

The early religious prohibitions against the taking of excessive interest influenced English law, which established a usury limit of 8 percent from 1624 to 1651 and 6 percent from 1651 to 1714.

RICHARD L. PETERSON *is the I. Wiley and Elizabeth Briscoe Professor of Bank Management in the Department of Finance at Texas Tech University. Previously, Dr. Peterson was associate director of the Credit Research Center at the Krannert Graduate School of Management and financial economist for the Board of Governors of the Federal Reserve System. He has published widely in professional journals and periodicals and is coauthor of several books, the most recent of which is* Financial Institutions, Markets, and Money.

This law was emulated by many colonies, beginning with Massachusetts in 1641. In 1971, all except two states, New Hampshire and Massachusetts (which repealed its law in 1867), had usury laws (NCCF, 1972A). England, however, suspended its law in 1854.

From colonial times, a major exception to usury laws was the "time-price doctrine," which recognized that retail merchants could legitimately charge a higher price for goods sold on an installment plan than for cash-and-carry sales. This procedure implicitly allowed interest to be charged. However, throughout the 1800s there was very little cash lending to U.S. consumers by legitimate lenders. Commercial banks primarily made loans to commercial customers, although some loans to proprietorships may have financed consumer purchases. Savings and loan associations primarily made loans secured by and related to real estate. Savings banks restricted their lending to safe "investments," such as bonds or real estate. While retailers sold goods on credit under the time-price doctrine, typical repayment patterns were relatively short. Nonetheless, at times consumers still needed to borrow cash. Thus, the common consumer had a difficult time obtaining small amounts of credit (credit unions were not started in this country until 1909, and even then were limited in scope).

Since consumers generally could not obtain cash credit from depository institutions, they were forced to borrow from lenders who operated outside the pale of the law. Such lenders often imposed harsh collection remedies on delinquent consumers, since they could not use the courts to collect debts.

Legislation was needed to encourage legal lenders to enter the market. Consumer credit had to be exempted from restrictive usury laws because the fixed costs associated with loans of small size and short maturity are large relative to the total amount of finance charges earned. In addition, losses and collection costs related to consumer lending are high relative to earned finance charges.

The Russell Sage Foundation studied the problems associated with consumer credit and supported the first small loan bill in the U.S., passed by New Jersey in 1914. Similar legislation followed in other states. This legislation recognized that consumer loans could not be profitably extended under existing rate ceilings and that protective laws were needed so consumers would not encounter collection abuses. These concerns are exemplified in the Uniform Consumer Credit Code (UCCC). This model code has been adopted in its entirety by less than a dozen states, but many more states have adopted provisions of the UCCC. The UCCC simultaneously sets rate ceilings, regulates collection activities, establishes state regulatory bodies, and sets chartering standards for consumer lenders.

There are two major sources of costs associated with consumer lending. First, there are costs of loan origination: filling out applications, reviewing the information provided by the consumer, obtaining credit reports, and ascertaining whether the consumer is likely to be able to repay the debt or not. Origination costs also include expenses incurred for posting consumer credit transactions, office space, and marketing.

The second type of costs relates to collection efforts. These include costs of obtaining and recording information on payments made on the loan; costs of telephones, letters, attorneys, bill collectors, and other resources used when a consumer does not pay promptly; and credit losses. These operating costs are ordinarily very large relative to the total finance charges. Consequently, consumer loans must be priced substantially above a lender's costs of funds.

The studies by Benston (1965) and Bell and Murphy (1968) found that the costs of consumer lending by commercial banks were between forty and fifty dollars per loan. In its 1978 "Functional Cost Analysis" the Federal Reserve found that bank costs of making consumer installment loans were approximately fifty dollars per loan. Benston (1973A) also conducted a study for the National Commission on Consumer Finance which found that the costs of consumer lending by consumer finance companies were approximately seventy dollars per loan. These costs have increased over time with inflation.

The effects of operating costs on the rate of return required to make consumer lending profitable are illustrated in Figure 1. That figure shows the interest rate lenders must charge to obtain a 12 percent rate of return on invested funds when the costs of loan origination are $50 per loan and collection costs average $2.50 per payment (which are low estimates). Figure 1 shows that if a lender is to earn a net rate of return of 12 percent on the money invested in making a one-year $100 loan, that lender

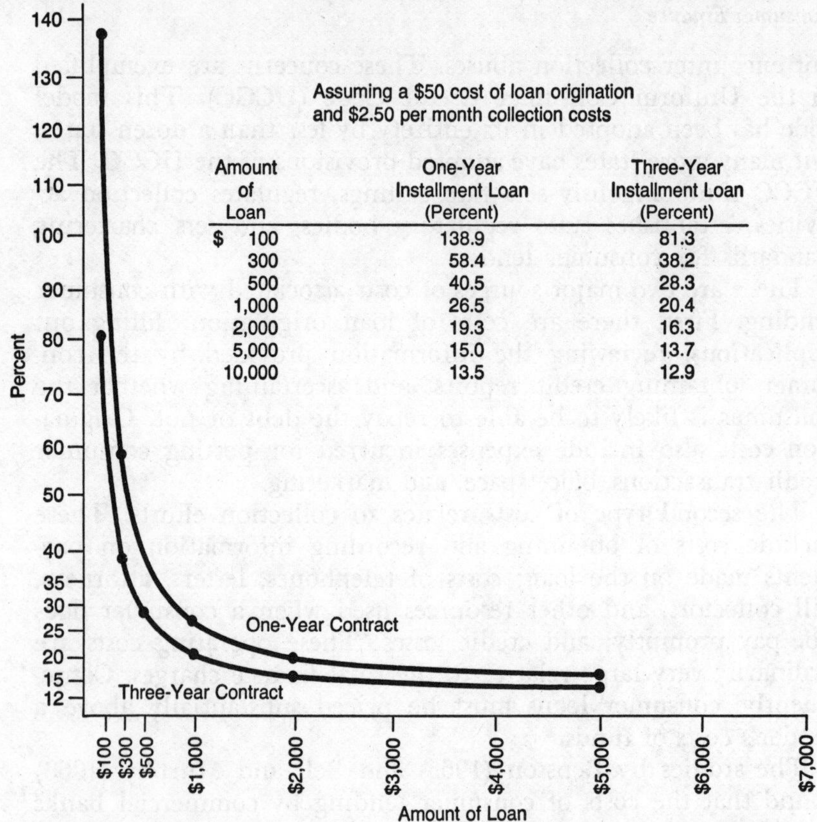

Amount of Loan	One-Year Installment Loan (Percent)	Three-Year Installment Loan (Percent)
$ 100	138.9	81.3
300	58.4	38.2
500	40.5	28.3
1,000	26.5	20.4
2,000	19.3	16.3
5,000	15.0	13.7
10,000	13.5	12.9

Fig. 1. Contract rates (annual percentage rates) required to generate a 12 percent return net of operating costs

would have to earn a contractual rate of return on the note of 138.9 percent. If the loan were stretched out to a three-year repayment period, the required contractual rate of return would fall to 81.3 percent. For larger loans and larger maturity loans, the rate required is closer to the net rate of return.

Since the smallest business loans are relatively large, most lenders assume that the markup for operating costs over the desired rate of return can be relatively small—.9 percent for a three-year $10,000 loan. However, for relatively small loans, such as consumer loans, the markup of the contract interest rate over the net rate of return that is required by the lender (if he is to stay in business) must be very substantial, as shown on Figure 1 (which uses highly conservative figures). This is why relief from usury ceilings applicable to business loans was necessary before legitimate consumer credit could expand in the United States.

THE DEVELOPMENT OF CONSUMER LENDING IN THE UNITED STATES

Table 1 summarizes the characteristics of consumer credit outstanding in the United States since 1920. In 1920 the predominant form of consumer lending was in the form of noninstallment credit extended by retailers and others. By 1930 installment credit had grown to the point where it was nearly as large as noninstallment credit. Also, finance companies had grown to where they held nearly as much installment credit as sellers of goods. Banks and credit unions were minor factors in the consumer credit markets.

In 1940 commercial banks had begun to expand their participation in the consumer installment credit market, although they still were third in importance behind finance companies and retailers. Noninstallment credit was smaller than installment credit in 1940—in part because automobile installment credit grew in importance during the 1930s. By 1950 the commercial banks had asserted their ascendancy as consumer installment lenders. Nonetheless, retailers still held a substantial amount of noninstallment credit and as a result still provided the largest single source of consumer credit.

The growth in bank lending from 1940 to 1950 was consistent with changes in banks' lending philosophy. After the depression, banks came to realize that the potential ability of a customer to repay a debt was more important than the marketability of the debt contract. As banks adopted the "anticipated income" theory of debt repayment, they acquired more consumer loans. Banks also found it easier to justify consumer lending in the 1940s because, due to the "accord" between the Federal Reserve and the Treasury Department that held interest rates on bonds below 3 percent, interest rates available on consumer credit were substantially higher than those paid on most other debt obligations.

From 1950 to 1960 consumer credit continued to grow rapidly and noninstallment credit decreased in relative importance. Banks expanded their credit share significantly and credit unions grew

TABLE 1. CONSUMER DEBT OBLIGATIONS

	1920[1]	1930[1]	1940[1]	1950[1]	1960[1]	1970[2]	1980[3]	1982[3] (June)
TOTAL CONSUMER CREDIT (in billions of dollars)	2.96	6.35	8.34	21.47	56.14	127.16	388.30	412.10+
INSTALLMENT CREDIT (as a percent of total consumer credit)								
Owed to:								
Commercial banks	1.0	3.1	18.0	27.1	29.7	37.3	37.9	35.6
Finance companies	6.1	21.1	18.9	17.3	19.2	21.1	19.8	22.6
Credit unions	0.3	0.3	2.0	2.7	7.0	10.0	11.3	11.1
Savings & loans and savings banks	—	—	—	—	—	1.8	3.3	3.7
Retailers and oil companies	25.7	23.0	19.2	13.6	11.2	10.6	8.5	7.5
Total Installment Credit	32.8	47.6	66.1	68.5	76.5	80.8	80.7	80.5
NONINSTALLMENT CREDIT (as a percent of total consumer credit)								
Owed to:								
Retailers, oil companies, and others	67.6	52.4	33.9	31.5	23.5	19.2	19.3	19.5
TYPES OF INSTALLMENT CREDIT (as a percent of installment credit)								
Auto	39.2	32.8	37.6	41.3	41.1	34.5	37.3	38.7
Mobile home	—	—	—	—	—	2.4	5.5	5.6
Revolving	—	—	—	—	—	—	18.6	17.9

[1] *Source:* Federal Reserve Board, *Banking and Monetary Statistics,* 1941–1970, pp. 1081 (Table 16.1) and 1087 (Table 16.2).

[2] *Source:* Federal Reserve Board, *Notice of Change in Series, Phase III,* Mortgage and Consumer Finance Section, December 1978.

[3] *Source:* Federal Reserve Bulletin, October 1982. Table A.42 (Consumer Credit Outstanding).

rapidly. In the 1960s new forms of consumer credit developed and credit unions had begun to gain market share from finance companies. Expanding forms of consumer credit included mobile home credit and revolving credit plans. While revolving credit plans started in the 1950s, they grew relatively slowly until the late 1960s, when bank credit card plans and other bank revolving credit plans stimulated substantial growth. Also, in the 1960s many retailers substituted revolving credit plans for other forms of credit.

The dollar value of consumer credit outstanding tripled from 1970 to 1980. Credit became much more widely acceptable for use in consumer transactions as members of the postwar baby boom came to a stage in their life cycle where they used credit extensively. During this decade, the assumption was made that credit was something that consumers needed and therefore had a right to have. In addition, because inflation rose faster than interest rates (and rate ceilings) on consumer loans, credit was relatively cheap. Laws were passed to ensure that consumers would have easy access to credit, and consumers borrowed heavily.

By 1980 banks had acquired nearly half of all consumer installment credit outstanding. Credit unions had acquired more consumer installment credit than retailers and were gaining ground on finance companies. Also, savings and loan associations and savings banks had become more aggressive in the consumer lending markets—in part because new legislation allowed them to make consumer loans, particularly mobile home loans and student loans, in addition to their traditional home improvement loans.

In 1980, as had been the case for fifty years, automobile credit accounted for the largest single form of consumer installment credit outstanding. Nonetheless, revolving credit had grown substantially in relative importance during the decade of the seventies, as it displaced both other consumer durable goods credit and personal loans at many lenders.

Consumer credit growth slowed after 1980. The incentive to supply consumer credit was reduced by high nominal interest rates coupled with restrictive rate ceilings. Since costs of funds rose faster than interest returns, numerous suppliers, particularly commercial banks, decreased their participation in the consumer credit markets. Since finance company subsidiaries of major automobile manufacturers provide credit to help the manufacturer sell cars, when the banks reduced their lending, these finance companies provided substantially more credit.

Overall, the consumer credit market has behaved in a highly competitive manner. As 40,000 depository institutions, several thousand finance companies, and over one million retail outlets have jockeyed for consumers' credit dollars, new contract arrangements have been developed, and the relative market position of various competitors has changed over time.

MORTGAGE CREDIT

Mortgage credit has had a long and checkered history in the U.S. In the 1800s, commercial banks sometimes made loans secured by real estate. However, such loans could go bad when speculative bubbles collapsed. Consequently, many banks and bank regulators viewed real estate lending to be a potentially risky activity for commercial banks. Savings and loan associations, in contrast, were established in order to provide funds to finance home construction.

In the 1900s, prior to the Great Depression, a wide variety of mortgage instruments was used. These included nonamortizing (interest only) loans of short maturity. Many of these went into default during the 1920s agricultural recession, the collapse of the Florida land boom of the 1920s, and the Great Depression of the 1930s. Consequently, mortgage lending became unpopular with financial institutions.

To support mortgages and restore confidence in the housing market, in the mid–1930s Congress formed the Federal Home Loan Bank System to assist and supervise savings and loan associations and the Federal Housing Administration (FHA) to insure low down payment self-amortizing loans. Subsequently, FHA, and later the Veterans' Administration (VA), insured mortgage loans became popular with lenders, such as insurance and pension funds, that preferred safety. In addition, savings associations (which received substantial tax breaks and regulatory support to encourage mortgage lending) became major holders of self-amortizing, long-term, uninsured conventional mortgages with relatively high down payments. Thus, in 1954, savings institutions held nearly half of all home mortgages outstanding and insurance companies and pension funds held an additional one-fifth (Table 2).

Savings institutions continued to expand their mortgage holdings rapidly through the remainder of the 1950s and 1960s. However, in the last half of the 1960s, market interest rates rose. Savings institutions, which had a hard time obtaining funds due to Regulation Q, were reluctant to put additional funds into

TABLE 2. HOME MORTGAGES: PRINCIPAL HOLDERS (ONE- TO FOUR-FAMILY MORTGAGES)

	1954[1]	*1970*[2]	*1980*[3]	*1982*[3] *(September)*
TOTAL MORTGAGES (by percentage)				
Held by:				
Commercial banks	17.6	15.2	16.2	16.0
Savings institutions	45.6	59.4	49.4	43.7
Insurance and pension funds	20.6	11.2	1.8	1.5
Individuals and others	12.5	6.8	14.0	16.8
Government sponsored agencies (and pools)	3.7	7.4	18.6	22.8
TOTAL MORTGAGES (in billions of dollars)	88.0	297.7	987.0	1,092.3
Holdings of:				
Commercial banks		42.3	160.3	175.1
Savings institutions		167.5	487.3	476.9
Insurance companies		31.4	17.9	16.6
Individuals and others		31.6	138.3	183.3
Government sponsored agencies (and pools) (subtotal)		24.7	183.3	248.5
FNMA (includes pools)			51.8	71.6
GNMA (includes pools)			92.3	112.0
FHLMC (includes pools)			17.4	39.6
Farmers Home Administration (includes pools)			17.6	20.1
Federal Land Banks			2.1	3.0
FHA and VA			2.1	2.2

[1] *Source:* Federal Reserve Staff Study: *Ways to Moderate Fluctuations in Housing Construction,* p. 446 (Table 8-data apply to all residential mortgages).

[2] *Source:* Flow of Funds Accounts: Assets and Liabilities Outstanding, 1968–78, p. 19 (Home Mortgages).

[3] *Source: Federal Reserve Bulletin,* January 1983. Table A.41 (Mortgage Debt Outstanding). Since September data are preliminary, totals do not add exactly.

mortgages—particularly since very few could make variable rate loans. As a result, the postwar growth in savings institutions' share of the mortgage market stopped in the 1970s and declined in the 1980s as savings associations lost funds and diversified into assets with shorter maturities.

In spite of the problems of the savings associations, mortgage credit (like consumer credit) grew extremely rapidly during the inflationary decade of the 1970s. In addition to changes in demand due to inflation and demographic changes, financing methods changed substantially after the late 1960s. The most important influence on the mortgage market in the 1970s and thereafter was federal government financing plans. Shares in mortgage pools issued by federally sponsored authorities provided substantial liquidity for holders of mortgage-related claims. Consequently, the government's share of the market expanded greatly as individuals, insurance companies, and pension funds acquired government mortgage pool participation certificates instead of home mortgages, per se (Table 2).

In addition to forming mortgage pools, government sponsored agencies directly picked up the slack when savings institutions reduced their mortgage lending in the 1980s. The Federal National Mortgage Association (FNMA) and Federal Home Loan Mortgage Corporation (FHLMC) acquired substantial amounts of mortgages on their own account and issued mortgage-backed securities to tap more funds for the mortgage market. While they also suffered declines in asset values when interest rates rose, their U.S. government credit lines let them attract funds to finance mortgage lending in the tight money periods.

CONSUMER CREDIT REGULATIONS

Consumer credit regulations have been in existence in the United States ever since the first usury laws were passed. They became more formalized and more specific to consumer credit when laws regulating rates applicable to consumer credit transactions were passed in the early 1900s. In addition, consumer credit has long been affected by bankruptcy legislation. However, until the late 1960s, consumer credit was primarily subject to state rather than federal government regulation. Then, responding to growth in the number of people of credit-using age, the "credit is a consumer right" philosophy, and a host of well-meaning, but misguided, consumer activists, Congress enacted a wave of legislation that affected the consumer credit markets.

The first of the new regulations, and the one with the most pervasive effect, was the Truth-in-Lending Act of 1968. It standardized the presentation of credit rate and contract information. Prior to the act, many creditors quoted rates on an "add-on" basis, others on a "discount" basis, and still others on a "simple interest" or a monthly interest basis. Consequently, consumers probably found it hard to identify the lowest cost source of credit. The Truth-in-Lending Act also established the National Commission on Consumer Finance (NCCF), which was charged with reporting to Congress on needed revisions in consumer credit laws. Its report was completed in 1972. Within a few years, Congress passed widesweeping legislation. This included the Equal Credit Opportunity Act (1974, amended in 1976), the Real Estate Settlement Practices Act (1974, amended 1976), the Fair Credit Billing Act (1975), the Fair Debt Collection Practices Act (1977), the Home Mortgage Disclosure Act (1975, renewed in 1980), and the Community Reinvestment Act (1977). In addition, the Federal Trade Commission Improvements Act (1975) gave the Federal Trade Commission (FTC) power to promulgate rules that affected all consumer creditors—including commercial banks —as long as no adverse influence of those regulations on the conduct of monetary policy was found. Finally, the Federal Bankruptcy Reform Act of 1978 became effective in 1979.

All these acts had a substantial impact on consumer credit markets. They affected both the cost and availability of consumer credit. Major changes in the structure of the consumer credit markets have occurred since the acts were passed. Those changes resulted, in part, from the effect of the acts on the credit markets and, in part, from the fact that the acts reflected major demographic and economic changes, the coming-of-age of the postwar baby boom, and the widespread entry of women into the labor force.

In general, the legislation passed during the 1960s and 1970s was intended to provide "fair credit" terms for consumers. The fairness, of course, differed with the interpretation of the legislators and the regulators who implemented the laws. While it was costly, the Truth-in-Lending Act seemingly increased consumer welfare by making sure people had fuller knowledge as to the true price of credit from various sources.

In other instances, it was less clear that credit markets would become more "fair" than they had been in the past. In particular, the Equal Credit Opportunity Act (ECOA) did not allow specified information to be used in credit evaluation if it was felt that such information might reflect unfavorably on certain "protected" groups. If the lack of relevant information caused credit losses to go up, creditors would either have to raise their rates, curtail credit availability, or leave the business. Consequently, members of "unprotected" groups who had to pay more to obtain credit, or could not get it at all, could have found the credit markets to be less "fair" after passage of the regulation.

Similar problems existed with the Home Mortgage Disclosure Act which was concerned only that credit be made available to inner city neighborhoods and did not consider whether that policy would reduce returns to savers or credit availability to others. Thus, in some cases, regulations were designed to ensure that credit markets were "fair" only to particular groups, while in other cases, such as the Truth-in-Lending Act, regulations were concerned with making credit markets work more effectively for all concerned.

The Effects of Regulation: Actual versus Intended Effects

Often the effects of regulations are quite different than the effects that were (ostensibly) intended by the regulators and legislators who drafted them. This section considers the actual versus the intended effects of major consumer credit regulations.

USURY LAWS: EFFECTS ON THE PRICE AND AVAILABILITY OF CREDIT

The stated intent of usury laws is straightforward. It is to prevent the payment of unconscionably high levels of interest by consumers who may be necessitous or otherwise be at a disadvantage relative to lenders. A second intent, often stated by advocates of usury laws, is that people should not borrow at high interest rates if they cannot afford to do so. Thus, if usury laws prevent credit from being made available to high-risk people who would have to pay high rates to obtain it, it is argued that those people will be better off.

The actual effects of usury laws are substantially different from the intended effects. The main reason for this is that usury laws do not prevent people who wish to obtain credit from obtaining that credit even when they are extremely high risks. This is so because many times the cost of credit is not differentiated from the cost of a related transaction. For instance, in a study conducted in the 1960s on the effect of the 8 percent usury law in Washington, D.C., the Division of Economic Analysis of the Federal Trade Commission (1968) found that many inner city merchants merely marked up the prices of goods to compensate for the deficiency in revenues realized on their credit sales. If a consumer were to pay more than the usual retail price for the good, the retailer could offer credit at low interest rates, or even at no interest rate, and still obtain a reasonable profit on the full transaction.

Along the same lines, Peterson (1983) has shown that Arkansas's 10 percent usury law (repealed in November 1982) did not prevent consumers from obtaining consumer credit. In fact, when all sources of credit, including retail sources and credit card credit, were considered, Arkansas consumers, including low-income and high-risk people, had just as much credit as did similar consumers located in other states. High-risk consumers in Arkansas, however, were more likely to use *retail* credit sources.

In addition, when usury laws are restrictive, pawnbrokers flourish. This was true in both Arkansas and Washington, D.C. Pawnbrokers can offer credit at low rates because, by under-appraising the value of a pawn and setting restrictive redemption terms, they can profit from the sales of goods left for pawn even if they do not profit from the extension of credit per se.

One problem from including credit charges in the price of goods sold is that cash buyers with limited shopping alternatives pay more for goods than would be the case if the credit costs were explicitly and fully embodied in the cost of credit. Such cash buyers "subsidize" credit buyers when usury laws cause goods' prices to rise.

While usury laws have little effect on total credit availability (since credit can still be obtained from retailers), they prevent high-risk borrowers from obtaining *cash* credit from regulated lenders. At the same time, low-risk consumers would find it easier to obtain cash credit at a lower rate if creditors incurred fewer losses on loans to high-risk consumers (such as young people) whom, in the absence of rate ceilings, creditors would serve by raising rates to all borrowers.

In addition, if cash credit supplies increase with interest rates, usury laws reduce the cost of credit to those who can still obtain it. This is shown in Figure 2, which illustrates that a usury law can force the highest cost cash credit suppliers out of the market, reducing the amount of credit available. However, even though available credit falls from DE to AB, as long as the number of people who benefit by obtaining cash credit at lower rates (i.e., the number of people who borrow credit amount AB) exceeds the number of people who lose by being rationed out of the credit market (i.e., the number of people who cannot obtain credit amount BC), usury laws may still be politically popular. Consequently, for political reasons usury laws may persist, even if overall they have little effect on the level of the credit, provided that a sufficient number of middle- and upper-class citizens believe the laws will help them obtain cash credit at lower rates and do not worry about where less fortunate customers obtain

Fig. 2. Effect of usury laws on cash credit costs and availability

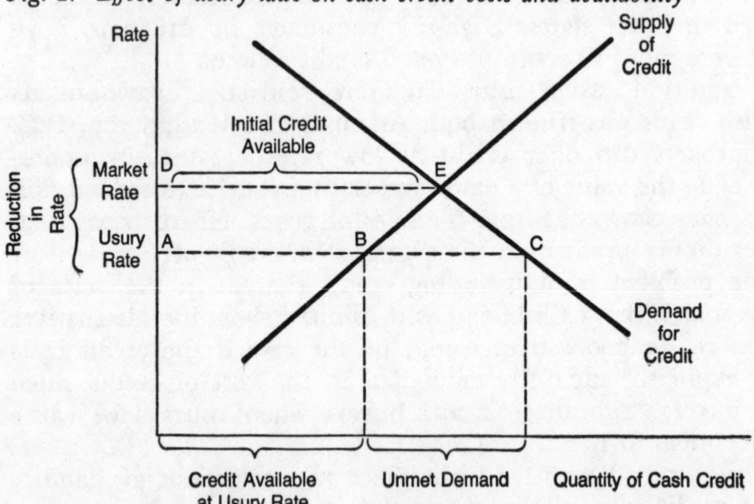

credit (from inner city merchants, pawnbrokers, illegal loan sharks, etc.).

However, frequently there are problems caused by usury laws that were set at low levels before interest rates rose to the point where lenders became unable or unwilling to extend credit at the existing rate ceiling. While the intent of a usury law might be to prevent only credit transactions that took place at unconscionably high rates, if interest rates rose sufficiently (probably as a consequence of inflation), the law could choke off all cash credit and interfere with the flow of commerce on a wide scale. Consequently, if usury laws are to exist, they should be set sufficiently above existing interest rate levels so that they do not interfere with the flow of commerce, and they should be adjusted to move up and down with market rates. In addition, Johnson and Peterson (1983) propose that the "break points" (above which graduated ceiling rates decrease for larger credit extensions) should be indexed to vary with the price level.

An interesting side effect of proposals to index rate ceilings and "break points" is that they would eliminate the need for legislators to make annual adjustments during periods when interest rates are rising or inflation is high. This would save resources since creditors would spend less on lobbying. Conversely, indexing proposals are likely to be politically unpopular with legislators who are reluctant to eliminate the political contributions and fringe benefits they obtain from lenders' lobbying efforts.

Because rate ceilings have been particularly troublesome in the housing market, the federal government preempted state mortgage rate ceilings in 1980 when it passed the Depository Institutions Deregulation and Monetary Control Act. Individual states were given a maximum of three years to reassert their right to impose rate ceilings on mortgage credit. Otherwise, their mortgage rate ceilings would be permanently voided. Similar federal legislation has been proposed, but not enacted, for the consumer credit markets. However, in the 1980–82 period a number of states either repealed their consumer credit rate ceilings, raised them substantially, or pegged them to market rate indexes. This alleviated some of the problems associated with consumer credit rate ceilings during high interest rate periods.

TRUTH-IN-LENDING

The intent of the Truth-in-Lending (TIL) Act was to provide full disclosure to consumers regarding the costs and terms associated with their credit transactions by requiring that credit rates be disclosed on a standardized, annual percentage rate basis. Seemingly, TIL had a beneficial effect on consumer behavior by making comparison shopping easier. After its passage, the market share of relatively low-rate consumer creditors—credit unions and commercial banks—rose relative to the market share of higher rate creditors.

However, the Truth-in-Lending Act was implemented with a set of very extensive and costly regulations. The regulations were so complex that it was almost impossible for lenders to comply in full with their requirements. Because the penalties for violations included legal default on the credit contract plus payment by the creditor of all attorneys' fees, the law generated an excessive number of lawsuits over technical and other trivial issues.

At one time, reportedly, a full quarter of all federal cases filed in Georgia consisted of Truth-in-Lending Act cases. In addition, the Connecticut Banking Commissioner, David Neiditz, reported that his office was threatened with a suit by a "consumer interest" law firm when it offered free forms and advice so that financial institutions could comply with the law. The firm that threatened suit had a profitable business selling forms and advice guaranteed to protect lenders against TIL suits; at the same time it was one of the most active law firms in the state for filing suits in the "consumer interest" against alleged violations of the Truth-in-Lending Act.

The large number of suits led to a call for revision in truth-in-lending regulations. This call was reinforced by the fact that compliance with the act was very costly. The regulations required all aspects of credit transaction to be spelled out in great detail, even though many details were unlikely to have an effect on consumers' borrowing decisions. Consequently the Depository Institutions Deregulation and Monetary Control Act of 1980 mandated that truth-in-lending disclosure be simplified. The Federal Reserve did so in 1981 by shortening TIL regulations by 40 percent, providing preapproved compliance forms, and combining all legal interpretations in a single document.

Nonetheless, in the opinion of this author, there still appear to be serious problems with TIL disclosure requirements. Two problems are of particular concern. First, because the primary objective of the act is to permit consumers to compare costs of funds readily from various sources, interest rates should be stated on an "annual compound rate" (A.C.R.) basis rather than on an annual percentage rate (A.P.R.) basis which is computed by merely multiplying the periodic rate by the number of periods in a year. This is necessary because, with current high rates, there is a substantial difference in the A.C.R. and the A.P.R. on a consumer loan. For instance, a consumer loan that charges 1.5 percent per month has an A.P.R. (disclosed under TIL) of 18 percent, but it has an A.C.R. of 19.6 percent. The annual compound rate is higher because it reflects the fact that the interest payments are available to be reinvested before the end of the year, while the annual percentage rate does not.

The discrepancy between annual percentage rates and annual compound rates can be important if a consumer is considering alternative costs of financing. For instance, a consumer might elect to borrow money on a credit card at 18 percent A.P.R. and invest that money in a stock venture promising a 19 percent return, not realizing that the borrowed money was costing 19.6 percent on an A.C.R. basis. Overall, the chronic rate understatement embodied in the A.P.R. may cause consumers to bias their budgets toward borrowing rather than saving. A loss of economic efficiency can result.

Another problem is that many mortgage lenders have been allowed to advertise "payment rates" that diverge from "contract rates" on variable rate loans. A "payment rate" of 11 percent indicates that the loan payments are computed as if the loan were an 11 percent loan, even though, in the short run, interest may be accruing at a higher rate, say, 16 percent. The residual 5 percent interest is not forgiven but instead is added to the outstanding mortgage debt. Thus, the advertised 11 percent "payment" rate is deceptive.

CREDIT AVAILABILITY REGULATIONS: THE EQUAL CREDIT OPPORTUNITY ACT AND "ANTI-REDLINING" LEGISLATION

The Nature of Credit Availability Regulation—The desired effect of credit availability regulations is to ensure that certain disadvantaged people, who might be discriminated against prejudicially, will be able to obtain credit. Thus, lenders are forbidden from denying credit on the basis of the applicant's sex, race, marital status, religious beliefs, political affiliation, receipt of welfare benefits, etc. The main problem faced by such regulations is that they must be carefully drafted to prevent discrimination based on prejudice while not preventing discrimination based on economic risk calculations. Such regulations can reduce economic efficiency if they cause creditors to "subsidize" members of "protected" groups by discontinuing or reducing discrimination based on economic risk assessments.

The Equal Credit Opportunity Act (ECOA) legislation was passed after Congress heard testimony that women had encountered discrimination in the form of unequal treatment in the credit markets. Some women could not obtain credit in their own names. In addition, women often were not considered to have stable incomes. Therefore, some lenders discounted the woman's contribution to joint family income on mortgage or other credit applications. The ECOA initially was designed to require equal treatment of women and men in the credit decision-making process, regardless of sex or marital status. It was later amended to include the aged, welfare recipients, and people of different religious faiths, nationality, or political affiliation.

The Home Mortgage Disclosure Act (HMDA) and the Community Reinvestment Act (CRA) were passed after Congress heard testimony that certain lenders engaged in "redlining activities." Redlining was said to be a lenders' drawing of a hypothetical "red line" around certain areas on the map and refusing to make loans in those areas. The effect was concentrated on inner city areas because properties in those areas most frequently were debilitated and often were populated by minority groups.

A possibly unstated objective of ECOA, CRA, and related credit allocation acts was to provide subsidies to certain classes of "protected consumers." For instance, the ECOA regulations required that the receipt of alimony be treated the same as other sources of income—even though, at times, its receipt is unreliable. Consequently, equal treatment of that income would allow a divorced person to qualify for credit more easily than would have otherwise been the case. Similarly, the requirement that major financial institutions extend credit to every area from which they obtain deposits (particularly older inner city areas), as embodied in the CRA, implies that funds should be channeled into these areas, thereby driving risk-adjusted interest rates in the riskier areas below those that would have prevailed in the absence of the regulation.

The Effects of Credit Availability Regulation—The actual effects of the credit availability regulations were quite different than their intended effects. For instance, Chandler and Ewert (1976) found that when women borrowers were evaluated under the same standards as males, they frequently would be less likely to qualify for credit. Incomes and the number of credit references are positively associated with creditworthiness. Usually women have lower amounts of each. Consequently, while a woman borrower might be a good credit risk with only two credit references, she might not obtain credit if evaluated on the same standards as a male borrower, for whom five good credit references would be required. The Chandler and Ewert study implies that profit-maximizing creditors could have used different credit evaluation standards for men and women before ECOA was passed, but such standards need not have discriminated against women. In contrast, forcing creditors to use equal standards could cause some qualified women to be denied credit.

While the Chandler and Ewert study indicates that ECOA could have reduced credit availability to women, a study by Peterson (1981) showed that commercial banks, in general, did not prejudicially discriminate against women before ECOA was passed. After ECOA was passed, separate evaluation procedures could be used only under restrictive conditions in "affirmative action" programs. It frequently was too expensive to develop such programs. Thus, if anything, ECOA may have made it harder for women to qualify for credit.

Nonetheless, ECOA did have some benefits. Prior to ECOA,

some creditors engaged in practices that were either offensive or unfair. For instance, testimony before Congress prior to the enactment of ECOA indicated that one major retailer discontinued the granting of credit to women when they got married and changed their names. After marriage, a woman could only obtain credit in her husband's name. Other lenders, particularly in mortgage markets, asked insulting or embarrassing questions about employed women's fertility and childbearing intentions. In addition, in a study conducted in Minnesota it was found that a couple who posed as an employed woman and a male graduate student spouse were able to obtain credit only in the husband's name (even though the wife earned the money) at a number of creditors to which they applied for an auto loan (NCCF, 1972A). Practices such as these were banned by the passage of ECOA.

Another effect of ECOA, which was not beneficial, was that it raised creditors' costs considerably. Extensive record-keeping requirements were imposed by the act, including the requirement that individuals be informed in writing why they were turned down for credit. In addition, because ECOA placed restrictions on creditors' abilities to obtain and use various information, creditors' potential credit losses were increased by ECOA as fewer good customers were accepted relative to the number of bad customers who could qualify for credit.

Overall, then, ECOA was costly and, while it undoubtedly had some beneficial effects, it is not clear that the effects were worth the cost. Also, ECOA potentially distorted credit flows since some people who previously could have qualified for credit could no longer qualify after ECOA was passed and others who should not have qualified could obtain credit more easily. Further, the Chandler and Ewert and Peterson studies indicate that ECOA may not have increased credit availability to the "protected" groups. Finally, a case can be made that, even though ECOA banned certain offensive practices, those practices would have been eliminated by market forces anyway when sufficient numbers of customers refused to patronize creditors who had insulted them.

The Home Mortgage Disclosure and the Community Reinvestment Acts were passed to induce lenders to make mortgage credit readily available in inner city neighborhoods. Those acts may have caused lenders to be more sensitive to eliminating practices that could be viewed as being discriminatory—even if those practices were based on economic risk assessments rather than on prejudice, per se. However, the acts also may have caused some lenders to bend over backwards in allocating credit to members of protected groups. In addition, the acts raised the costs of mortgages for lenders in general. Furthermore, both Benston (1979) and Canner (1982) have reviewed the extensive literature on mortgage credit discrimination. Neither found any evidence that members of protected groups could not obtain credit prior to the passage of those acts because of systematic discrimination against them. In general, research studies show that, regardless of location, people who desired credit could obtain it based solely on their credit qualifications and the risk of the loan.

Continuing Issues: Are Credit Availability Regulations Cost-Effective?—The evidence suggests that in a highly competitive marketplace, systematic discrimination against any particular class of borrowers will not persist for long. If one group becomes more creditworthy than before, intense competition among the multitude of potential lenders ensures that at least one lender will perceive that he can improve the performance of his loan portfolio by extending credit to such a group. Consequently, as long as there are many suppliers of credit services, it is unlikely that systematic credit discrimination against one group will persist. This phenomenon drastically limits the potential gross gain that can be achieved from regulation. Consequently, the most that credit availability regulations can achieve in a competitive market is to ensure that the market will provide credit more readily to a group whose credit status has changed more quickly than many lenders recognized. For instance, testimony on ECOA suggested that the growing acceptance of women in the labor force seemingly improved women's general creditworthiness faster than several creditors were willing to acknowledge. ECOA, then, may have encouraged some lenders to extend credit to women faster than would have occurred from competition alone.

Regulation clearly raises the cost of credit. Direct costs of complying with the regulations can be substantial. In addition, in order to avoid trouble with the regulators, creditors may be willing to extend more credit than is warranted to certain groups. If so, creditors' earnings would be lower or their losses greater than would otherwise be the case.

Rather than impose compliance costs on all creditors, a more cost-effective approach to problems of credit discrimination would focus directly on those creditors who allegedly were engaged in discriminatory practices. If a creditor were accused of discrimination, statistical techniques could be used to determine if that creditor had, in fact, discriminated against a particular class of individuals. Meanwhile, institutions that did not engage in discriminatory practices would be spared the costs necessary to comply with a blunderbuss regulation.

Another alternative to omnibus regulation that should be considered is fostering increased competition so that members of disadvantaged groups would have many vendors offering them credit on competitive terms. Research indicates that people can obtain the credit they desire in competitive markets, regardless of whether or not they belong to a "disadvantaged" group.

CREDITORS' REMEDIES

Regulations that restrict the methods creditors may use to collect on delinquent or defaulted loans have existed for many years. Among other things, such regulations may limit the attorneys' fees that the creditor can assess if the creditor must sue to recover payment on a debt and the late charges that may be assessed. They also may affect creditors' abilities to repossess property purchased on credit; garnish the wages or the savings of a delinquent debtor; or contact either the debtor, or the debtor's employer, friends, or relatives about a delinquent debt.

Regulations restricting creditors' remedies primarily are imposed by individual states. However, the Federal Trade Commission (FTC) has restricted the use of "holder-in-due-course" clauses and proposed a "Trade Regulation Rule on Credit Practices" that would restrict other creditors' remedies on a national basis. In hearings on the FTC's credit practices rule, evidence was presented on the impact of these restrictions on the price and availability of consumer credit. In addition, the National Commission on Consumer Finance (1972B) presented substantial evidence of the impact of creditors' remedies on the price and availability of credit of various types.

Generally, restrictions on collection remedies are likely to increase creditors' costs and, where rate ceilings are binding, reduce their willingness to extend credit to the riskiest classes of customers. Because credit losses are generally relatively low and creditors' remedies only have an effect in cases where a debt is not repaid, restrictions on creditors' remedies cause interest rates to rise by only a small amount. The increase in rates is greater on riskier loans, however. Barth and Yezer (1977) found, for instance, that interest rates on consumer finance company loans were several percentage points higher in states with restrictive remedies—partially because consumers were willing to pay more for such credit.

Overall, restrictions on creditors' remedies act much like an insurance policy. Individuals who default on their debts are less frequently subject to harsh remedies if remedies are restricted. However, all individuals who borrow pay a "premium" in the form of higher rates and less favorable credit terms. If rate ceilings are binding, cash credit availability to high-risk borrowers is additionally reduced.

The overriding policy issue is whether or not insurance against creditors' exercise of harsh remedies should be mandated by law, or be individually arranged by negotiation between customers and creditors. Johnson (1978) has argued that consumers would pay to eliminate contract clauses that involve harsh debt collection methods if those clauses were worth more to the consumer than to the creditor. In contrast, the FTC staff (1974) has argued that individual negotiation over remedies was not feasible. Peterson and Falls (1981), however, have presented evidence that creditors may forego the use of harsh collection methods because they do not wish to lose customer good will. The evidence shows that creditors place the least value on collection remedies that are most disliked by consumers.

Because many creditors voluntarily restrain their use of remedies, it is possible for consumers to select creditors who have good reputations for not using harsh collection remedies when they borrow. If they do so, they also may be willing to pay higher rates to borrow from such creditors. In that way they implicitly purchase insurance against the exercise of harsh collection remedies. Through this mechanism, the private market can provide protection against the use of harsh collection remedies without explicit bargaining over the use of remedies.

A continuing issue that exists with regard to creditor remedy regulation is whether or not restrictions on creditors' remedies should be regulated at the national or state level. At the present time individual states provide for substantial regulation of creditors' remedies. Because of that fact, and because of the market forces described above, national regulation is not needed to ensure that creditors do not use harsh collection practices.

CONSUMER BANKRUPTCY LAWS

Over many years, bankruptcy laws have evolved from the concept that debtors should either pay their debts or be punished, to the current concept that debtors who are *hopelessly* behind on their debts should be able to discharge them and obtain a fresh start. Unfortunately, there is no standard in the law to define when debts are sufficiently oppressive that a consumer can file for bankruptcy. Rather, consumers can file whenever they wish, provided they have not filed in the previous seven years.

Studies of bankruptcy filings after the Federal Bankruptcy Reform Act of 1978 became effective have shown that a substantial percentage of consumers who had filed for personal bankruptcy under the Federal Bankruptcy Act, in fact, could have repaid a very substantial portion of their debts—in many cases in their entirety (Johnson, Peterson, and Schick, 1982). Some of those consumers had filed for bankruptcy because they were angry at particular creditors. Others seemingly filed for bankruptcy because, for a number of years, they had used credit to live above their incomes. Then, as their indebtedness grew, they found it easier to declare bankruptcy than to live below their income until they had repaid their debts.

In part because of abuses of the Federal Bankruptcy Reform Act of 1978, creditors' losses increased sharply. Subsequently, creditors altered their willingness to extend credit to various classes of customers. In particular, since unsecured creditors frequently lose their entire claim under the Federal Bankruptcy Reform Act, the major personal finance companies in the United

States frequently require that consumers pledge security, in the form of second mortgages, for a substantial portion of their loans. In addition, even when they do not require collateral, the major consumer finance companies now only lend to people who are well established and highly creditworthy. As a result, young people and people without home equity have found it increasingly difficult to obtain cash credit since the act was passed. As a remedy, lenders have suggested that the law be changed to include a "means test" to determine whether bankrupt consumers could, in fact, repay a substantial portion of their debts. If judged able to repay, consumers would be required to do so rather than to discharge their debts under Chapter 7 of the Federal Bankruptcy Act.

Potential Changes in the Consumer Credit Market: Changes in Market Structure

Substantial changes are occurring in the structure of the consumer credit markets. Because of the recent change in bankruptcy laws and inflation, the growth of second mortgages has been substantial, and other secured debt has grown at the expense of unsecured debt. Revolving credit also has grown substantially. It is convenient for consumers, and the costs of credit origination need only be borne once, even though the credit line can be used many times. However, the unsecured nature of revolving credit poses problems when a consumer files for bankruptcy. Thus, some lenders have offered revolving credit tied to second mortgages.

An additional change in market structure is the exit of lenders from highly regulated markets. Consumer finance companies no longer operate in Arkansas, which for many years had a 10 percent usury ceiling, and they have withdrawn operations from many other states, such as Maine (Benston, 1972) where usury ceilings are low and credit regulations are extensive. In general, in recent years finance companies have shifted lending activities from the consumer credit market to the business credit market. Regulations affecting business lending are not extensive, and few restrictions, if any, exist on rates of return that can be charged on business loans.

Since high-risk lenders are the most affected by regulations, consumer finance companies have been most affected by regulations restricting creditors' remedies, rate ceilings, and recoveries from bankrupt debtors. Thus, consumer finance companies have been more prone than other lenders to abandon the consumer credit market when regulations and rate ceilings are binding. As a result, their share of the consumer credit market has declined substantially over time.

Another recent phenomenon is the entry of less regulated consumer lenders. More institutions have attempted to become "financial supermarkets" in recent years. Merrill Lynch has offered credit cards which let wealthy customers borrow at margin account interest rates. Sears, Roebuck, through its acquisition of Dean Witter and Co., is tapping the "upscale market" for consumer financial services. Both Sears and Merrill Lynch offer investment services as well as credit services to their customers. Many major banks have acquired brokerage firm connections while continuing to make traditional consumer loans. Also, many savings and loan associations have diversified their traditional mortgage lending by granting second mortgages and making other consumer loans.

In general, these structural changes involve a shift of credit availability from the poor to the wealthy. Regulations on creditors' remedies and the Federal Bankruptcy Reform Act of 1978 have made creditors' losses greater if they lend to poor, high-risk customers who have difficulty repaying their debts or elect not to do so. At the same time, greater ability to collateralize margin accounts and obtain second mortgage loans has meant that credit has become more readily available for people with stocks, bonds, and houses.

A final factor that has begun to influence the consumer financial markets has been the growth of remote (electronic) funds transfer services. Nationwide automatic teller machine systems will provide consumers with cash at various points, while credit cards can be used to obtain both point-of-sale credit from cooperating merchants and cash credit from cooperating financial institutions. As home computer use grows and more consumers acquire interactive cable television or phone capabilities, credit buying through home terminals will become more popular. At present, such credit use is relatively limited because of the limited availability of appropriate mechanisms.

Summary and Conclusions

Consumer finance markets are characterized by two major attributes. First, there are large numbers of vendors who provide services in the consumer financial markets. In general, this means that, left to their own devices, those markets will generate substantial competition. The existence of substantial competition tends to keep prices down or, at least, keep prices in line with costs. In addition, competition ensures that credit and other financial services are made widely available to all potential customers.

Another attribute of consumer finance markets is that they periodically are subject to intensive regulation. This regulation attempts to redress presumed imbalances between the superior knowledge and market power of financial institutions and the inferior knowledge of consumer borrowers. Such regulations have erroneously assumed that financial institutions will engage in any collection activity on delinquent or defaulted debts that is allowed by law, that they will arbitrarily and capriciously deny credit to certain classes of borrowers, and that they will exploit to the maximum any knowledge advantage they may have vis-à-vis consumers.

Because consumer financial markets are quite competitive, many regulations have not had their intended effects. Rate ceilings on consumer cash loans have led to the growth of retail credit, where prices of goods can be marked up to compensate for reduced credit revenues. Credit availability regulations have been applied to markets that previously acted in a competitive fashion, in that the markets generally provided consumer and mortgage credit to all customers who were qualified on the basis of risk, regardless of race, sex, marital status, or location—even before the regulations were passed.

Overall, consumer credit market regulation appears to result from a tug-of-war between idealistic social reformers and practical people who feel excessive regulations have had adverse consequences on competitive markets. In the late 1960s and into the 1970s, social reformers passed extensive legislation affecting consumer credit markets, much of which did not have its intended effect. As evidence accumulated that much legislation was unnecessary or ineffective in competitive markets, starting in 1980 procompetitive forces gained the upper hand.

In the future, legislation that is based on the assumption that consumer financial markets are not competitive should not be enacted unless prior careful study shows that a systematic problem, in fact, exists. In addition, steps should be taken to undo unnecessary costs imposed on competitive markets by overzealous and ineffective legislation. Particular care should be taken to ensure that regulation does not primarily serve the vested interest of legislators, attorneys, or other special interest groups. At the same time, effective legislation, such as the Truth-in-Lending Act, should be targeted more precisely and, if possible, made more effective by requiring credit interest rates to be stated on a basis that is comparable to interest rate quotations in the savings market.

Stuart I. Greenbaum and Bryon Higgins 

8
Financial Innovation

Introduction

Financial evolution is a process by which the financial system adapts to environmental shocks such as changes in technology, demand, and public regulation. This adaptation is manifested in the mix of claims produced, the delivery systems through which these claims are marketed, and the organizational forms and industrial structure of the financial services industry. When external shocks are moderate relative to the adaptive capability of the financial system, we observe smooth passages from one

STUART I. GREENBAUM *is the Harold L. Stuart Professor of Banking and Finance and director of the Banking Research Center at the J. L. Kellogg Graduate School of Management, Northwestern University. He has consulted for numerous professional organizations, financial institutions, public regulatory agencies, and management consulting and public accounting firms. He has testified before committees of both houses of Congress as well as other legislative bodies. He serves on the Board of Directors of two financial institutions. Dr. Greenbaum publishes in economics and finance journals, as well as in journalistic outlets. He has served on the editorial boards of five academic journals.*

BRYON HIGGINS *is assistant vice president and economist at the Federal Reserve Bank of Kansas City. He has taught macroeconomics at the University of Missouri at Kansas City and was visiting assistant professor of economics at the University of Iowa, where he headed courses in money and banking. Dr. Higgins has published numerous articles on monetary policy.*

state to the next without disruption of financial or related "real-sector" activities. However, when shocks are large or when the financial system's adaptive capability is impaired, disturbances result in financial crises, recessions, and related symptoms that capture public attention and often ignite social upheaval. Whether disturbances result in trauma or smooth transitions, the process of adaptation inevitably affects the prices and availability of financial services, the allocation of other resources, and the distribution of income and wealth.

The adaptive process is illustrated by the U.S. experience of the past decade, during which massive real resources were diverted to financial applications such as cash management. In addition, credit contracts were redesigned, shortening durations in line with the eclipse of capital markets. At the same time, deposit-type intermediaries lost their "core" deposits, a major source of bank capital, thereby impairing their ability to withstand external shocks. These changes have been spurred by a stubborn inflation and by technological advances in data processing and telecommunications. The upshot is a financial system undergoing profound change with its future contours only vaguely defined. The questions raised by this flux transcend the financial services industry. Property rights are affected, of course, as is the distribution of risk among the public, industry, and government. In addition, the industry's traditional role as a conduit of monetary policy casts the issues in a still more expansive context. These issues motivate this chapter on the causes and consequences of financial innovation.

This chapter is organized in seven sections. For background, the next section describes the traditional functions of the financial system. This is followed by a description of the financial system in terms of the claims produced, the delivery systems used to market these claims, and the organizational forms and structure of the financial services industry. The subsequent section addresses inflation's effects on the financial system in terms of the allocation of real resources, the conduct of monetary policy, the pace of technological advance in the financial system, the subversion of public regulation, and the public's growing financial sophistication. The next section addresses the rationale and appropriate scope for public regulation of financial institutions. In particular, we examine the government's role as guarantor of the financial system and then consider the implications of sanctioning this government intervention in financial arrangements. The next to last section describes three theories of the financial innovation process, all of which are linked to inflation and public regulation. The final section presents conclusions.

Functions of the Financial System

Financial intermediaries perform two closely related functions: they process information and risk. The informational function is illustrated by the "best-efforts" contract of the investment banker. As a broker, the banker matches transactors but need not incur risk. A broker simply produces information for resale. The broker's only possible risk arises from uncertainty regarding the demand for the information it supplies.

The potential reuseability of information is the broker's raison d'être. By centralizing the collection and processing of information, the broker reduces resources used in search and related informational activities. Viewed in this way, the need for brokerage is both compelling and fundamental, especially in large and complex environments. When the object of search is well-defined and readily observable, the brokerage function can be performed mechanically and quite simply. Only if the attributes about which information is desired are subtle, as in the cases of personality or default risk, do the brokers' skills and reputation become important. Thus, the larger the grid over which the search is to be performed, the more compelling the need for brokers, irrespective of skills. The less observable or well-defined the object of search, for any given grid, the greater the return to search skills and reputation.

Risk-processing, the second basic function of the financial system, relates to qualitative asset-transformation. Whereas a broker can maintain a balance sheet with perfectly matched assets and liabilities, the asset-transformer has a mismatched balance sheet, thereby altering the attributes of the claims held by its clientele. Furthermore, in accepting the mismatched balance sheet, the asset-transformer incurs interest rate risk. The widely noted withdrawal risk faced by depository institutions is a special form of interest rate risk, often resulting from a ceiling on deposit interest rates. If the transformation is across currencies, the risk relates to exchange rates. Credit risk, still another form of exposure, arises when the intermediary fails to shift default risk directly from borrowers to ultimate lenders. For example, the depositor does not directly or completely assume the credit risk inherent in the bank's earning assets.

The qualitative asset-transformer may shift risk to a third party, in which case it evolves toward the hedged position of the broker. Alternatively, the asset-transformer may simply absorb risk or dissipate it through diversification. In general, asset-transformation encompasses a variety of processes, forms of exposure, and claim attributes (e.g., liquidity, divisibility, reversibility, use as a unit of account, acceptance in exchange, and degree of default risk). However, the standard example is that of a depository intermediary funding long-term loans with short-term liabilities. In this case, the asset-transformer accepts default risk and also shortens the duration of publicly held claims. Setting aside default considerations, the intermediary assumes the risk of rising short-term interest rates and is presumably compensated by a liquidity premium imbedded in the term structure of interest rates. Indeed, the liquidity premium provides the incentive for duration-reducing asset-transformation which, in turn, reduces the premium in the term structure of interest rates. Thus, duration transformation evidences an underlying liquidity premium, but it also confounds its measurement.

Still another, perhaps even more basic, rationale for asset-transformation derives from indivisibility of claims. Suppose a fixed cost inhibits all but the largest nonfinancial firms from fractionating their liabilities. That is, only if the potential number of claim holders is very large can average costs be low enough to warrant the distribution of many small dividend and interest checks and the maintenance of necessary ownership and tax records. Because of these fixed costs, smaller firms find it optimal to issue their claims *en bloc,* as in private placements or bank loans. In such a setting, asset-transformers emerge for the purpose of purchasing the issues of smaller nonfinancial firms with the proceeds of their own, more divisible, liabilities. The asset-transformer thereby permits constrained wealth-owners, the ultimate investors, to diversify without financial leverage. In performing this service, the asset-transformer accepts a form of balance sheet mismatching owing to the need for an inventory in any such activity (Deshmukh, Greenbaum, and Kanatas, 1983).

Although many taxonomic treatments of financial intermediation focus on other services, such as the maintenance of the payments mechanism (provision of a medium of exchange) or the temporal transfer of consumption, the broker/asset-transformer description subsumes most of these alternative descriptions as special cases. For example, moneyness can be viewed as a claim attribute that asset-transformers provide by assuming various forms of exposure, particularly funding and credit risk. Alternatively, money can be viewed as an intermediary in its own right, directly providing brokerage services as in the case of J. Niehans's (1971) trading-stations argument. Similarly, Irving Fisher's (1930) explanation of credit markets as instruments for the temporal adjustment of consumption to arbitrarily timed endowments is readily interpreted as a form of brokerage activity. Still another example is provided by the specialist in the organized exchange or the market-maker in any "over-the-counter" market. The market-maker typically provides a combination of brokerage and asset-transformation services. Without an inventory, the client obtains a pure low-skill brokerage service. With an inventory, the market-maker sustains risk and provides liquidity, divisibility, and price-smoothing services.

Three Facets of the Financial System

As mentioned earlier, we view the financial system as being composed of claims, delivery systems, and organizations. Claims can be thought of as embodiments of various combinations of attributes. Thus we can visualize an attribute continuum with as many dimensions as there are relevant attributes. Each produced claim can be represented as an address, in this hyperspace, and the introduction of a new claim is nothing more than a change of the attribute mix to occupy a previously vacant address. The proliferation of claims reduces the gaps between existing claims and tends to complete the market. The menu of produced claims may increase because of interest rate or wealth increases, technological advances, or because public regulation provides incentives to innovate. The production of a new claim imposes a new mix of exposures on the intermediary and thereby presents a new risk-management challenge. However, it is difficult to imagine that this form of innovation can generate inordinate fixed costs. Nor are the welfare implications of claim proliferation entirely clear.

In contrast, a delivery system is a nonfinancial asset used for marketing purposes. In the present context, financial claims are the objects being marketed. Delivery systems typically involve substantial development costs along with subsequent depreciation costs. A system is usually capable of distributing a wide array of financial services to a particular market. Thus, delivery systems tend to be market-specific rather than product- or service-specific.

Retail commercial banking has traditionally employed a brick and mortar delivery system that many now believe to be obsolete. Life insurance companies and commercial lending have relied for the most part on labor-intensive personalized selling. Mutual funds use phone, mail, and wire distribution systems. Credit and debit cards represent yet another distribution technology, whereas automated teller machines (ATMs) are a robotic substitute for full-service branches. Each of these systems is designed to serve a particular niche in the market, with inevitable overlap resulting in competition and even potential eclipse of outmoded systems. Since the functional rationalization or coalescence of the older delivery systems has been inhibited by legal and regulatory barriers, circumvention of these barriers has resulted in the development of newer systems in much the same way that interest rate ceilings have led to development of new claims.

Public regulatory restrictions on organizational forms, particularly spatial and functional limitations, have constrained the types of delivery systems. Without these restrictions, the technology of brick and mortar probably would have led to the development of extensive branching systems such as those in the United Kingdom, Canada, and Israel. Similarly, real estate securities distribution, accounting and legal services, and insurance might have been distributed through the same brick and mortar delivery system were it not for legal restrictions. However, the American financial tradition has been characterized by narrowly focused delivery systems with sharp product line and geographic distinctions. This has led to excessive investment in banking plant and equipment, and also to low market entry barriers. Indeed, regulatory entry restrictions can be viewed as compensating for the artificially low market entry barriers resulting from regulation-mandated spatial and functional restrictions and from governmental deposit insurance.

Relaxation of public regulation of organizational forms seems to be a major contemporary theme. The recent expansion, some would say rationalization, of delivery systems has been variously ascribed to technological advances and to the growing impotence of public regulation, both of which are attributable in part to inflation. Whatever the ultimate explanation, the restructuring of organizational forms and delivery systems has had far-reaching manifestations, including franchising, networking, and shared ATM systems. The interstate expansion of thrifts and bank loan production offices (LPOs) and the entry of both thrifts and banks into discount brokerage provide still other examples. On yet another level, the striking international integration of banking is a manifestation of the changing relationship between organizational form and delivery systems. Money market mutual funds and credit (debit) card systems, perhaps the first nationwide retail banking distribution systems, constitute yet other examples.

The continuation of this trend toward increased scale and scope of delivery systems points to an industry organized around tiers of firms, with a small number of worldwide systems challenging the regulatory hegemony of nation states. A small number of nationwide delivery systems will serve mass markets without brick and mortar or labor-intensive technologies. These nationwide systems will be complemented by a larger number of specialized distribution systems for specialized segments of the market. Routine financial services will undoubtedly be delivered electronically, but commercial lending, underwriting, and many forms of insurance will continue to require more labor-intensive distribution methods. Banks engaged in commercial lending will find it increasingly compelling to offer fixed-rate term loans in order to permit their commercial borrowers to achieve a tolerable degree of protection against interest rate exposure. Unable or unwilling to fund these loans with short-term purchased money, the banks will come under increasing pressure to develop markets for term liabilities. The most likely candidates are insurance and pension liabilities. Thus we can expect a powerful tendency for coalescence between commercial banks on the one hand and insurance companies and pension fund managers on the other. Although this coalescence would be achieved indirectly through the use of futures markets, the more direct joining of complementary functions is less likely to be less costly, especially for larger institutions. The traditional separation of banks and their trust departments is likely to be reexamined.

Brick and mortar will continue to play a significant role in serving "downscale" markets where verification requirements are substantial, credit lines are small, and educational levels are low. Nevertheless, the development of national and even transnational delivery systems will raise serious questions of public policy. Retail intermediation services may come to look increasingly like public utilities. Entry costs will undoubtedly escalate, perhaps reducing the degree of competition. Furthermore, multinational financial institutions are uniquely equipped for arbitrage across regulatory domains, thus requiring a higher degree of international cooperation among governments.

Organizational form, the third facet of the financial system, is perhaps most ephemeral. It can be viewed as the outcome of tension between the technology of production and public regulation. A wide variety of organizational designs is probably consistent with almost any technology. Thus a nationwide electronic funds transfer system could be a monopoly, as in the case of our telephone system, or a competitive industry with several firms. Decisions regarding organizational forms are often substantially political but have important economic implications. The tradition of mutuality in the thrift industry provides a good example. Despite deep historical roots, the mutual form of organization among thrifts seems to be in eclipse as a result of a moderately sustained period of economic adversity. The relative disadvantage of mutual institutions is their unfavorable access to capital markets and their high operating costs (Deshmukh, Greenbaum, and Thakor, 1982). Some argue that the mutual form of organization also impedes adaptation because of the division between de jure and de facto ownership.

In any case, we are confronted with difficult political choices regarding organizational forms, including choices between public and private ownership. However, these choices will need to be made in light of more fundamental economic considerations relating to delivery systems and claim menus.

Inflation's Effects on the Financial System

The U.S. financial system is based on contracts written in nominal rather than real terms. Moreover, many financial assets offer more or less fixed nominal returns. In such a setting, inflation—especially if unanticipated—inevitably savages the system by encouraging substitution away from those claims offering lower real rates of return. Since interest rate ceilings are applied to existing claims, whereas yields on unproduced claims are unconstrained, inflation typically spurs proliferation of claims. This is perhaps the most fundamental effect of inflation on the financial system. It explains the proliferation of money substitutes, such as money market mutual funds, as well as the growth of federal funds, repurchase agreements, C/Ds, and the like.

The counterpart of this claim proliferation is the increasing use of real resources for cash management. The combination of legal reserve requirements and interest rate ceilings induces efforts to reduce the holding of rate-constrained claims, thereby increasing the velocity of money (Niehans, 1982). This explains the Federal Reserve's recent frustration in its conduct of monetary policy. The heightened volatility of interest rates and the confusion regarding monetary aggregates are the concomitants of the massive substitution away from traditional monetary forms. Hence, we have observed the elevation and expansion of the financial function in nonfinancial firms as well as the dramatic growth in the past decade in all manner of financial service enterprises.

Interest and exchange rate volatility has also contributed to the striking growth of risk-shifting instruments, such as forward exchange, options, financial futures, loan commitments, letters of credit, and bankers acceptances (Wolkowitz, et al., 1981). The implications of bank contingent (and often off-balance sheet) liabilities for banks' management of solvency risk and the central bank's monetary management are serious, but barely grasped. For a discussion of the management issues, see Thakor, Hong, and Greenbaum (1981). The perverse effects of loan commitments on monetary policy are explained by Deshmukh, Greenbaum, and Kanatas (1982) and Ricart i Costa and Greenbaum (1983A).

Less widely appreciated are inflation's effects on technological advances and the speed of their adoption. Basic computer and telecommunications technology probably was not substantially influenced by recent inflation. However, financial applications certainly were stimulated by high nominal interest rates and the associated turbulence in financial markets. Illustrations include the development of same-day clearing for international payments, the spreading use of ATM systems, improved wire-transfer systems, videotex systems, and money market mutual funds. Many of these advances simply speed payments and reduce float. They are merely symptoms of the cash management syndrome referred to earlier. Thus many innovations thought to be exogenous are in part the result of inflation. Innovative applications of new technology are often responses to the more basic motive to husband assets bearing diminishing real returns because of inflation.

Just as inflation hastens the application of new technology, it also stimulates the search for means of circumventing regulation. These two phenomena are closely related in that both technology and regulation constrain the transformation of inputs into financial services. They differ in that technological constraints are natural in origin, whereas regulatory constraints are artificial. With both, inflation elevates the shadow price of a constraint and thereby stimulates the search for means of circumvention. Illustrations include the expanded use of nonreservable bank liabilities such as Eurodollars, federal funds, and repurchase agreements. Claims also were designed to circumvent Regulation Q, and even the modest deposit insurance premium. The growth of bank contingent liabilities, particularly off–balance sheet items, resulted in part from attempts to avoid regulatory constraints relating to liquidity and financial capital.

The nationwide spread of LPOs was a palpable circumvention of the intent of the McFadden Act and the Douglas Amendments to the Bank Holding Company Act, although the connection with inflation is somewhat oblique. The spread of LPOs was part of a broader phenomenon involving the international integration of financial markets (Porzecanski, 1981). Nonetheless, this integration was rooted in the inflationary pressures that varied across countries and were so important in escalating the volatility of exchange rates.

Differences between the financial regulatory agencies of the

1960s and those of today are also striking. Whether correct or not, public regulators previously believed they could shape the direction of change. All acknowledged regulators' power to discipline their constituents. Today we find the central bank unable to define money and uncertain of its ability to control it, however defined. We find regulators preoccupied with financial institutions seriously weakened by the loss of core deposits and deterioration of asset quality. For the first time in forty years, failing institutions are an overriding concern. Even the vaunted governmental deposit insurance system is being challenged for the first time in its history. Moreover, major pieces of the financial system have either drifted away from regulatory control or have grown up outside the regulators' sphere of influence. We find a severely shaken community of public regulators, with badly strained and overextended resources, especially in examination, supervision, and deposit insurance.

Some would add yet another effect of inflation to our list. Investors of all stripes have allegedly begun to ascend a learning curve that irreversibly sensitizes them to financial change. Financial markets may become increasingly erratic, reacting to every scintilla of information, misinformation, or disinformation. The increased awareness of asset-holders helps explain the increase in real resources dedicated to financial management. It also suggests that important aspects of financial change are irreversible (i.e., the system is permanently destabilized by the heightened sensitivity and growing sophistication of investors). The learning curve paradigm implies that a return to lower inflation and lower nominal interest rates may not reverse the flow of resources into financial management or allow return to a financial system stabilized around idle balances together with some lender exploitation.

Public Regulation of the Financial System

In the span of U.S. history, the financial system has always been the object of substantial public regulation. Despite numerous explanations, there remains considerable controversy as to the motive and necessity for public intrusion into private financial arrangements. The currently fashionable view of regulation as an instrument for organizing commerce in governmentally dispensed privileges seems incomplete at best (Stigler, 1975). More localized forces seem to explain pervasive public regulation of the financial sector. Special treatment of the financial sector is almost certainly traceable to the putative fragility of the financial system and to its monetary functions. The system's strategic position is further heightened by its role as a conduit for monetary policy, although activist monetary policy is a recent phenomenon extending back at most to the formation of the Federal Reserve System.

This interpretation raises two questions. Is the financial system unstable? If it is unstable, does its monetary role warrant regulation? The latter question can be formulated in terms of the real costs of turbulent financial markets. Some scholars have argued that the financial system performed without catastrophe for protracted periods, such as from the demise of the Second Bank of the U.S. in 1836 to the Civil War period, with only minimal governmental intervention (Hammond, 1957; Friedman and Schwartz, 1963). To be sure, bank failures were quite common during this period. Nevertheless, the effects were more or less isolated without the major externalities associated with contagious and cumulative runs (Rolnick and Weber, 1983; Rockoff, 1974). Moreover, firms come and go in other industries without major social costs. If markets work, as they assuredly do most of the time, firms that choose to operate with high risk are evaluated accordingly by investors. Thus, even if failures of financial firms are numerous, the money and capital markets should price deposits and other financial assets appropriately, and the public can exercise its preferences without impediment. The failure of firms need not imply the failure of markets. It is the latter type of failure that must be demonstrated to justify public intervention.

An alternative view is that informational asymmetries inhibit the working of the financial system as just described. Information costs and consequent informational asymmetries among potential transactors are thought to be especially important in rental markets, among which labor and financial markets are notable examples. The services traded in these markets tend to be especially heterogeneous, thus posing problems of observability, breaches of contract, and moral hazard. These problems tend to undermine the efficient working of rental markets and inhibit trade. The singular vulnerability of rental markets to failure owing to informational asymmetries provides a brokerage role for government. In the financial realm, this role has been expressed in a variety of ways, e.g., "to provide a stable environment to facilitate private contracting," "to maintain a stable money," "to stabilize the financial system," and "to provide a uniform commercial code." These are all means of resolving informational asymmetries that frustrate contracting and thereby impede commerce and production. Moreover, long placid periods without public regulation did not preclude occasional explosive disruptions, such as those in 1907 and 1929, that not only paralyzed commerce and production, but also threatened political upheaval.

We turn now to the question of why the financial system may be singularly unstable. First, it should be noted that generations of business cycle theorists have explained economic instability in terms of the periodic collapse of the financial system (Mitchell, 1927). Thus, the idea of financial sector fragility is not novel. There seem to be two related reasons for this alleged fragility. First, as explained by Diamond and Dybvig (1982), a fractional reserve banking system is characterized by multiple equilibriums: one is a tenable equilibrium whereas another is characterized by a "run," the ultimate form of withdrawal risk. According to this analysis, the process of liquidity production via private asset-transformation inherently gives rise to the possibility of a "runs equilibrium" because of the associated limited liability and credit risk. A 100 percent reserve banking system, as recommended by Simons (1948), would remedy the problem but would also preclude private production of liquidity.

A second reason for the alleged instability of the financial system arises from the technology of intermediation. Financial intermediation requires little specific physical or financial capital. To see this, one need only compare the balance sheet of a randomly selected financial institution with that of a similarly selected nonfinancial firm of the same asset size. Entry into financial intermediation requires little more than the ability to borrow. The low natural barriers to entry have meant that considerable adjustment in the industry's equilibrium output is effected by the entry and exit of firms. This method of adjusting output is considerably more disruptive than output changes by existing firms, since it involves breaches of contracts. Indeed, one advantage of permitting the industry to become more concentrated is that the number of firms might be stabilized because of the associated increase in barriers to entry. It is presumably more difficult to enter an unprotected market and compete directly with Citicorp than it would be to open a bank next to The First Bank of Hazard in a countywide market area. Thus the nexus between private liquidity production and bank runs on the one hand, and the low natural barriers to entry, on the other, helps explain the fragility of the financial system. Moreover, informational asymmetries can result in market failures that may warrant a role for government as a broker and guarantor in financial markets. However, the extent of governmental intervention justified by informational considerations is an open question.

We now turn to the locus of governmental intervention in financial markets and its implications. The most basic governmental intrusions are those of lender-of-last-resort and guarantor of bank liabilities. To be sure, bank regulation has many other manifestations, but most can be understood as deriving from these two basic activities. Moreover, these two activities are inextricably linked in much the same way as liquidity and solvency are linked. The history of public regulation and guarantee of the banking system reflects the same confusion and contradictions found in the economics literature on the relationship between liquidity and solvency. For example, Keynes (1936) tried with limited success to define precisely what liquidity is. Tobin (1958), one of Keynes's foremost interpreters, clarified the issues. However, there is still no clearly accepted definition of liquidity and no clear distinction between the concepts of liquidity and solvency. Moreover, the concept of solvency of financial institutions, is itself subject to disparate interpretations.

The lender-of-last-resort is the most time-honored of central banking functions. Indeed, it was the unquestionable need for such a facility that led to the creation of the Federal Reserve System. The introduction of the quasi-governmental lender-of-last-resort in 1913 immediately raised questions regarding the appropriate terms and availability of credit extended through this facility.

Two questions were uppermost. First, given that the discount window was intended to augment liquidity rather than to remedy problems of asset quality, what were the appropriate availability restrictions? Second, in light of the narrowly circumscribed role of the discount window, how should advances be priced? The first question was addressed by defining eligible paper—essentially an asset quality restriction related to solvency—and by delimiting the legitimate purposes of discount borrowing, which proved difficult to administer in all but the most egregious cases. The pricing issue is traceable to the idea that the window was to serve as an emergency facility. Consequently a "penalty" discount rate would discourage abuse. It was thought that banks should never be presented with arbitrage opportunities involving discount window advances. However, the Federal Reserve has never accepted this pricing principle, preferring to post a lower rate and thereby placing a heavier burden on "administration" of the discount window. Certainly, this facet of Federal Reserve behavior is consistent with Stigler's (1975) theory of public regulation.

However, even with a penalty discount rate, a subsidy inheres in the discount window giving rise to a moral hazard problem that helps explain many other facets of bank regulation. Given the possibility of a bank being "rationed out of the market," any discount facility guaranteeing a finite rate of interest presents its clientele with a subsidy. By eliminating the possibility of banks being confronted with an infinite marginal borrowing rate, the discount window inevitably reduces banks' voluntary holdings of liquidity reserves. This reduction in reserves, attendant to the introduction of the discount window, shifts part of the profit from money creation to the private banks and thereby constitutes a form of moral hazard (Greenbaum, 1983).

The Federal Reserve is in much the same position as the fire insurance carrier whose clients do not install sprinkler systems. The introduction of a lender-of-last-resort provides an incentive for banks to substitute earning assets for cash. This substitution not only shifts deposit seigniorage from government to the banks, but also results in increased risk of insolvency for any given level of bank capital. To be sure, the shift in seigniorage tends to increase bank capital, offsetting to some extent the greater risk of insolvency. Nevertheless, the government is faced with a loss of tax revenue together with increased bank risk as a result of its accepting the lender-of-last-resort responsibility. It therefore responds by introducing risk-abatement regulations together with monitoring of compliance. The discount window therefore provides a rationale for reserve requirements, asset proscriptions, capital requirements, bank examinations, and entry restrictions. If one accepts the argument that high funding costs lead banks to acquire riskier assets, then the discount window can also explain deposit interest rate ceilings.

After twenty years of experience, it was agreed that the lender-of-last-resort was not the panacea some of its most ardent supporters had thought. It became apparent that the public's confidence in banks could be eroded despite the presence of a discount facility with virtually unlimited resources. The problem was one of solvency, not liquidity; the discount window was confined to a narrowly defined role. Political forces demanded that government's role in banking be expanded from deep involvement to total immersion. This meant guaranteeing bank liabilities in addition to liquefying bank assets. The introduction of federal deposit insurance meant that the government's risk exposure arising from private decisions took a quantum leap. Banks were no longer borrowing against their own liabilities. They were now selling contingent liabilities of the U.S. government, much like the debt issues of U.S. government agencies such as the Federal National Mortgage Association. The expanded guarantor role resulted in additional moral hazard and thereby subjected the government to further potential exploitation and abuse.

Before the introduction of deposit insurance, bank capital served three distinct functions. It provided a buffer against bankruptcy costs associated with insolvency, a direct source of funds, and an indirect source of funds. In this last role, capital reduced the cost of selling debt by reducing the default risk sustained by depositors. In principle, each bank would weigh the cumulative benefits of capital against its cost in order to determine the optimal amount of financial capital. The introduction of deposit insurance virtually eliminated the indirect-source-of-funds function of bank capital by eliminating default risk on deposits. Insured deposits became perfectly interchangeable across banks because they were seen as contingent liabilities of the U.S. government. The elimination of one of its three functions meant that capital became less valuable. As a result, banks would be expected to reduce their capital and thus increase their financial leverage.

This phenomenon is equally apparent from another point of view. Bank capital serves as a deductible on the deposit insurance policy in that the government sustains losses only after the bank's capital is exhausted. Hence, at an unchanged insurance premium, the value of the policy is increased with a reduction in bank capital. The introduction of deposit insurance, therefore, provided banks with an incentive to reduce their capital and incur higher risk of insolvency, while at the same time increasing the government's contingent liability. This moral hazard problem is aggravated by the structure of deposit insurance premiums, which are approximately proportional to a bank's total (not insured) deposits.

Despite criticism of the insurance pricing system and frequent calls for more risk-sensitive pricing, the regulators have until very recently not endorsed such proposals. To be sure, many of the recommendations have been unduly facile in failing to recognize the difficulties of risk measurement (Ricart i Costa and Greenbaum, 1983B). On the other hand, the regulators' demonstrated lack of enthusiasm for risk-sensitive premiums—most recently in response to the deposit insurance study mandated by Section 712 of the Garn–St Germain Depository Institutions Act of 1982—is probably related to their similar lack of enthusiasm for a penalty discount rate. This seems to reflect a regulatory preference for administrative rather than pricing remedies for incentive compatibility problems. Rather than attempting to price the risk and thereby reduce the necessary scope of regulation, the regulators choose to deal with moral hazard problems by employing rules and proscriptions with the attendant necessity for monitoring through supervision and examination. This, of course, expands the resources dedicated to regulatory activities.

To summarize, the government's guarantee system involves two related activities, the lender-of-last-resort function and deposit insurance. Although these guarantees are separated for administrative, and even occasionally for analytical, purposes, the two are conceptually inextricable because liquidity protection is inseparable from solvency protection. Any liquidity-augmenting innovation reduces the probability of insolvency. Similarly, any measure to protect depositors against default risk increases banks' liquidity. Indeed, when considered as a single entity, the pricing of the government's guarantee is less risk-insensitive than focusing exclusively on deposit insurance premiums would suggest.

Both guarantees provide banks with incentives to assume added risk which could be mitigated, but probably not eliminated, by alternative pricing structures. This residual moral hazard provides the most compelling justification for public regulation and monitoring of banks. As long as the government serves as guarantor of the financial system, there will be moral hazard warranting some regulation and monitoring. However, the scope of regulation has been unnecessarily magnified by the regulators' bias against incentive-oriented pricing policies.

The necessity for public regulation, given the government's role as guarantor of the financial system, provides a basic motivation for financial innovation. To the extent that regulation constrains private initiatives, entrepreneurs will weigh the cost of compliance against the cost of circumvention. This cost comparison serves as the trip-switch for the introduction of new claims, new delivery systems, and new organizational forms.

Theories of Financial Innovation

The recent turbulence in financial markets has stimulated academic interest in explaining financial evolution. This work is still in an embryonic stage of development. Much of it is fragmentary and conjectural, and to speak of theories of financial evolution is a form of intellectual hyperbole. Nevertheless, three related strands of thought are identifiable: the linear programing approach, associated with Silber (1975); the Hegelian dialectic, associated with Kane (1981); and the regulatory explanation, associated with Greenbaum and Haywood (1971). These three explanations are by no means mutually exclusive. Indeed, they differ more in explanatory style and emphasis than in substance.

Silber's explanation is clearly most general. It is virtually axiomatic and probably also is incapable of being empirically rejected. He views the financial system as maximizing some (linear) objective function, subject to a set of constraints. The constraints have shadow prices, i.e., implicit prices of violating (or just satisfying) the constraints. These constraints can be regulatory in origin, like a legal reserve requirement or a capital requirement; they may be technologically based, like a production function parameter; or they may be rooted in the tax code. In Silber's view, financial innovation is a systemic response to rising shadow prices. Thus, as the cost of satisfying a particular constraint increases, resources are devoted to circumventing or overcoming it. The culmination of this effort is a change in the financial system in the form of a new claim, delivery system, or organizational form.

The generality of Silber's approach derives from the fact that shadow price increases can be attributable to a wide variety of stimuli, including changes in demand, tax laws, regulation, or technology. The theory, therefore, says little more than that financial innovation is an adaptive response by the financial system to some external shock that expresses itself in terms of an increase in the system's cost of satisfying some constraint. As such, the theory is difficult to quarrel with; however, it provides limited illumination.

Kane explains innovation in dialectical terms. The protagonists are the financial system on the one hand and public regulators on the other. The latter seek to restrain the financial system through the imposition of some constraint—a price ceiling, a reserve requirement, or an asset proscription. The system adapts in order to circumvent the regulatory initiative. The regulators respond by imposing yet another restriction, thereby prompting yet another adaptive initiative. The process continues ad infinitum resulting in an ever-expanding regulatory system together with an increasingly complex financial system. The implication is that both represent a squandering of societal resources with a welter of perverse effects.

Kane's characterization of innovation focuses on the undeniable tension between the governmental and private participants in the financial system. It constructively suggests, but does not pursue, a game-theory approach to explaining both regulation and the system's adaptation to regulation. But it also leaves a good deal unanswered. For example, why doesn't the regulator eventually learn to anticipate the system's responses and vice versa? Why doesn't the process converge to an equilibrium? Why is there public regulation to begin with, and what makes the system so readily adaptable? Periods of rapid change, including occasional crises, seem to alternate with others that are relatively placid. Can the theory explain the conditions giving rise to alternate periods of rapid and gradual evolution?

Greenbaum and Haywood argue that new claims are brought into existence largely because of secular increases in real income and cyclical increases in interest rates. The growth of real income creates a demand for a wider variety of financial claims, and the system duly responds by producing an ever-wider array of claims. This explanation merely asserts that increasing income results in increased demand for all claims, whether produced or not. Hence, rising income should gradually pull more and more claims from the unproduced to the produced category.

Rising interest rates also increase the demand for unproduced claims, because these are the claims without ceiling interest rates. As rates rise and we substitute away from claims with constrained rates, new claims come into existence. The problem with this substitution-effect argument is the absence of any clear long trend in interest rates that would help explain a secular proliferation of claims. Cyclicality in interest rates presumably should carry some of the burden of expanding the secular growth in the menu of claims. The explanation originally offered by Greenbaum and Haywood was that after claims are brought into existence, owing to high interest rates, they become candidates for regulatory protection. More plausibly, claims do not become candidates for regulatory protection, but firms producing claims do. Thus, claims can disappear as readily as they appear, provided their disappearance does not threaten the population of firms in the financial system. When new claims are produced by specialized new firms, there will be a tendency toward irreversibility. However, when new claims are produced by existing firms that provide a wide array of claims, we would expect a cyclical reversal in interest rates to lead to the disappearance of the new claim. Thus, a drop in interest rates is much more likely to eclipse the federal funds, retail repurchase agreements, and sweep accounts of commercial banks than it is to lead to the disappearance of, say, money market mutual funds.

Because regulation is skewed toward protecting firms in the financial system, it tends to relegate innovation to the periphery. The proscriptions that are central to regulation inhibit existing firms from leading the innovation process. New claims, therefore, tend to spawn new firms and sometimes even new delivery systems. By pushing innovation to the system's periphery and then protecting financial firms, the public regulator may foster secular proliferation of claims growing out of interest rate cyclicality. This view of the innovation process also suggests a financial and regulatory system of ever-increasing complexity and fragility. One might imagine this process culminating in collapse owing to the sheer weight of the system's elephantine structure. Collapse and crisis can be expected to prompt basic reform as illustrated by the Banking Act of 1933 (creating the FDIC), the Federal Reserve Act, the National Bank Act, and the legislation giving birth to the First and Second Banks of the U.S.

Before leaving this topic we should note that government and public regulation are not the sole possible sources of irreversibilities in the financial system. Others have emphasized the importance of investor learning, as mentioned earlier. Once the public has learned about money market mutual funds, it is claimed that they are not likely to return to passbook savings accounts, even if interest rates retreat quite considerably. Although there may be considerable force in this argument, it incorporates an element of implausibility. Rather than prompting an educational revolution, high interest rates dictate a diversion of real resources to financial management, and low rates can be expected to reverse the resource flow. It would therefore seem plausible to anticipate the reemergence of idle balances and even our traditional, civilized obliviousness to issues of "float." This reversion is not a return to naivete; rather it constitutes a rational response to altered opportunity costs. Indeed, we have forgotten how to ride horses, except in Hollywood movies and on polo fields. The concept of float only became *au courant* in the frenetic 1970s.

Still another possible irreversibility stems from the recent development of costly and expansive delivery systems. In order to avoid the discarding of these assets, their owners have an incentive to maintain the system's level of throughput. Thus, one might imagine operating the system even at a loss in order to avoid redevelopment costs the next time a profitable product opportunity becomes available. Effectively, this is what Citicorp was doing for years with their credit card system. They correctly anticipated that the card would become the foremost mass market delivery system for financial services and that it would ultimately operate profitably. They did not shrink from this vision, despite years of negative spreads and huge operating losses.

Conclusion

In a brief ten years, inflation has destabilized our financial system and set it on an evolutionary path of uncertain direction and terminal points. Although inflation has abated, at least temporarily, the financial system continues to lurch erratically, posing a variety of disquieting policy questions. Barring new governmental initiatives and fundamental reform, we will need to learn to live with a financial system stripped of much of its financial capital, a system much more akin to that of the 1920s than to that of the 1950s or 1960s. This will mean more frequent failures among financial institutions, together with a growing tendency toward concentration among financial firms. It will also mean less scope for subsidizing socially mandated investment in housing and other areas. In addition, we can anticipate higher credit standards in general and less unsecured lending (the recent growth of asset-based lending is symptomatic). Total deregulation is unlikely, but the locus of regulation can be expected to shift toward the major sources of exposure in intermediation, i.e., credit and funding risk. This may well mean an expanded intrusion of public regulation into the treasury function of financial institutions, perhaps in lieu of legal reserve requirements.

These changes may necessitate compromises in public convenience and in managerial prerogatives, and they will almost certainly elevate the importance of management skills. The industry will have to husband and rationalize these resources much more intensively. But this more fragile financial system may prove workable and may even allocate society's resources more intelligently. The great danger is that a return to higher inflation may result in major disruptions with attendant economic trauma and chaos.

Almarin Phillips and Donald P. Jacobs

9

Reflections on the Hunt Commission

Introduction

New and restrictive regulations were imposed on the deposit financial intermediaries in the 1930s. Whatever the original rationale for those regulatory constraints, considerable sentiment for change developed among academicians, many regulators, and

---

ALMARIN PHILLIPS *served as a visiting professor at a number of national and international universities and was professor at the University of Virginia before joining the faculty of the University of Pennsylvania, where he is now Hower Professor of Public Management. He has consulted for several organizations, including the Board of Governors of the Federal Reserve System, the Department of the Treasury, and the RAND Corporation. Dr. Phillips was a codirector of the President's Commission on Financial Structure and Regulation (the Hunt commission) and is currently director of the National Bureau of Economic Research. He has written numerous articles in professional journals and other publications and has served as editor and author of several books.*

DONALD P. JACOBS *is the dean and the Gaylord Freeman Distinguished Professor of Banking at the J. L. Kellogg Graduate School of Management at Northwestern University. He has served as a consultant to a wide range of corporations, institutions, and government agencies. Dr. Jacobs was a codirector of the President's Commission on Financial Structure and Regulation, and from 1975 to 1979, he was chairman of the board of Amtrak. He is a member of the board of directors of several private corporations, including Commonwealth Edison, Hart Schaffner and Marx, Union Oil Company of California, and First Chicago Corporation. An author and researcher, Dr. Jacobs has published numerous articles and papers.*

a number of executives of depository financial institutions during the 1960s. They recognized that new, competitive relationships were emerging within and among the markets of the deposit intermediaries and other providers of financial services. They believed that the existing set of regulations could no longer protect the institutions from competition. Deregulation was needed to allow them to compete with other less heavily regulated sectors of the broader financial services market.

Regulatory change would require congressional action, however, and it was recognized by those advocating change that there would be strong opposition to almost any form of deregulation. There was no unified view or even a clear consensus as to the particulars of deregulation. Indeed, many in the affected industries did not share the view that deregulation was needed. A few officials in the Treasury Department were among those favoring a legislative thrust toward deregulation. They urged that an overall plan be developed that considered the social, political, and economic aspects of regulatory change. The emphasis should be on the public interest with an orderly transition away from regulation.

A presidential commission was formed in June 1970 at the behest of the Treasury Department. The commission was to develop recommendations that would serve as guidelines for a broad legislative proposal for regulatory reform, with the main focus on the deposit financial institutions. The commission was designated "The President's Commission on Financial Structure and Regulation," but soon became known as the Hunt commission, after its chairman, Reed O. Hunt. The commission was composed of twenty members with loose but not official representation from commercial banks, mutual savings banks, savings and loan associations, life insurance companies, state regulators, home builders, business, labor, and academia. The chairman was an industrialist of very broad experience that included the financial intermediaries. The authors of this chapter were the codirectors. The commission completed its task in slightly less than eighteen months and submitted its report to the President in December 1971.

The *Report of the President's Commission on Financial Structure and Regulation* was the basis of draft legislation presented by the administration for discussion to Congress, the financial industries, and the public. A wide-ranging debate and the introduction of several bills followed, but no significant deregulation legislation was enacted for almost ten years. Now, looking back more than a decade after the report was submitted, it is clear that a substantial part of the recommendations has finally become law. It is also clear the long delay in the implementation of the report's recommendations imposed substantial costs on the deposit intermediaries and, more importantly, on the public. This chapter has the dual aims of analyzing why legislative change was so long delayed and of assessing the costs of that delay.

The analysis in this section focuses on the activities and discussion that followed the submission of the Hunt commission report. This is not meant to suggest that the Hunt report was the only road map to reform that has been developed or that this report was unique in calling for reform. The Commission on Money and Credit developed a set of recommendations in 1961 that argued for much the same changes. So did the Heller committee in 1963. Another broad study was undertaken in the House of Representatives subsequent to the Hunt commission. The report, *The Financial Institutions and the Nation's Economy* (FINE), argued for reforms in the same general direction. The same set of forces greeted all of these proposals. Thus, although this discussion is particularized to the Hunt report, it is for the most part a description of the difficulties of enacting any broad reform program in the area of deposit institution regulation in the 1960s and 1970s.

Attempts at Regulatory Reform

During the period of discussions and decisions leading to the recommendations, the senior staff of the commission kept Treasury Department officials informed of the direction the commission members seemed to be taking. The staff also met with other federal agency and cabinet officials, as well as with trade associations and academics. Moreover, commission members kept the officers of trade associations informed about the subjects and, on occasion, the specifics of the deliberations.

A number of papers were prepared at the request of the commission, and industry groups submitted position papers. There were no hearings. No industry group other than credit unions—

which had no representation on the commission—was permitted to make a presentation at a meeting.

The principal recommendations of the report were (1) a five-year phase-out of ceilings on savings and time deposits (Regulation Q); (2) broader liability, loan, and investment powers for the thrifts; (3) a lifting of certain loan and subordinated debt restrictions on commercial banks; (4) the sale and distribution of mutual funds and commingled agency accounts by commercial banks; (5) limited revenue bond underwriting by commercial banks; (6) a central liquidity fund and broader loan, share account, and service powers for credit unions; (7) chartering and conversion options for all of the thrift institutions; (8) statewide branching for commercial banks; (9) mandatory Federal Reserve membership for all institutions with third-party payments; (10) lower and uniform reserve requirements on third-party payment accounts; and (11) the abolition of reserve requirements on time and savings deposits.

Some tax reforms and modest reorganization of the federal regulatory agencies were also suggested. The commission found it extremely difficult to reach a consensus recommendation concerning the prohibition of interest on demand deposits. After noting the adverse effects the prohibition was then having and forecasting that these would become of increasingly greater consequence, the only positive recommendation was for a future review of the issue.

It was obvious to those familiar with inner workings of the Hunt commission that the accord reached on the recommendations contained elements the general membership of the applicable industries would find objectionable. As the December 1971 deadline approached, each meeting required a redesigning of previously settled positions. When the members identified with the objective of the commission—and with the public interest in such reforms—they concurred with the basic thrusts of the draft report before them. When these same members spent time with industry associates between formal meetings, a few saw the transition problems for their own extracommission constituencies as being too grave for full endorsement of the report.

It was not a complete surprise, then, that November and December of 1971 brought rumors of possibly dissenting, modifying, or supplementary statements. The dissent of the labor representative had been foreseen for some time. Another dissent argued that tax credits on interest on residential mortgage to the lender would, to a degree, result in a diversion of funds from existing tax-exempt securities. Not unexpectedly, there was also a relatively mild, but nonetheless important, dissenting comment that wider powers for the thrifts and the removal of ceilings on interest rates would either dry up mortgage funds, cause increased volatility in this sector of the funds markets, or both.

When this report was published, reservations such as those found in the dissents exploded into vocal and sometimes bitter criticism. The report met with widespread disapproval from the vast majority of commercial banks, savings and loan associations, and credit unions. Its reception by the mutual savings banks was warmer, but not by many degrees.

Actually, it was the *strategy* underlying the commission's report that gave rise to the disagreements and, in turn, to the failure to gain legislative support. The commission looked carefully at the history of the existing regulatory framework. It assessed the present operations of the industry groups and developed a view of the market and technological environment that these firms would face in the future. The commission members unanimously accepted the view that whatever had been the conditions giving rise to the existing regulatory framework, economic conditions had changed in fundamental ways. The market and regulatory structures as constituted in 1971 contained elements that would cause great difficulties in the future. Commission members were convinced that the forecasted economic conditions and technological advances would greatly increase the severity of interindustry disintermediation, add to system inefficiencies, and create greater crises than had been experienced up to that time. There was a very strong belief, it should be noted, that technological advances had to be factored into the recommendations.

In light of these beliefs, the commission very early in its deliberation concluded that the major emphasis of its recommendations would be to reduce the scope of existing regulations. The major problem was that those regulations, as well as having developed a set of "mission-oriented industries," had also erected market protections for many of the established firms performing these missions. With some regulatory costs, each had been prohibited from expanding from its prescribed areas of business. For the most part, the deposit institutions saw deregulation as a removal of the protective cloak each wore with respect to the others. They largely ignored the fact that these same cloaks make them vulnerable to what was then a less obvious threat—competition from both new and old forms of nondeposit financial intermediaries.

From the point of view of each of the "mission-oriented" groups, it appeared that deregulation meant several others could play on their hitherto reserved playing field. Thus, each individual group could muster arguments against deregulation since none wished to act on what, from a broader perspective, would have appeared as a collective benefit. Moreover, the elimination of the regulations would have had short-term negative effects on their operations. These effects loomed very importantly when contrasted with the long-term and far less clearly defined benefits promised by deregulation.

To break through these impasses, the commission's strategy was to develop a set of recommendations that contained a balance of competitive costs and benefits for each of the industries. The balance had to be seen in each case as positive enough to produce wide support for the entire package. A resolution of this sort was reached by the commission itself and, in this vein, it urged others to view the recommendations as a coherent "package." The report, with the exception of the suggested organizational changes for the regulators, was to be treated as a whole. The commission was not setting forth an array of recommendations designed to be picked over by the various financial industries and their clients.

The strategy of fashioning sets of costs and benefits producing surpluses of benefits for all depended on being able to convince the affected groups that they were, in essence, not "on the contract curve" that existed among them. More practically, it depended on demonstrating that eliminating regulations provided trade-off options such that each would be better off. Thus, to be successful, the commission's *modus operandi* depended on whether there would be agreement by the regulated industries that (1) the conclusions concerning the market and technology environmental scans were correct, (2) a package of deregulation recommendations could be developed that would produce benefits in excess of costs to the entire complex of groups, and (3) the package would distribute these benefits so that the individual industry groups would see it in their self-interest to favor passage of the package. The members of the commission were convinced of the correctness of the first two of these requirements. The major problem came with the third.

Even within the commission, the problem of the distribution of gains and losses at times led to temporary impasses. The long-term gains from the enlarged asset and liability powers for the thrifts were not uniformly seen as a large enough reward for surrendering the short-term protections of Regulation Q. When the parochial interests of the home builders in mortgage financing were joined with the thrifts on this question, successful resolution even within the commission was threatened. Any time the related question of interest on demand deposits arose, agreement within the commission became impossible. It was, in fact, due only to the timely and forceful intervention of Mr. Hunt that the commissioners agreed on the recommendations that finally appeared. He directed that interest on demand deposits be removed from the agenda, and he figuratively "locked in a room" the principal parties among whom agreement seemed impossible until an accord was reached.

It was obvious all along that once outside the milieu of commission meetings and of Mr. Hunt's ministrations, the commissioners would be subject to different pressures. Identification with the short-term goals of the respective industries would rise, and the long-term gains from trade-offs would be less defensible. Thus, early in its tenure the commission decided that immediately after the report was accepted it should be an administration bill. A strong lobbying effort was to be mounted to get it enacted into omnibus legislation. It was these considerations that caused the codirectors, Mr. Hunt, and Treasury Department officials to maintain liaison with key members of Congress, the staffs of key congressional committees, and the heads of the regulatory agencies during the tenure of the commission. There were also efforts to maintain the interest of President Nixon in regulatory reform for financial institutions. Immediately after the report was issued, a number of the commissioners—not all—and the codirectors traveled extensively for the purpose of "selling" the package.

In late 1972 and early 1973, the Treasury Department developed working drafts of legislation based on the Hunt commission's report. Indeed, the codirectors of the commission became "weekend consultants" to the Treasury Department in connection with the project. The push for legislation was on. And, interestingly, it was immediately apparent that the report was already outdated. Negotiable order of withdrawal (NOW) accounts had been started in Massachusetts and spread almost at once to New Hampshire. This innovation was an extremely visible event. Less visible to both the public and most of the smaller financial institutions was the appearance of the first money market mutual fund. Mr. Hunt's edict that interest on transactions accounts was off the commission's agenda could no longer apply to the proposed legislative agenda.

In August and September of 1973, the Treasury Department issued original and then revised "Recommendations for Change in the U.S. System." These contained NOW account powers for corporations, as well as for individuals. Many of the provisions of the Hunt commission's proposals were incorporated in the document that went forward under a presidential message to Congress.

Here the clear track of the Hunt commission ends. It was not the NOW account or the money market fund that stopped the administration's thrust, however. Rather, it was the escalating concern of the administration about the Watergate matter. As is well known, Watergate effectively neutralized the executive branch of government. The Ford administration, while pushing deregulation in other areas, did not revive the momentum for omnibus financial reform. The initiative moved to Congress and, more particularly, to the Senate.

In October 1973, Senate Bill 2591, the Financial Institutions Act of 1973, was introduced and referred to the Committee on Banking, Housing, and Urban Affairs. Companion legislation was introduced in the House and referred there to the Committee on Banking, Finance, and Urban Affairs. The House subsequently undertook the FINE study and, pending completion of that study, was not receptive to passage of omnibus financial reform legislation. On the Senate side, the Subcommittee on Financial Institutions, under Senator Thomas McIntyre, had begun exploratory work on reform legislation early in 1973. The Senate committee prepared a number of omnibus reform bills, and at least one was passed by the Senate. Companion measures were not even seriously championed in the House.

Before considering the question of why the legislative attempts at omnibus deregulation of financial markets were unsuccessful, it should be noted that some less general legislation was enacted. Prior to the Hunt commission's report, the Bank Holding Company Act of 1970, the National Credit Union Administration Act of 1970, and the National Credit Union Share Insurance Act of 1970 were enacted.

Public Law 93–100, enacted in 1973, authorized NOW accounts for all deposit institutions except credit unions in Massachusetts and New Hampshire. Public Law 94–222, passed in 1976, gave similar powers in the other New England states and in New York. The Financial Institutions Regulatory and Interest Rate Control Act of 1978 established the type of central discount fund the Hunt commission had recommended for credit unions.

Still, it was not until passage of the Deposit Institutions Deregulation and Monetary Control Act of 1980 and the Garn–St Germain Depository Institutions Act of 1982 that packages anything like the Hunt commission's recommendations became law.

The Resistance to Reform Financial Legislation

Why was general reform so difficult? Was the Hunt commission's assessment incorrect? We think not. An examination of the characteristics of the several types of deposit institutions indicates that other political factors were at work.

COMMERCIAL BANKS

As is well known, the commercial banking industry is composed of some 14,000 separately chartered banks. Legislative lobbying by the industry is conducted by a number of associations of which three are the most important. The first is the American Bankers Association (ABA), which has virtually all banks as members.

Second, there is the Independent Bankers Association of America (IBAA) whose main membership and constituency is with the smaller, unit banks. And finally, there is the Reserve City Bankers Association (RCBA) whose members are the large money market and regional banks. The first two associations have strong lobbying programs. The third organization has not historically supported a unified lobbying effort, but many of its members have the resources and the desire to be heard directly.

The commercial banks covered a wide spectrum of views with respect to costs and benefits to be derived from the commission's recommendations. Rather than being a single industry, commercial banks can be more aptly categorized as local banks, regional banks, money center banks, and international banks. With regard to the commission's recommendations, the position of each of these subgroups can be viewed as along two interrelated dimensions: first, the composition of their liabilities, and second, management's views about how future technology would affect the markets they serve.

An important component of the commission's recommendations was the phase-in period for the changes that could produce the largest impacts on the institutions. The phase-in was designed to give institutions time to adapt to altered market conditions and implement new strategies in an orderly fashion. The phase-in period alleviated the danger of massive shifts that could be very costly to institutions inexperienced with intense competition.

The perceived competitive costs of the phasing-out of Regulation Q to the various commercial banks depended upon the proportion of liabilities acquired under the rate maximum. For the smaller institutions and others operating in markets where thrift institution competition was not intense, this change was seen as a major cost. At the other extreme were the money center institutions that, by 1970, were already acquiring a substantial portion of their liabilities at market rates. For them the phasing-out of Regulation Q was perceived as an immediate benefit. They would gain freedom to compete more effectively in a market that was by then already very competitive. Medium-sized institutions and bank holding companies of substantial size but operating in many local markets fell in between the two extremes.

The commission's report suggested that improving technology—computer and communication—would increase the geographic size of the market served by an office, permit new products to be offered, and create stronger competition among the deposit institutions. The benefits of rate regulation were rapidly disappearing. This meant that institutions that relied on Regulation Q to contain the cost of funds would shortly discover that such reliance was misplaced. There is little evidence, however, that banking institutions then benefiting from Regulation Q ceilings in fact forecast a continuing sizable decline in these benefits.

The same technological advances were also predicted to bring new competitors into the markets that historically had been the province of the deposit institutions. These entrants would offer new or redesigned products, greater convenience, and other attractive and unregulated terms. But the vast majority of banks were unconcerned about the potential market erosion that could arise because of the new technology. This reasoning then led to a position where they were unwilling to forego any present benefits to attain a better position in the future.

In the lobbying efforts, therefore, the IBAA was flatly opposed to the commission's proposals. The IBAA perceived the expanded powers to the thrifts as the real competitive threat and saw the elimination of deposit interest rate ceiling as a cost, not a benefit. They did not view any expansion in their operating powers as an important benefit. Of course they would have preferred to get rid of the positive rate differential held by the thrifts, but not at the price of losing Regulation Q and increasing the powers of the thrifts.

The ABA, probably because of the wide spectrum of its membership, seemed neither clearly in favor of nor clearly against the package. The leadership discussed the issues and at times seemed to favor some sort of legislation. Problems of reserve requirements occupied their attention. There always seemed to be some hesitation and an indication that the ABA was assuming a bargaining stance. It never pushed for specific legislation and opposed parts of all the proposals. Unfortunately, the strongest potential proponent voice in the banking industry, the RCBA, did not take a lobbying position. On the whole, the banking industry was not an important force pushing for omnibus deregulation.

THRIFTS

Thrifts are of two distinct types: savings and loan associations (S&Ls) and Mutual Savings Banks (MSBs). The former are spread throughout the nation. A few S&Ls are large, but most are quite small. The MSBs are located primarily in the Northeast and, on the average, are considerably larger than the S&Ls. Both have strong industry associations.

The United States League of Savings Associations was widely reputed to be a very effective lobbying group, particularly in the House of Representatives. This lobbying power is probably attributed to three factors. First, the very narrow and uniform range of products produced by thrift institutions meant that management of these institutions had very similar perceptions of their own best interests. Thus, the association leadership found very little dissension or disagreement to contend with in reaching an appropriate policy stance. Second, the thrifts, again because of their asset structure, formed a natural alliance with the home builder/real estate lobby. The National Association of Home Builders was itself very powerful, again probably more so in the House. Finally, the mutuality and "little guy" and "Populist" aspects of the S&Ls and home building/home ownership can be blended into very emotional and patriotic themes.

The political strengths of the S&Ls and the home builders caused problems when the commission's recommendation to permit broader asset powers for the thrifts came under discussion. The S&L industry had grown rapidly in the years after World War II, largely because the structure of interest rates had a strong positive slope until the mid–1960s. This yield curve was ideal for an industry that bought short maturity funds and made long-term loans. The inflationary conditions after the mid–1960s and predictions for the 1970s suggested that such conditions would not continue. That this posed serious threats to the continued prosperity of the S&Ls had been obvious since at least 1966. But, unfortunately, the majority of the industry's managers were myopic. The previous prosperity, the "fix" occasioned by Regulation Q, and the fact that few of them had experienced disintermediation to nondeposit segments of the market made them unwilling to forego their interest rate advantage and the protection of regulatory rate maximums in exchange for greater asset freedom. In addition, the real estate lobby was strongly opposed to permitting thrifts greater product freedom. The home builders were not convinced by the argument that a crippled, yet captive, thrift industry would provide smaller amounts of mortgage funds than would a healthy industry that also provided other financial services.

The National Association of Mutual Savings Banks, sometimes with and sometimes without an alliance with the Savings Bank Association of New York State, represented the position of the MSBs. The MSBs were chartered and regulated by the state in which they were domiciled. There was considerable variance among states with respect to operating powers. In general, the MSBs had broader operating freedom than S&Ls, and they were less tied to the home builder and real estate interests.

Probably because of their location in the eastern part of the country, their concentration in urban areas, and their larger asset size, the MSBs were the group most in favor of expanded asset and liability powers. Because of the relative sophistication of depositors in their markets, they were already exposed to deposit shifts when market rates went above deposit interest rate ceilings, and they were also feeling the first effects of new technology. In some states the MSBs were also restricted by the strength of commercial banks in the state legislative process. These MSBs were very much in favor of being permitted direct access to the third-party payment system. They clearly signaled their willingness to forego the differential rate advantages under deposit interest rate ceilings and to phase out the ceilings entirely in exchange for permission to offer checking accounts and the ability to shift to a federal charter. At the federal level, however, only a few legislators had great interest in the position of the MSBs.

REAL ESTATE LOBBY

Real estate interests are divided into two major groupings—the home builders and the real estate agents. Both are numerous and distributed throughout the country. Because the members of these groups are characterized by relatively small capitalization, they tend to have close ties to grass-roots politics. In addition to numbers and dispersal, the high social priority accorded housing has made the housing lobby extremely potent.

These groups were the most adamantly opposed to implementation of the commission's recommendations. The local thrift institution was the backbone of their traditional financing vehicle. They often formed and controlled the S&Ls. Because they were not familiar with changes, actual and prospective, in the market for consumer financial services, the changes predicted by the commission were almost completely ignored. As a whole, the industry was unwilling to forego any part of the existing financial relationship for some other untried and untested arrangements.

CREDIT UNIONS

At the time of the commission's deliberations, credit unions (CUs) were the most rapidly growing, least professionally managed, least regulated, and, operationally, the most rapidly changing of the deposit intermediaries. The CUs were not subject to formal deposit interest rate ceilings, but neither were they usually permitted to guarantee a percentage return on share accounts. Company sponsored CUs, in the main, were supported operationally by their host firms and used the privilege of payroll reductions for deposits and loan repayments. Occasionally they had full-time, salaried employees, but for the most part they were managed by volunteers. In their early history, the CUs largely made personal installment loans. They then moved into durable goods financing. As interest rates rose in the late 1960s, they gradually and selectively moved into housing-related finance. Their growth accelerated during the years as their dividends rose above those offered by other institutions constrained by interest rate ceilings while, at the same time, the CUs' loan rates remained below those of other institutions.

The major disadvantage of the CUs in the marketplace was erased in 1970 when they were accorded National Credit Union Share Insurance. They perceived their main remaining need to be a centralized source to provide help when individual organizations came under liquidity strains. The commission's recommendations provided for the establishment of such a liquidity source. The recommendations also endorsed a full range of consumer financial services for the CUs. On the other hand, the commission recommended only limited third-party payment powers unless the CUs held reserves equal to those of the other providers. Quite realistically, the CUs felt they could achieve their objectives outside of the general realignment proposed by the commission. They did not actively take part in the discussion and have achieved most of what they wanted without reference to omnibus reform.

THE FEDERAL REGULATORY AGENCIES

The federal regulatory agencies would have been affected by the report in two ways. First, a segment of the recommendations was devoted to a plan to reorganize the federal regulatory system. Second, the agencies, whether reorganized or not, would have been influenced because of the operational changes in the deposit intermediaries they regulate.

The redesign would have affected all of the agencies, but the major impact would have been on the Board of Governors of the Federal Reserve System. The commission believed that the regulatory activities of the Federal Reserve diverted its resources and energies away from its proper major charge—framing monetary policy and performing the function of lender-of-last-resort. Thus, the commission recommended that, with a few exceptions, the Federal Reserve should not be involved in the regulatory process. Indeed, all of the agencies would have experienced a substantial reduction in their regulatory influences with the commission's recommendations. Regulation, as far as the commission's recommendations were concerned, was to be a far less important force in the markets for financial services.

The behavior of the regulatory agencies with respect to the Hunt commission's recommendations lends credence to the view that regulatory organizations act so as to protect and enlarge their own spheres of influence. There was no open campaign by the agencies against the commission's recommendations, but neither was there substantial support. Yet these agencies all had staffs of well-trained, qualified economists who, in the vast majority, individually supported the general thrust of the recommendations. In retrospect, it is regrettable that the regulatory agencies did not take a leading position in pushing for change.

THE TREASURY DEPARTMENT

The Treasury Department staff was designated in the planning stages as the group that would receive the recommendations, develop an administration legislative proposal, and work with the interested parties and Congress to get legislation enacted. As noted above, this is just what happened until late 1973. In the absence of Watergate, it might have worked. However, the strength of the IBAA, the thrifts, and the housing groups in the House make it questionable whether the administration could in fact have gotten the legislation passed.

THE CONGRESS

Although the Treasury Department staff did not continue to push for passage, the commission staff, the Democratic chairman of the Senate Banking, Housing, and Urban Affairs Committee, the Democratic chairman of the Subcommittee on Financial Institutions, and some of their Republican colleagues took over the sponsorship of financial reform legislation. A bill was passed by the Senate, only to flounder in the House. The various factions described above presumably succeeded in impressing House committee members that the legislation was not needed, was untimely, or was unfair. The House mounted its own study to determine what changes were needed. This was a time-consuming effort to develop another package of proposals for restructuring the regulatory system.

THE DELIBERATIONS

Clearly the loss of the Nixon administration as the coordinator of negotiations and as the major force endorsing and pressing for legislation guaranteed defeat of the omnibus bills. The description of the forces at play suggests that even if the administration had moved as forcibly as had been projected, there was at least an even chance that the proposals would have been emasculated or defeated outright.

The "mission-oriented" design of the regulatory system, when large numbers of firms are involved, almost guarantees defeat for far-reaching changes that are supported primarily by projections of altered conditions, improved social performance, or forecasts of new technology. Nothing changes substantially unless there is an obvious crisis at hand. Managers in regulated industries do not seek out opportunities for change so that more competition will appear.

The Costs of the Failure to Deregulate

Evaluating costs involves a comparison of alternatives. The alternatives we consider are the events as they actually occurred since 1973 and a less certain scenario of what might have occurred in the same period had significant deregulation transpired in 1973. It is obvious that this evaluation contains substantial elements of judgment. We know of no other way to assess the importance of deregulation and the costs imposed by the political inaction described above.

The discussion considers two types of costs. The first centers on allocative efficiency, noting market distortions caused by the retention of regulation. The second type of cost—less commonly thought of as a social cost—concerns system instability, the creation of uncertainty, and possible other macroeconomic effects. We note also some distributional considerations which may or may not be thought of as costs.

What happened? Table 1 summarizes some of the events from 1973 through 1982 in the regulated environment. The inflation rate, compared to the recent historical experience, was high but not accelerating in the first part of the decade (Column 3). From 1977 on, the inflation rate was much higher and accelerating until 1981. Inflation appeared to be far more serious when measured by the popularly reported Consumer Price Index (CPI) than when seen in terms of the gross national product (GNP) deflator. The CPI rose by 13.3 percent between 1978 and 1979, with the home ownership elements (interest, taxes, insurance) rising by

27.5 percent, motor fuel rising by 52.2 percent, and energy, generally, by 37.4 percent.

Interest rates were also high by historical standards (Column 4). Nonetheless, from 1974 through 1976 rates eased. After 1976, but particularly after 1978, interest rates rose sharply.

In addition to the high and generally rising rates, there was extreme vacillation in their levels. The yield on three-month Treasury bills, for example, rose from 9.26 percent in July 1979 to 15.53 percent in March 1980 and then fell to 8.13 percent by

TABLE 1. SUMMARY DATA ON MONEY FINANCIAL INSTITUTIONS AND MARKETS, 1973–1982

(Dollar Figures in Billions)

Year	*M1* * (Dec.) [*1*]	*Nominal GNP* [*2*]	*GNP Deflator, % Change* [*3*]	*Yield, 90-Day Treasury Bills (Yr.)* [*4*]	*Savings Deposits (Dec.)* [*5*]	*Small Time Deposits (Dec.)* [*6*]	*Large Time Deposits (Dec.)* [*7*]
1973	$264.4	1,326.4	5.8%	7.04%	$322.2	$266.4	$110.9
1974	277.4	1,434.2	8.8	7.89	337.6	290.0	144.4
1975	291.0	1,549.2	9.3	5.80	387.7	340.9	129.8
1976	310.4	1,718.0	5.2	4.00	451.7	396.5	118.4
1977	335.5	1,918.3	5.8	5.27	490.4	454.1	145.2
1978	363.2	2,163.9	7.4	7.22	479.9	533.9	194.6
1979	389.0	2,417.8	8.6	10.04	421.7	652.6	221.8
1980	414.5	2,633.1	9.3	11.51	398.9	751.7	257.9
1981	440.9	2,937.7	9.4	14.08	343.6	854.7	300.3
1982	478.4	3,057.6	6.0	10.67	359.0	859.1	333.9
Percent change 1973–77	26.9%	44.6%	—	—	52.2%	70.5%	30.9%
Percent change 1978–82	31.7%	41.3%	—	—	(25.2%)	60.9%	71.6%

Sources: Board of Governors of the Federal Reserve System; *Economic Indicators,* Department of Commerce.

* All checkable deposits.

† Estimate.

** Percent change 1973–77.

July 1980. By December 1980 that yield was back to 15.66 percent. Prime rates announced by major banks lost much of their meaning as indicators of actual loan rates; in March 1980 they varied from 16.75 to 19.5 percent. They had been in the 11.5 to 11.75 percent range in July 1979 and reverted to 11 percent by August 1980. A market in "interest rate futures" developed, partly for sheer speculation and partly for risk-reducing hedging operations.

The prohibition of interest on demand deposits applied through-

(Dollar Figures in Billions)				
Overnight Repurchase Agreements & Overnight Eurodollars (Dec.) [8]	*Money Market Mutual Funds (Dec.)* [9]	*Commercial Paper & Bankers' Acceptances (Dec.)* [10]	*Demand Deposit Turnover Rate, NYC (Year)* [11]	*Income Velocity of M1 (Year)* [12]
$6.8	$0.1	$50.0	248	5.02
7.2	2.3	60.7	296	5.17
7.5	3.6	56.4	357	5.32
13.7	3.4	60.5	412	5.53
18.8	3.8	74.7	503	5.40
24.1	10.2	100.6	542	5.96
26.3	43.7	123.5	646	6.22
35.0	75.8	129.9	814	6.35
38.1	184.9	143.9	1100	6.66
44.2	229.7	152.5	1200†	6.39
176.5%	65.2%**	49.4%	102.8%	7.6%
83.4%	152.0%	51.6%	121.4%	7.2%

out the period. Regulation Q ceilings on savings deposits were 5 percent and 5.25 percent by commercial banks and thrifts, respectively, from July 1973 to July 1979, when they were raised by a quarter of a percentage point.

The ceilings on various maturity small time deposits rose gradually, with the larger denomination and longer maturity deposits generally being permitted the higher of the maximums. Rates on large denomination time deposits—those of $100,000 or more—were unregulated. After June 1978, six-month, nonnegotiable "money market" time deposits of $10,000 or more were permitted, with rate maximums varying with the six-month Treasury bill rate. In July 1979 minimum denomination regulations were dropped on deposits with maturities of four or more years. This regulation was changed in January 1980 to apply to maturities of 2.5 years or more. Rate ceilings were variable based on yields of similar maturity Treasury securities. It is important to note that the pattern of the "deregulation" that did occur was designed to *avoid* the payment of market rates of interest on the short-maturity, negotiable, small "money-like" deposits. Early redemption penalties were imposed for just this purpose.

Savings account balances rose from 1973 through 1977, but then declined (Column 5). The .25 percent differential in the ceiling for thrifts did not prevent a continuous outflow from what had been their primary source of funds. Concomitant with the loss of savings account balances was a dramatic rise in both small (less that $100,000) and large time deposits (Columns 6 and 7). As this occurred, and given the pattern of deregulation, the marginal cost of funds for the deposit institutions rose dramatically.

Contrary to what seems to be general opinion, the growth in M1 (all checkable deposits) was fairly steady and at a rate significantly below that of nominal GNP throughout the 1973–82 years (Columns 1 and 2). The largest rates of growth were in 1977 and 1978, when M1 rose by 8.1 and 8.3 percent, respectively. In other years the growth rate ranged from 4.4 to 7.1 percent. Checkable deposits other than demand deposits—NOW and automatic transfer service (ATS) accounts, share drafts, etc.—amounted to only $4.2 billion in 1977 but grew to over $100 billion by the end of 1982. After 1970, the variance in M1 or M2 explains virtually none of the variance in prices or GNP. Vastly varying reserve requirements that depended on deposit type, deposit size, city classification, and institutional form, together with changes in float, off-shore banking practices, and delayed reserve requirement computations, made the relationship between M1 and "high-powered money" (currency plus reserves) less stable than it had previously been.

A number of relatively new money market institutions grew rapidly in this setting. The commercial and finance paper and bankers' acceptance markets were almost "reinvented" in the 1969–70 period. From 1973 to 1982, outstandings in these markets rose threefold, from $50 billion to $151 billion with only a small hesitation in 1975–76 when short-term rates of interest were relatively low (Column 10). The use of overnight repurchase agreements and overnight Eurodollar borrowings started at a nearly negligible $6.8 billion in 1973. By 1982, these balances had grown to $44 billion. Money market funds (MMFs) were started in 1972 but grew little from 1973 through 1977. When market rates of interest rose thereafter, MMF balances grew rapidly. The rate of increase in the MMFs was particularly sharp after October 1979 when the Federal Reserve announced that its "new" monetary policy would be oriented exclusively toward control of the growth in monetary aggregates regardless of the effects of that policy on interest rates.

Table 1 shows a seldom noted consequence of the expansion in holdings of short-term time deposits, negotiable C/Ds, commercial and finance paper, repurchase agreements, Eurodollars, MMFs, and other nondeposit obligations. Non-interest-bearing demand deposits became much more purely transactions accounts; the demand to hold balances in these accounts decreased. As demand deposits were used increasingly for effecting exchanges among the other types of holdings, the turnover rates on demand deposits increased. Thus, in New York City the turnover rates on demand deposits rose from about 150 times per year in 1970 to almost 250 times per year in 1973 and—with the large post-1977 increase in interest rates—to over 1,200 times per year by 1982 (Column 11). For all standard metropolitan statistical area (SMSA) commercial banks, the turnover rate on demand deposits rose from about 100 in 1973 to nearly 300 in 1982.

Just as nondemand deposit assets were converted momentarily to demand deposits for the purpose of exchanging one nondemand deposit asset for another, so could such assets be converted to demand deposits to facilitate expenditures for final goods and services. That is, with lower transactions costs based on new technologies, the appearance of new markets, and the high opportunity costs of demand deposit balances in a high market interest rate regime, a given demand deposit balance could be used to accommodate higher levels of total expenditures. This change appears in Table 1 as the increase in income velocity from 5.02 in 1973 to 6.39 in 1982 (Column 12). Recall that the M1 data used here include checkable deposits other than demand deposits, which grew by about $100 billion over the period. For bank demand deposits plus currency alone, the income velocity growth was from about 5.0 in 1973 to over 8.0 in 1982.

From the point of view of an individual bank, there is no difference between higher deposit turnover for asset exchanges and for purchases of goods. The higher turnover rates, however, have affected bank operations and bank risk exposure. As an example, think of a New York commercial bank with demand deposit liabilities equal to eight times its capital. If that bank has a demand deposit turnover rate of 1,200 per year, say three times per day, the bank has daily commitments to pay out twenty-four times its capital on average. An amount equal to its total capitalization must be paid out every hour of the twenty-four-hour day. The bank clearly must rely on receiving payments from others that very nearly balance these obligations both in amounts and in timing.

Juxtaposed against needs to satisfy customer demands for loans, improved cash management services, and other new services, these higher turnover rates appeared operationally through:

1. more extensive use of the federal funds market, with inclusion of member banks, nonmember banks, domestic offices of foreign banks, Edge Act corporations, S&Ls, MSBs, the FHLBB, other U.S. agencies, and investment bankers in that market;
2. more extensive use of Eurodollar borrowings from foreign branches of U.S. banks and from foreign banks;
3. greater use of overnight and term repurchase agreements;
4. more extensive use of bankers' acceptances;

5. sales of loans to nonbanking holding company affiliates;
6. sales of commercial and finance company paper by banking holding company affiliates;
7. private placements and, as permitted, underwriting of commercial and finance company paper;
8. encouraging the shifting of deposits from those with higher reserve requirements and low interest rate ceilings to those with lower reserve requirements and higher ceilings;
9. increased use of subordinated, nondeposit debt instruments;
10. extended offerings and internal operations based on account "sweeping";
11. service as the managing institution and/or transfer agent for NOW accounts, share drafts, MMFs, and other nonbank institutional offerings;
12. extended services in connection with correspondent banks.

As a consequence of many of these changes, default risk and interest rate risk increased. In particular, default risk and the risk of technologically-related transaction breakdowns rose tremendously for the commercial banks at the center of the transaction process. Interest rate risk was especially pronounced for institutions borrowing or lending for long terms and, of course, for those with existing assets composed of long-term instruments. Thus, from 1978 through 1982 the thrifts experienced enormous deposit outflows on accounts paying substantially less than market rates and earned negative returns on those deposits paying market rates. The viability of that entire industry—the S&Ls and the MSBs—was, and continues to be, truly threatened.

Similarly, home building, real estate sales activity, and mortgage financing experienced critical downturns after 1978–79. Housing starts fell from over 2 million units in 1978 to an annual rate of less than 1 million in May 1980. By mid–1981, after some recovery, the number of starts again dropped below a million per year. The intermediaries through which private funding had been transacted could not bear the interest rate costs involved in buying funds; their traditional borrowers were detracted by both the cost and the interest rate risks of long-term financing.

There were other developments that require only brief note. At the retail level, automated teller machine (ATM) deployment grew, and toward the end of the period local, regional, and national networks were in operation. Credit card use expanded.

Pricing of card services tended to change toward greater payments by the cardholder (to cover credit extension during the grace period), and there was exploration, if not wide use, of the debit card. Electronic clearing networks grew through automated clearing houses (ACH), BankWire, and Fed Wire. The Clearing House Interbank Payments System (CHIPS) and Society of Worldwide Interbank Financial Telecommunications (SWIFT) expanded as high interest rates increased the opportunity value of avoiding regulations through international transactions. In some sense, especially when the interinstitutional aspects of "sweep balance accounts" and cash management services are included, the time and money costs of exchanging one asset for another fell rapidly.

WHAT MIGHT HAVE HAPPENED

Whether deregulation in 1973 would have made a difference obviously depends on the character and extensiveness of the deregulation under consideration. Ignoring the political realities that prevented enactment of the modified Hunt commission recommendations in Senate Bill 2591, the deregulation we consider here exemplifies the spirit of the reform proposals, not a particular set of actual recommendations. More specifically, what would the 1973–82 period have looked like if, by late 1973, it had been clear that:

1. The prohibition of interest on demand deposits was to be eliminated.
2. Regulation Q was being rapidly phased out.
3. All deposit institutions would have third-party payment powers.
4. The thrift institutions (including credit unions) had the broad asset powers recommended by the Hunt commission and as enacted in the Garn–St Germain Act of 1982.
5. Reserve requirements were being phased out, the Federal Reserve had initiated payment of interest on reserve balances, and all deposit institutions were required to keep reserve balances at the Federal Reserve.
6. Broad intrainstitutional and interinstitutional branching powers were granted, including ATM deployment.
7. Trust departments were permitted to offer commingled agency accounts, and banks were permitted to underwrite, sell, and distribute mutual funds.

8. Defined national housing goals and other social priority financing programs were to be met through direct taxation and direct subsidization programs rather than through restraints and incentives affecting particular lending institutions

The first and least controversial observation about the difference such deregulation would have wrought is that a number of instruments designed specifically to "go around" the old regulations would not have appeared. The NOW account innovation is one of these. In markets unfettered by the prohibition of interest on demand deposits and the rate maximums of Regulation Q, competitive forces would have established rates (prices) for deposits that reflected underlying supply (cost) and demand conditions. In general, charges would have been made for transactions, and interest would have been paid on deposit balances. Lower interest rates would have been paid on highly liquid (shorter term, more negotiable) balances than for less liquid balances. That some institutions would "bundle" their prices would be of no concern so long as both the institutions and their customers were free to arrange unbundled services. Whatever early redemption penalties existed would be based on private contracting, not on regulatory fiat.

In this unregulated environment, the historic classifications of demand, savings, and time deposits would lose their meaning. The terms of deposit account contracts—negotiability, maturity, redeemability, minimum balances, minimum payment orders, etc.—would be effectively determined in the market itself. This would not, however, have meant that all deposit institutions would be identical in their offerings. As is true in other markets, broad operating powers permit specialization as well as "department store" approaches. We suspect a good deal of specialization would in fact have occurred. Some banks would have moved toward the large corporate and interbank accounts and others to more retail-oriented household and small business specialization. How far this would have gone is difficult to assess.

A side aspect of specialization is worth noting, however. Commercial banks, because of their historic operations and the technologies employed, have clear cost advantages in intrainstitutional and interinstitutional clearings of transactions. Further, efficient clearing takes on the characteristics of a hierarchical network,

One thing that would have spread more rapidly is bank-correspondent clearing arrangements, with smaller banks making more extensive use of the services of larger banks for transaction deposit offerings. This would reflect greater efficiency, with the clearing network arranged by the market for that purpose.

Just as the NOW account would not have made its appearance, so would the MMFs not have arisen in the form they took. That is, on a continuing basis, there would not have been numerous large and small holders of deposit balances seeking higher return, deposit-like assets. If a nondeposit institution began providing, say, a mutual fund with terms attractive to holders of any type of deposit, the outflow from such deposits to the alternative would have prompted the deposit institutions to increase rates, decrease transactions fees, or change other terms to retain the deposits. The market equilibrating forces would have been such that in the end any institution—deposit or nondeposit—could sustain only those services for which it had a comparative cost advantage. The MMFs as they are used for transacting incur higher costs than do banks.

That the MMFs of the present type would not have arisen does not mean that new and innovative mutual funds would not have emerged. The point is that the advantage of such funds would not have been in their third-party payment and quick redeemability features. Banks have the comparative cost advantage with respect to these features. It is not at all clear, however, that the banks possess any advantages in organizing, managing, and distributing funds with other attractive features—portfolios of equity securities, commercial paper, real estate paper, tax-exempt issues, Treasury securities, etc. Under deregulation, some banks might have attempted to sell products such as these, but they might not have succeeded. Indeed, just as it seems that other institutions would contract with banks for transactions services, it is likely that banks would have contracted with securities firms and investment companies for many types of securities and fund offerings. With unregulated deposits and the technology and expertise of the securities industry, we believe that the powers of banks to offer commingled agency accounts and mutual funds would not have been of great significance. In fact, as presented in the *ICI v. Camp* case, the commingled accounts were themselves designed primarily to avoid Regulation Q and the prohibition of interest on demand deposits.

Deregulation would have aided the thrift institutions only to the extent that the latter were capable of mixing the new asset, liability, and service powers into packages in which they had comparative cost and marketing advantages. Just where those advantages would have existed is not clear. We suspect, however, that some thrifts would have broadened their operations to serve more fully the financial needs of consumers; some would have become much like bank branches, as a consequence either of mergers or of contractual arrangements with banks or large thrifts. Others would have continued their specialized role in real estate and housing-related financing, with new types of liabilities (less liquid, with offsetting rate advantages) that matched their assets. A good number of the thrifts—especially those in competitive urban areas—would not have survived as independent institutions when the quasi subsidies inherent in the old regulations were removed.

Thus, while deregulation would have prevented the global disintermediation from the thrifts (and the banks) to the nondeposit sectors of the financial markets, it would not have prevented—indeed, it would have caused—significant market restructuring. The restructuring would have cut two ways. First, there would not have been the entry of almost 300 transactions-oriented MMFs, since deposit institutions could more efficiently have performed transactions services. Second, the same competitive pressures that would have prevented the growth of the MMFs would have weeded out inefficient deposit institutions. That, of course, is the ultimate reason the thrifts and many of the banks opposed the attempts at regulatory reform.

In terms of Table 1, several effects of the deregulation are then apparent. Since the various types of deposits would have had terms and conditions reflecting their costs and the demands for them, by 1982 it would have been impossible to define meaningful distinctions among checkable deposits (M1), savings deposits, small time deposits, large time deposits, and all of the subcategories of such deposits as have existed by regulation. In truth, the distinctions were not very meaningful in the marketplace well prior to 1982, despite the regulations. Funds moved among account types as the regulations changed and interest rates escalated. The difference with deregulation is that a market equilibrating mechanism, not regulations, would have been paramount in determining the funds shifts. Shifting within and among institutional types, and within and among deposit and nondeposit liabilities, would result in price and nonprice changes that would dampen and control the intermediation process. There would be more, not less, stability in the intrainstitutional and interinstitutional flows of funds.

A very important consequence of deregulation, then, would have been a much lower rate of growth in demand deposits–or just transaction deposits–turnover rates. With explicit pricing individuals and businesses would be able freely to adjust asset portfolios such that their holdings of particular assets, given prices, matched the various needs for which the portfolio is held. While cash management accounts, sweep balances, automatic transfer accounts, etc. might still exist, the concept of a zero-balance account would apply only to assets that could not be sold at a price to cover their costs. No one would be forced by regulation to move funds inefficiently to avoid regulatorily-imposed interest rate penalties.

It has been argued–mostly by the Federal Reserve itself–that mandatory reserve requirements and a clearly defined monetary aggregate (M, M1, M1A, M2–depending on the day) are necessary for effective monetary control. These arguments are wrong, and rest on central bank experience and monetary theories predicated on the regulations. In the deregulated regime, we consider monetary policy would have been more, not less, effective.

While deregulation would have abolished mandatory reserves—reserve balances presumably beyond those that member banks would voluntarily hold–it would also have allowed financial institutions to hold balances at the Federal Reserve and have the Fed pay interest on such balances. Individual institutions would, in effect, choose between Federal Reserve balances, interbank balances, and other assets as optimizing portfolio choices. Collectively, the balances at the Federal Reserve would nonetheless remain at the discretion of the Federal Reserve. Absent use by the Federal Reserve of the traditional means of increasing or decreasing reserves (primarily open-market operations), the total of the voluntarily-held reserves of all institutions would remain fixed. Action by one institution to increase its reserves (i.e., by selling, calling, or not renewing another asset) would be identically matched by losses in reserves held by other institutions.

Note, nonetheless, that the Federal Reserve could affect the amount of reserves institutions wished to hold by altering the rate it paid on reserve balances. Raising that rate would precipitate demands to hold more reserves and result in the sale of other assets by individual banks. Systemwide, however, those sales would wash out, but with lower prices and higher rates of interest on those assets.

In the deregulated regime, the higher Federal Reserve rate on reserve balances would be reflected in higher loan rates, higher deposit rates (including those on interbank deposits), and higher market rates for nondeposit negotiable instruments. The effect would spread through all financial markets as new market equilibriums were found. The disequilibrating and destabilizing effects of disintermediation would be avoided since each of the submarkets would reach its own adjustment. Thus, the aggregate of all "money-like" instruments would bear a more stable relationship to higher powered money with deregulation than it has in the last decade with regulation. And indeed, the policy consequences of quantitative controls would be far more predictable.

We are of the opinion that with even a modicum of good sense at the Federal Reserve, deregulation would have ameliorated the severe and unpredictable vacillations in interest rates we have experienced since 1972. To a considerable degree, the latter have been the result of unpredictable reactions taken *because* of regulations. The "Fed watcher" syndrome in financial markets since the early 1970s has been characterized by gross inaccuracies in short-term forecasts that exacerbated short-term rate fluctuations.

The generally upward trend in rates and inflation would, we suspect, not have been greatly affected. The underlying reasons for inflation were not of a financial character. They originated in the fiscal policies attendant to the Vietnam War; in other fiscal excesses; in world petroleum, energy, and commodity markets; in declining labor productivity; in "learned" and institutionalized nominal wage-price behavior; and in other factors. Perhaps the fact that new money substitutes could so easily circumvent monetary and interest rate controls contributed to some of this story. Still, while the upward drift in income velocity was abated by ineffective monetary regulation, the latter did little to cause the inflation.

Finally, we note some differences that are, for the most part, of a distributional nature. Both the new money market instruments and the gradual relaxation of rate maximums that occurred since 1982 were of a sort that accommodated the runs of "big money." Large corporations and wealthy individuals have been little affected by interest rate ceilings for nearly two decades. Both as borrowers and as asset holders, they have had the advantage of new and innovative services provided by banks and nonbanks.

The costs of moving "small money," however, have not warranted the same regulatory relaxation or private market accommodations. As borrowers, small businesses have not had easy access to nonbanking markets. As holders of funds, most households have not had realistic alternatives that yielded market-determined rates of interest. On both scores deregulation would have reduced the discriminatory effect.

Conclusion

We are reminded of the time-worn adages of "If, If, If." If only there had not been Watergate; if only the trade association leaders had adopted a long-term point of view; if only there had been deregulation.

By the 1970s, it was obvious that the nation's financial regulatory system was in desperate need of substantial reform. Modifications, however, came about slowly throughout the decade. Then, in the early 1980s, massive changes in the system occurred. But the size and magnitude of those changes were so sweeping that the hitherto remote possibility of serious or major disruptions in the system loomed larger. Disaster scenarios were not only discussed in the popular press, but bankers and other finance professionals began thinking about the unthinkable. Clearly these discussions had an impact on financial decisions reached by laypersons as well as professionals. Fortunately, the degree of chaos contemplated by doomsayers has not recurred. But the fact remains, based on both the public and private discussion, that the system could have failed. There could have been chaos. This has created a serious concern, a concern that must be measured as a cost of immense proportions.

But is that the hollow lesson? We hope not. The implementation of new economic, political, and social directives is not easy. Still, to the extent that this story makes clear that long-term problems are only exacerbated by a policy of no change or a propping up of an old system, its telling has some worth.

George J. Benston 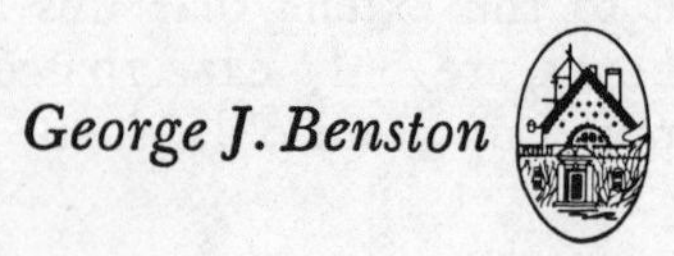

A Summary of Public Policy Questions

Though each author of the chapters presented in this book has given or could give answers to the following public policy questions, we think it best for readers to supply their own. The future of the financial services industry depends in large measure on what these answers are and how they are implemented. However, in proposing one or another answer, readers should consider the reaction of individual suppliers and consumers of financial services to legal and other changes, and they should also recognize that laws and regulations are only partial determinants of events.

TRANSACTIONS SERVICES

Entry

1. Should any firm be legally prohibited from offering depository services to the public?
2. Would the public benefit from having many suppliers of these services? In particular, should special charters be required?

Geographic Restrictions

3. Should suppliers of financial services (including depository services) be permitted to establish branches or affiliates anywhere they wish?

Interest on Deposits

4. Should ceiling rates or other constraints be imposed on the terms offered to the public for their funds?

5. In this regard, should any type of liability, such as a transactions or savings deposit, be distinguishable?
6. Similarly, should the source of funds, such as individual or corporation, be distinguishable?
7. In particular, should minimum balance requirements, restrictions on the number of transactions, and early withdrawal penalties be imposed?
8. In addition, should the prohibition of interest payments on demand deposits imposed by the Banking Act of 1933 be repealed?

Interest on Required Reserves

9. Should deposit balances at Federal Reserve banks receive interest?
10. Should required reserves be treated differently with respect to interest payments?

Deposit Insurance

11. Under what conditions should depository financial institutions be permitted to fail?
12. Should there be federal deposit insurance?
13. If so, how should the insurance contracts be designed and priced? (For example, which types of liabilities should be insured, what powers should a governmental insurer have, and what constellation of agencies—public and private—should offer the contracts?)
14. In this regard, should this policy differ according to the size of the institutions?

PAYMENTS SYSTEM

Federal Reserve Involvement

15. Should the Federal Reserve continue to provide payments clearing services?
16. If so, should any of these services be subsidized?
17. Should the government attempt to direct the evaluation of the payments system?

Risk in the Payments System

18. Should a uniform legal code that establishes the responsibilities and rights of participants in the payments system be enacted?

Electronic Funds Transfer Systems

19. Are the present antitrust laws adequate to assure competition in the establishment and use of these facilities?

POWERS OF FINANCIAL SERVICES FIRMS

Financial Services

20. Should any institution be legally constrained from offering securities services, including underwriting and any type of financial service?

21. In particular, should the Glass–Steagall Act provisions that attempt to separate commercial and investment banking be repealed?
22. Should depository institutions continue to be prohibited from providing nonfinancial services?
23. If not, should they be permitted to provide these services directly, through subsidiaries, or as affiliates of a holding company?
24. Should depository institutions be permitted to hold corporate equities as investments?

ANTITRUST AND MERGERS

Antitrust Laws

25. Should there be special antitrust laws for any or some categories of financial services firms?

Merger Actions

26. Should mergers be restricted to similarly regulated financial institutions (e.g., commercial banks only with other commercial banks), or should mergers be permitted among such institutions as commercial banks, savings and loan associations, and savings banks?

CONSUMER FINANCE

Usury Laws

27. Should usury laws be repealed?
28. Failing that, should the interest rate ceilings on loans be indexed?

Protection Laws

29. Do the costs of consumer protection laws (such as the Truth-in-Lending Act, Equal Credit Opportunity Act, and Community Reinvestment Act) outweigh their benefits?

Bankruptcy Laws

30. Should the Federal Bankruptcy Reform Act of 1978 be amended?

Bibliography

AHARONY, JOSEPH, AND ITZHAK SWARY, "Effects of the 1970 Bank Holding Company Act: Evidence from Capital Markets," *Journal of Finance,* 36 (September 1981), 841–53.

ARTHUR D. LITTLE INC., *Report on the Payments System,* Report to the Association of Reserve City Bankers, Washington, D.C., 1982.

ATKINSON, THOMAS R., *Trends in Corporate Bond Quality.* New York: National Bureau of Economic Research, 1967.

BAKER, DONALD I., "Competition, Monopoly and Electronic Banking," in *The Economics of a National Electronic Funds Transfer System,* Federal Reserve Bank of Boston Conference Series #13, 1974, pp. 47–64.

BALDERSTON, FREDERICK E., "The Savings and Loan Mortgage Portfolio Discount and the Effective Maturity on Mortgage Loans," Institute of Business and Economic Research, University of California, Berkeley, Working Paper 81–41, November 19, 1981.

BARTH, JAMES, AND ANTHONY YEZER, "Economic Impact of the Federal Trade Commission Proposals for Credit Contract Regulations on the Cost and Availability of Consumer Credit," Bureau of Social Science Research, Inc., George Washington University, Washington, D.C., Research Paper, 1977.

BELL, FREDERICK, AND NEIL MURPHY, *Costs in Commercial Banking,* Federal Reserve Bank of Boston, Research Report #41, 1968.

BENSTON, GEORGE J., "Economies of Scale and Marginal Costs in Banking Operations," *National Banking Review,* 2 (June 1965), 507–49.

———, "An Analysis of Maine's '36 Month Limitation' on Finance Company Small Loans," *National Commission on Consumer Finance Technical Studies,* Vol. 2, Washington, D.C.: U.S. Government Printing Office, 1972.

———, "The Costs to Consumer Finance Companies of Extending Consumer Credit," *National Commission on Consumer Finance Technical Studies,* Vol. 2, Washington, D.C.: U.S. Government Printing Office, 1973A.

———, "Bank Examination," *The Bulletin,* New York University Institute of Finance, Nos. 89–90, May 1973B.

———, "Mortgage Redlining Research: A Review and Critical Analysis," *The Regulation of Financial Institutions,* Federal Reserve Bank of Boston Conference Series #21, October 1979.

———, "Mortgage Redlining Research: A Review and Critical Analysis," *Journal of Bank Research,* 12 (1981), 8–23.

———, "Federal Regulation of Banking: Analysis and Policy Recommendations," *Journal of Bank Research,* 14 (1983A), 216–44.

———, "Bank Failure and Deposit Insurance," *Economic Review,* Federal Reserve Bank of Atlanta, March 1983B, pp. 4–17.

Benston, George J., Gerald A. Hanweck, and David B. Humphrey, "Scale Economics in Banking: A Restructuring and Reassessment," *Journal of Money, Credit, and Banking,* 14 (November 1982), 435–56.

Bleeke, Joel, and James Goodrich, *Capitalizing on Opportunities Created by Deregulation of the Banking Industry,* McKinsey & Company, Inc., September 1981.

Boyd, John H., Gerald A. Hanweck, and Pipat Pithyachariyakul, "Bank Holding Company Diversification," in *Proceedings of a Conference on Bank Structure and Competition,* Federal Reserve Bank of Chicago, 1980, pp. 105–21.

Canner, Glenn B., "Redlining: Research and Federal Legislative Response," *Staff Studies,* Board of Governors of the Federal Reserve System, Summarized in *Federal Reserve Bulletin,* October 1982.

Canner, Glenn, and Joe M. Cleaver, "The Community Reinvestment Act: A Progress Report," *Federal Reserve Bulletin,* 66 (February 1980), 87–96.

Chandler, Gary G., and David C. Ewert, "Discrimination on the Basis of Sex under the Equal Credit Opportunity Act," Credit Research Center, Krannert Graduate School of Management, Purdue University, Working Paper 8, 1976.

Chase, Samuel B. Jr., "The Bank Holding Company as a Device for Sheltering Banks from Risk," in *Proceedings of a Conference on Bank Structure and Competition,* Federal Reserve Bank Holding Companies, Golembe Associates, Inc., February 1978.

Christophe, Cleveland A., *Competition in Financial Services.* New York: First National City Corporation, 1974.

Citicorp, *The Old Bank Robbers' Guide to Where the New Money Is.* New York: Citicorp, undated.

Cox, Edwin B., "Developing an Electronic Funds Transfer System: Incentives and Obstacles," in *The Economics of a National Electronic Funds Transfer System,* Federal Reserve Bank of Boston Conference Series #13, 1974, pp. 15–31.

Darnell, James, "A Study of the Costs of Complying with Government Regulation," *Issues in Bank Regulation,* 5 (Winter 1982), 14.

Deshmukh, Sudhakar D., Stuart I. Greenbaum, and George Kanatas, "Bank Forward Lending in Alternative Funding Environments," *Journal of Finance,* 37 (September 1982), 925–40.

———, "Lending Policies of Financial Intermediaries Facing Credit and Funding Risk," *Journal of Finance,* 38 (June 1983).

Deshmukh, Sudhakar D., Stuart I. Greenbaum, and Anjan V. Thakor, "Capital Accumulation and Deposit Pricing in Mutual Financial Institutions," *Journal of Financial and Quantitative Analysis,* 17 (December 1982), 705–26.

Diamond, Douglas W., and Philip H. Dybvig, "Bank Runs, Deposit Insurance and Liquidity," *Journal of Political Economy,* 1982.

Eisenbeis, Robert A., *Financial Innovation and the Role of Regulation: Implications for Banking Organization, Structure and Regulations,* Board of Governors of the Federal Reserve System, February 1980.

———, "How Bank Holding Companies Should Be Regulated," *Economic Review,* Federal Reserve Bank of Atlanta, January 1983.

Eisenbeis, Robert A., Robert S. Harris, and Josef Lakonishok, *Benefits of Bank Diversification: The Evidence from Shareholder Returns,* School of Business Administration, University of North Carolina, October 1982.

Federal Trade Commission, *Economic Report on Installment Credit and Retail Sales Practices of District of Columbia Retailers.* Washington, D.C.: Federal Trade Commission, 1968.

Federal Trade Commission Bureau of Consumer Protection, "Memorandum in Support of a Trade Regulation Rule on Credit Practices." Washington, D.C.: Federal Trade Commission, 1974.

Fischer, Gerald C., and Carter H. Golembe, "The Branch Banking Provisions of the McFadden Act as Amended: Their Rationale and Rationality," in *Compendium of Issues Relating to Branching by Financial Institutions,* Subcommittee on Financial Institutions of the Committee on Banking, Housing, and Urban Affairs, United States Senate, 94th Congress, 2nd Session. Washington, D.C.: U.S. Government Printing Office, October 1976.

Fisher, Irving, *The Theory of Interest as Determined by Impatience to Spend Income and Opportunity to Invest It.* New York: Macmillan, 1930.

Flannery, Mark J., "A Method for Empirically Assessing the Impact of

Market Interest Rates on Intermediary Profitability," in *Proceedings of a Conference on Bank Structure and Competition,* Federal Reserve Bank of Chicago, 1980A, pp. 1–15.

———, "How Do Changes in Market Interest Rates Affect Bank Profits?" *Business Review,* Federal Reserve Bank of Philadelphia, September/October 1980B, pp. 13–22.

FLANNERY, MARK J., AND JACK M. GUTTENTAG, "Problem Banks: Examination, Identification and Supervision," in *State and Federal Regulation of Commercial Banks,* Federal Deposit Insurance Corporation, Washington, D.C., 2 (1980), 169–226.

FORD, WILLIAM F., "Banking's New Competition: Myths and Realities," *Economic Review,* Federal Reserve Bank of Atlanta, January 1982, pp. 3–11.

FRIEDMAN, MILTON, AND ANNA J. SCHWARTZ, *A Monetary History of the United States, 1867–1960.* Princeton, New Jersey: Princeton University Press, 1963.

GREENBAUM, STUART I., "Legal Reserve Requirements: A Case Study of Bank Regulation," *Journal of Bank Research,* 14 (Spring 1983).

GREENBAUM, STUART I., AND CHARLES F. HAYWOOD, "Secular Change in the Financial Services Industry," *Journal of Money, Credit and Banking,* 3 (May 1971), 571–89.

HADAWAY, BEVERLY L., AND SAMUEL C. HADAWAY, "An Analysis of the Performance Characteristics of Converted Savings and Loan Associations," *Journal of Financial Research,* 4 (Fall 1981), 195–206.

HAMMOND, BRAY, *Banks and Politics in America: From the Revolution to the Civil War.* Princeton, New Jersey: Princeton University Press, 1957.

HAWKE, JOHN D., JR., "Are State Laws Prohibiting Interstate Banking Constitutional?" *American Banker,* December 15, 1982.

HAWKE, JOHN D., JR., WILLIAM J. SWEET, JR., AND MICHAEL B. MIERZEWSKI, "Revised BSC Act Offers Banks New Opportunities, *Legal Times,* December 20, 1982.

HICKMAN, BRADDOCK, *Corporate Bond Quality and Investor Experience,* National Bureau of Economic Research, Studies in Corporate Bond Financing No. 2. Princeton, New Jersey: Princeton University Press, 1958.

HOMER, SIDNEY, *A History of Interest Rates.* New Brunswick, New Jersey: Rutgers University Press, 1963.

HUMPHREY, DAVID B., "Scale Economies at Automated Clearing Houses," *Journal of Bank Research,* 12 (Summer 1981), 71–81.

INTERAGENCY TASK FORCE ON SMALL BUSINESS FINANCE, "Overview of a Series of Papers on Financing Small Business," in *A Report to Congress,* Board of Governors of the Federal Reserve System, Comptroller of the Currency, Federal Deposit Insurance Corporation, Washington, D.C., February 1982.

JAFFE, NAOMI L., AND RONALD B. HOBSON, *Survey of Interest-Rate Futures Markets,* Commodities Futures Trading Commission, Washington, D.C., December 1979.

JAFFEE, DWIGHT M., "Housing Finance and Mortgage Market Policy," in *Government Credit Allocation,* Institute for Contemporary Studies, San Francisco, 1975, pp. 93–122.

JBR ASSOCIATES, *Final Report to the Federal Financial Institutions Examination Council, Section 340(e) Fair Housing Lending Study,* July 30, 1982.

JOHNSON, ROBERT W., *Cost/Benefit Analysis of Creditors' Remedies: Monograph No. 12,* Credit Research Center, Purdue University, 1978.

JOHNSON, ROBERT W., AND RICHARD L. PETERSON, *Indexing Rate Ceilings: Monograph No. 25,* Credit Research Center, Purdue University, 1983.

JOHNSON, ROBERT W., RICHARD L. PETERSON, AND BLAIR C. SCHICK, *Consumer Bankruptcy Study, Volume 1: Monograph No. 23,* Credit Research Center, Purdue University, 1982.

JONES, SIDNEY L., *The Development of Economic Policy: Financial Institution Reform.* Ann Arbor, Michigan: University of Michigan Press, 1979.

KANE, EDWARD J., "Accelerating Inflation, Technological Innovation and the Decreasing Effectiveness of Banking Regulation," *Journal of Finance,* 36 (May 1981), 355–67.

———, *The Gathering Crisis in Federal Deposit Insurance: Origins, Evolution and Possible Reforms* (in progress).

KEYNES, JOHN M., *The General Theory of Employment, Interest and Money.* New York: Harcourt Brace, 1936.

KING, THOMAS A., *Discrimination in Mortgage Lending: A Study of Three Cities,* Monograph Series in Finance and Economics, #1980–4, Salomon Brothers Center for the Study of Financial Institutions, Graduate School of Business, New York University, 1980.

LONG, ROBERT H., "Discussion," in *The Economics of a National Electronic Funds Transfer System,* Federal Reserve Bank of Boston Conference Series #13, 1974, pp. 32–38.

MARTIN, J. D., AND A. J. KEOWN, "Market Reaction to the Formation of One-Bank Holding Companies," *Journal of Banking and Finance,* 5 (December 1981), 383–93.

MAYER, THOMAS, "Credit Allocation: A Critical View," in *Government Credit Allocation,* Institute for Contemporary Studies, San Francisco, 1975, pp. 39–92.

MCAFEE, JAMES, *Regulatory Analysis of Revised Regulation Z,* Board of Governors of the Federal Reserve System, Washington, D.C., March 26, 1981.

METZKER, PAUL F., "Future Payments System Technology: Can Small Financial Institutions Compete?" *Economic Review,* Federal Reserve Bank of Atlanta, November 1982, pp. 58–67.

MITCHELL, WESLEY C., *Business Cycles: The Problem and Its Setting.* New York: National Bureau of Economic Research, 1927.

MURRAY, WILLIAM J., "Bank Holding Company Centralization Policies," study prepared for the Association of Registered Bank Holding Companies, Golembe Associates, Inc., February 1978.

NATIONAL COMMISSION ON CONSUMER FINANCE, *Consumer Credit in the United States: Report of the National Commission on Consumer Finance.* Washington, D.C.: U.S. Government Printing Office, 1972A.

NATIONAL COMMISSION ON CONSUMER FINANCE, *Technical Studies Volume V: Creditors' Remedies and Contract Provisions: An Economic and Legal Analysis of Consumer Credit Collection,* by Douglas F. Greer. Washington, D.C.: U.S. Government Printing Office, 1972B.

NIEHANS, JÜRG, "Money and Barter in General Equilibrium with Transactions Cost," *American Economic Review,* 61 (December 1971), 773–83.

———, "Innovation in Monetary Policy: Challenge and Response," *Journal of Banking and Finance,* 6 (March 1982), 9–28.

PETERSON, RICHARD L., "An Investigation of Sex Discrimination in Commercial Banks' Direct Consumer Lending," *The Bell Journal of Economics,* 12 (Autumn 1981), 547–561.

———, "Usury Laws and Consumer Credit: A Note," *Journal of Finance,* 39 (September 1983).

PETERSON, RICHARD L., AND GREGORY D. FALLS, "Costs and Benefits of Restrictions on Creditors' Remedies," Credit Research Center, Purdue University, Working Paper 41, 1981.

PORZECANSKI, ARTURO C., "The International Financial Role of U.S. Commercial Banks: Past and Future," *Journal of Banking and Finance,* 5 (December 1981), 5–16.

RHOADES, STEVEN A., "The Effect of Bank-Holding-Company Acquisitions of Mortgage Bankers on Mortgage Lending Activity," *Journal of Business,* 48 (1975), 344–48.

———, "The Performance of Bank Holding Companies in Equipment Leasing," *Journal of Commercial Bank Lending,* 63 (1980), 53–61.

RHOADES, STEVEN A., AND GREGORY E. BOCZAR, "The Performance of Bank Holding Company-Affiliated Finance Companies," Board of Governors of the Federal Reserve System, Division of Research and Statistics, Washington, D.C., Staff Study 90, 1977.

RICART I COSTA, JOAN E., AND STUART I. GREENBAUM, "Bank Forward Lending: A Note," *Journal of Finance,* 39 (September 1983A).

———, "The Pricing of Deposit Insurance," Banking Research Center, J. L. Kellogg Graduate School of Management, Northwestern University, Working Paper 88, 1983B.

Rockoff, Hugh T., "The Free Banking Era: A Re-examination," *Journal of Money, Credit and Banking,* 6 (May 1974), 141–67.

Rolnick, Arthur J., and Warren E. Weber, "The Free Banking Era: New Evidence on Laissez Faire Banking," *American Economic Review,* 73 (1983).

Rose, John T., "Bank Holding Companies as Operational Single Entities," in *The Bank Holding Company Movement to 1978: A Compendium,* Board of Governors of the Federal Reserve System, Washington, D.C., September 1978.

Rosenblum, Harvey, and Diane Siegel, "Competition in Financial Services: The Impact of Nonbank Entry," Federal Reserve Bank of Chicago, Staff Study 83–1, 1983.

Savage, Donald T., "A History of the Bank Holding Company Movement, 1900–78," in *The Bank Holding Company Movement to 1978: A Compendium,* Board of Governors of the Federal Reserve System, Washington, D.C., September 1978.

Schafer, Robert, and Helen F. Ladd, *Discrimination in Mortgage Lending.* Cambridge, Massachusetts: MIT Press, 1981.

Shay, Robert P., and William K. Brandt, "Public Regulation of Financial Services: The Truth in Lending Act," in *Regulation of Consumer Financial Services,* ed. Arnold A. Heggestad. Cambridge, Massachusetts: Abt Books, 1981.

Shay, Robert P., William K. Brandt, and Donald E. Saxon, Jr., "Public Regulation of Financial Services: The Equal Credit Opportunity Act," in *Regulation of Consumer Financial Services,* ed. Arnold A. Heggestad. Cambridge, Massachusetts: Abt Books, 1981.

Silber, William L., "Towards a Theory of Financial Innovation," in *Financial Innovation,* ed. William L. Silber. Lexington, Massachusetts: D. C. Heath, 1975.

Simons, Henry C., "A Positive Program for Laissez Faire: Some Proposals for a Liberal Economic Policy," in *Economic Policy for a Free Society.* Chicago: University of Chicago Press, 1948.

Smith, Lee, "Merrill Lynch's Latest Bombshell for Bankers," *Fortune,* April 19, 1982, pp. 67–72.

Stigler, George, *The Citizen and the State: Essays on Regulation.* Chicago: University of Chicago Press, 1975.

Stover, Roger D., "A Re-examination of Bank Holding Company Acquisitions," *Journal of Bank Research,* 13 (1982), 101–8.

STRACHAN, S., " 'Congenerics' Draw Enough Buyers to Spark Sound Rally in Equities," *American Banker,* July 8, 1968.

STROVER, ROBERT, "The Single Subsidiary One-Bank Holding Company," in *Proceedings of a Conference on Bank Structure and Competition,* Federal Reserve Bank of Chicago, April 27–28, 1978.

TALLEY, SAMUEL H., "Bank Holding Company Performance in Consumer Finance and Mortgage Banking," *Magazine of Bank Administration,* 52 (1976), 42–44.

THAKOR, ANJAN V., HAI HONG, AND STUART I. GREENBAUM, "Bank Loan Commitments and Interest Rate Volatility," *Journal of Banking and Finance,* 5 (December 1981), 497–510.

TOBIN, JAMES, "Liquidity Preference as Behavior Towards Risk," *Review of Economic Studies,* 25 (March 1958), 65–86.

U.S. Congress House of Representatives, Committee on Banking and Currency, 91st Congress, 1st Session, *The Growth of Unregistered Bank Holding Companies—Problems and Prospects.* Washington, D.C.: U.S. Government Printing Office, February 1969.

WEISBROD, STEVEN, "Economics of Scale in Commercial Banking," unpublished paper, 1980.

WESTIN, ALAN F., "Privacy Aspects in EFT Systems," in *Issues in Financial Regulation,* ed. Franklin Edwards. New York: McGraw-Hill Book Company, 1979.

WHALEN, GARY, "Multibank Holding Company Organizational Structure and Performance," Federal Reserve Bank of Cleveland, Working Paper 8201, March 1982A.

———, "Operational Policies of Multibank Holding Companies," *Economic Review,* Federal Reserve Bank of Cleveland, Winter 1981–82B.

WOLKOWITZ, BENJAMIN, PETER LLOYD-DAVIES, BRIAN C. GENDREAU, GERALD A. HANWECK, AND MICHAEL A. GOLDBERG, "Below the Bottom Line: The Use of Contingencies and Commitments by Commercial Banks," Board of Governors of the Federal Reserve System, Washington, D.C., Staff Study 113, 1982.

Index

The American Assembly

COLUMBIA UNIVERSITY

About The American Assembly

The American Assembly was established by Dwight D. Eisenhower at Columbia University in 1950. It holds nonpartisan meetings and publishes authoritative books to illuminate issues of United States policy.

An affiliate of Columbia, with offices in the Sherman Fairchild Center, the Assembly is a national educational institution incorporated in the State of New York.

The Assembly seeks to provide information, stimulate discussion, and evoke independent conclusions in matters of vital public interest.

AMERICAN ASSEMBLY SESSIONS

At least two national programs are initiated each year. Authorities are retained to write background papers presenting essential data and defining the main issues in each subject.

A group of men and women representing a broad range of experience, competence, and American leadership meet for several days to discuss the Assembly topic and consider alternatives for national policy.

All Assemblies follow the same procedure. The background papers are sent to participants in advance of the Assembly. The Assembly meets in small groups for four or five lengthy periods. All groups use the same agenda. At the close of these informal sessions, participants adopt in plenary session a final report of findings and recommendations.

Regional, state, and local Assemblies are held following the national session at Arden House. Assemblies have also been held in England, Switzerland, Malaysia, Canada, the Caribbean, South America, Central America, the Philippines, and Japan. Over one hundred forty institutions have cosponsored one or more Assemblies.

ARDEN HOUSE

Home of The American Assembly and scene of the national sessions is Arden House which was given to Columbia University in 1950 by W. Averell Harriman. E. Roland Harriman joined his brother in contributing toward adaptation of the property for conference purposes. The buildings and surrounding land, known as the Harriman Campus of Columbia University, are 50 miles north of New York City.

Arden House is a distinguished conference center. It is self-supporting and operates throughout the year for use by organizations with educational objectives.

AMERICAN ASSEMBLY BOOKS

The background papers for each Assembly are published in cloth and paperbound editions for use by individuals, libraries, businesses, public agencies, nongovernmental organizations, educational institutions, discussion and service groups. In this way the deliberations of Assembly sessions are continued and extended.

The subjects of Assembly programs to date are:

1951—United States-Western Europe Relationships
1952—Inflation
1953—Economic Security for Americans
1954—The United States' Stake in the United Nations
—The Federal Government Service
1955—United States Agriculture
—The Forty-Eight States
1956—The Representation of the United States Abroad
—The United States and the Far East
1957—International Stability and Progress
—Atoms for Power
1958—The United States and Africa
—United States Monetary Policy
1959—Wages, Prices, Profits, and Productivity
—The United States and Latin America
1960—The Federal Government and Higher Education
—The Secretary of State
—Goals for Americans
1961—Arms Control: Issues for the Public
—Outer Space: Prospects for Man and Society
1962—Automation and Technological Change
—Cultural Affairs and Foreign Relations
1963—The Population Dilemma
—The United States and the Middle East
1964—The United States and Canada
—The Congress and America's Future
1965—The Courts, the Public, and the Law Explosion

1965—The United States and Japan
1966—State Legislatures in American Politics
—A World of Nuclear Powers?
—The United States and the Philippines
—Challenges to Collective Bargaining
1967—The United States and Eastern Europe
—Ombudsmen for American Government?
1968—Uses of the Seas
—Law in a Changing America
—Overcoming World Hunger
1969—Black Economic Development
—The States and the Urban Crisis
1970—The Health of Americans
—The United States and the Caribbean
1971—The Future of American Transportation
—Public Workers and Public Unions
1972—The Future of Foundations
—Prisoners in America
1973—The Worker and the Job
—Choosing the President
1974—The Good Earth of America
—On Understanding Art Museums
—Global Companies
1975—Law and the American Future
—Women and the American Economy
1976—Nuclear Power Controversy
—Jobs for Americans
—Capital for Productivity and Jobs
1977—The Ethics of Corporate Conduct
—The Performing Arts and American Society
1978—Running the American Corporation
—Race for the Presidency
1979—Energy Conservation and Public Policy
—Disorders in Higher Education
—Youth Employment and Public Policy
1980—The Economy and the President
—The Farm and the City
—Mexico and the United States
1981—The China Factor
—Military Service in the United States
—Ethnic Relations in America

1982—The Future of American Political Parties
—Regrowing the American Economy
1983—Financial Services
—Improving American Innovation
1984—Alcohol Use in America
—Public Policy for the Arts
—Canada and the United States

Second Editions, Revised:

1962—The United States and the Far East
1963—The United States and Latin America
—The United States and Africa
1964—United States Monetary Policy
1965—The Federal Government Service
—The Representation of the United States Abroad
1968—Cultural Affairs and Foreign Relations
—Outer Space: Prospects for Man and Society
1969—The Population Dilemma
1973—The Congress and America's Future
1975—The United States and Japan